A new
CERTIFICATE OF
PROFICIENCY
ENGLISH COURSE

with
PRACTICE AND TEST PAPERS

THIRD EDITION

ONA LOW

SALOP(E)

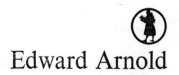

Edward Arnold

© Ona Low 1975

First published 1966 by
Edward Arnold (Publishers) Ltd
25 Hill Street, W1X 8LL

Reprinted, 1968, 1969, 1970
New edition 1973 (incorporating the 2nd edition of
Certificate of Proficiency English Course for Foreign Students).
Third edition 1975
Reprinted 1975 (twice), 1976, 1977, 1978

ISBN 0 7131 1922 5

A **Key** containing answers to all the exercises in this book, along
with notes for teachers, is published separately and should be
available from booksellers. Further information may be obtained
from the publishers.

By the same author:

Certificate of Proficiency English Course: Key

First Certificate in English Course
First Certificate in English Course: Key

First Certificate in English Practice
First Certificate in English Practice: Key

Speak English Fluently 1
Speak English Fluently 2

Printed in Great Britain by Butler & Tanner Ltd, Frome and London

Preface to the First Edition

The student who embarks on a course leading to the Cambridge Certificate of Proficiency in English Examination should already have an adequate command of English to be able to deal simply but reasonably correctly with most everyday situations.

Preparation for the Certificate involves above all two aspects of more advanced language study:

(i) An extension of the student's vocabulary and power of comprehension to cover a wide variety of subjects ranging over cultural, scientific, all kinds of intellectual and utilitarian topics.

(ii) The acquisition of such facility in expression that he is able to present his ideas not only in correct English but in the language best adapted to his subject and likewise to appreciate the skilful use of language in the texts he studies.

A student who passes the Proficiency Examination at a satisfactory level should be sufficiently at home in the language to derive from any kind of study course in English a benefit equal to that of an English student of comparable educational background.

While this book has the primary purpose of preparing the student for the examination, it should prove useful to any advanced learner who wishes to achieve the foregoing aims.

Throughout the text there is no attempt at simplification as at this stage the student should be learning new words of all kinds in their contexts the whole time and should be developing confidence in his ability to understand fully English of a reasonably advanced level.

Preface to the Third Edition

Considerable changes now introduced into the Certificate of Proficiency examination syllabus have necessitated the replacement of a good deal of the material in the existing edition of this book.

Here is a summarised version of the requirements of the new syllabus:

1. COMPOSITION (3 hours)
   A Two compositions
   B A passage to test understanding of its contents and the writer's technique
2. READING COMPREHENSION (1¼ hours)
   A Forty multiple-choice vocabulary items
   B Twenty multiple-choice items based on 2 or 3 passages
3. USE OF ENGLISH (3 hours)
   A Exercises to test control of English usage and structure
   B Prose passage(s) to test the ability to understand, interpret and summarise
   C A composition (letter, report, etc.) based on information provided
4. LISTENING COMPREHENSION (30 minutes)

5. INTERVIEW (12 minutes)
    A Questions based on or related to a photograph
    B A two-minute speech
    C Reading aloud of a character part in a play
    D An appropriate and socially acceptable response to a situation.

   With the exception of Listening Comprehension exercises, and of essay-writing (Composition A), the latter fully covered in existing chapters, material representative of all other sections of the examination is provided in the eight new Practice Papers. In addition model Composition, Reading Comprehension and Use of English test papers now conclude the book.

   A *Key* to this course is published separately, and the material is presented clearly enough for the student working alone to benefit from it.

Contents

viii

Part I   Comprehension and Practice

PRACTICE PAPER 1

I   READING COMPREHENSION

Section A

In this section you must choose the word or phrase which best completes each sentence. Write down each number and beside it the letters **A, B, C, D** and **E**. Then in each case cross through the letter before the word or phrase you choose. Give one answer only to each question.

1. Only hotel guests have the ——— of using the private beach.

    A occasion   **B** possibility   **C** privilege   **D** habit
    E permission

2. The lorry was travelling at a high ———.

    A rate   **B** quickness   **C** acceleration   **D** speed
    E rapidity

3. The children were having a wonderful time ——— on the frozen lake.

    A slipping   **B** gliding   **C** slithering   **D** skidding
    E sliding

4. Our new house is very ——— for the office as I can get there in five minutes.

    A comfortable   **B** suitable   **C** available   **D** convenient
    E pleasant

5. Beside washing that cut, put some —— on it in case you have got some dirt in it.

    A medicine   **B** disinfectant   **C** antiseptic   **D** antidote
    E deodorant

6. The Fosters believe so firmly in family equality that they never go to visit their friends without their children's ——.

    A allowance   **B** permit   **C** admission   **D** concession
    E permission

7. She had just —— the shell of the hard-boiled egg and was starting to peel it off.

    A snapped   **B** cracked   **C** fractured   **D** shattered
    E burst

8. New mineral resources may be discovered during the forthcoming Antarctic ——.

    A excursion   **B** voyage   **C** expedition   **D** migration
    E campaign

9. Although he was neat and well-groomed, he was slightly unattractive in ——.

    A outlook   **B** look   **C** appearance   **D** expression
    E feature

10. The bishop preached a farewell sermon to a(n) —— that filled the church to overflowing.

    A congregation   **B** audience   **C** procession   **D** crowd
    E reunion

II READING COMPREHENSION

Section B

In this section you will find after the passage a number of questions or unfinished statements about it, each with four suggested ways of answering or finishing it. You must choose the one which you think fits best. Write the numbers 1–10 and beside each, the letters **A, B, C** and **D.** Then in each case, cross through the letter you choose. Give one answer only in each case. Read the passage right through before choosing your answers.

One of the oldest seafaring ships in the world has been reconstructed after seven years' patient archaeological work. The ship, a 60-foot sailing vessel, sank off the coast of Cyprus in the days of Alexander the Great around the year 300 B.C. Its discovery and restoration have now thrown new light on the
5 ancient trade routes and shipbuilding techniques.

What makes the Cyprus ship so informative is the remarkable state of preservation—mainly due to an unusual feature of its design. The hull was sheathed on the outside with lead that was fixed to the timber with bronze tacks which helped the wooden frame survive 2000 years under the sea.

10 The first clue to the wreck's existence came in 1964 when a sponge diver from the present-day resort of Kyrenia came across a pile of amphorae (ancient storage jugs). Unfortunately his diving air supply ran out just at that moment, so that he had no time to mark the spot. It took him three more years and hundreds of dives before he chanced upon them again.

15 He reported his find to an underwater archaeological team from the University of Pennsylvania, which was surveying the Cypriot coasts for wrecks. After checking his description, the team decided to concentrate their resources on the Kyrenia ship, and over the next two years a team of no fewer than 50 archaeologists and divers took part in the excavation.

20 With the help of a metal detector, the team discovered that wreckage lay scattered over a 2000-square-feet area, often buried beneath sand and seaweed. Each item was carefully photographed in its place, and a system of plastic grids stretched over the whole site so that it could be accurately mapped.

25 More than 400 amphorae lay buried in the sand. The ship had been carrying a cargo of wine and almonds. More than 9000 of these were found in or nearby the amphorae, their outer shells still perfectly preserved. As well as

2

these, there were 29 stone grain mills, being carried both as cargo and as ballast. These were carefully stowed in three rows parallel to the axis of the keel. 30

As well as the main cargo, there were other small finds. Four wooden spoons, four oil jugs, four salt dishes and four drinking cups suggested the number of crew on the ship's last voyage. There was an axe, and near the intricately carved mast lay a wooden pulley, used to raise and lower the yard. A bronze cauldron, used perhaps to prepare the crew's meals, was also lying 35 in the wreck.

Of five bronze coins found, none dated earlier than 306 B.C. Carbon-14 analysis of the almond cargo pinpointed their date at about 288 B.C., but that of the ship's planking suggested an earlier date of 370 B.C. Thus the Kyrenia ship was more than 80 years old the day she sank—a long life for a wooden 40 hull and proof of the good craftsmanship of her builder.

Raising the delicate timbers of the ship presented grave problems. The archaeologists decided that trying to lift them out in one piece would be too risky. Instead the hull was cut into sections on the site by an electric under-water saw. Then each carefully labelled piece was raised to the surface by a 45 lifting balloon. Once out in the air again, each timber section was treated with a preservative called polyethylene glycol. This replaces the water in the weak-ened wood so that the timbers do not disintegrate when they dry.

Until the discovery of the ship, little was known of the Eastern Mediterran-ean trading vessels, their routes or their cargoes. Thanks to the different 50 shaped amphorae, the Kyrenia ship's last voyage can be traced. She had been threading her way southwards along the coast of Anatolia, stopping at the islands of Samos, Kos and Rhodes, before continuing eastwards to the north coast of Cyprus.

What calamity caused her to sink about a quarter of a mile east of the 55 horseshoe harbour of Kyrenia remains a mystery. There are no traces of fire on board, which rules out the possibility of lightning. Perhaps a sudden autumn storm simply caught her four-man crew unawares. They seem to have abandoned ship, for no human remains were found on board.

1. The discovery of the ship is important to students of early ships and their routes because

   A as the oldest surviving ship it is a valuable source of information
   B it is a useful means of extending their existing knowledge
   C its discovery has changed completely their existing ideas
   D this provides the only information about early Mediterranean trading ships that has come their way.

2. Archaeologists were able to learn a lot about the construction of the ship because

   A it was discovered only a short distance from land
   B there were various forms of tools and equipment
   C it was in a surprisingly good condition
   D a lot of its cargo still remained

3

3. How was the first discovery of the ship made?

   A by chance
   B as a result of an archaeological survey
   C with the help of a metal detector
   D by underwater photography

4. When informed of the discovery the archaeological team decided

   A to narrow down their investigation to this ship
   B to include this research in their programme
   C to organise a team to search for other wrecks in this area
   D to examine at the same time other nearby wrecks

5. Which of the following tasks is not stated as having formed part of the research?

   A recording pictures of the finds
   B making an exact plan of the position of the finds
   C locating all the parts of the ship and its cargo in that area
   D storing everything carefully in rows

6. The stone grain mills were being carried to

   A provide flour for food for the crew
   B contain stores of corn
   C keep the ship low enough in the water
   D strengthen the structure of the ship

7. The approximate date of the shipwreck could be decided from

   A the dates on the coins found
   B the analysis of the age of the materials from which the ship was built
   C the scientifically-determined age of some of the cargo
   D a knowledge of the date of the building of the ship together with her known age

8. The archaeologists faced a considerable problem in raising the ship because

   A the structure would be extremely heavy to bring to the surface as a whole
   B raising all the separate parts would be a long and tedious job
   C the materials were very frail and could be damaged
   D the raising of such a large structure might involve some of the men in accidents

9. The ship's route could be determined from

   A the discovery that she had been travelling southwards and eastwards
   B the various containers she was carrying
   C the types of wines on board
   D the fact that she had sunk just near Kyrenia

4

10. Which of the following items of information is quite certainly correct?

    A there were no survivors of the shipwreck
    B the disaster took the crew by surprise
    C no member of the crew was drowned as a result of the wreck
    D a considerable amount of the cargo remained on board

III USE OF ENGLISH

Section A

1 Fill each of the numbered blanks in the passage with one or two suitable words.

We were having such —— (1) weather in London that Roberta suggested —— (2) Christmas week in an Italian seaside resort we had visited the previous summer. We thought this idea —— (3) for —— (4) day or two and then —— (5) our minds to go. When I asked my brother whether I could —— (6) some money from him, he advised me —— (7) anywhere —— (8) that time of year but finally —— (9) help us when I promised faithfully —— (10) him back the loan from my next month's salary. The manager of a local tourist office gave us some advice and a lot of useful —— (11) about our —— (12) from London to Italy, hotels and the type of clothes —— (13) with us for Christmas week. "You'd better —— (14) London at —— (15) two days before Christmas if you can, if not earlier, so —— (16) be —— (17) plenty of time for the Christmas Eve celebrations," he said. "I hope you enjoy —— (18) much."

Now we are looking forward —— (19) in a warm sunny country for a few days. But we have just heard —— (20) radio that icy gales are sweeping Southern Europe while London is now enjoying blue skies and warm sunshine.

2 Finish each of the following sentences in such a way that it means exactly the same as the sentence printed before it.

Example: Everybody present found fault with the committee's decision.
            Nobody present ....

Answer: Nobody present approved of the committee's decision.

    He had never been on board a ship before.
1. This was the ....
    He kept making angry comments during the reading of the radio news.
2. While ....
    It was your father's wish that you should become an engineer.
3. Your father wanted ....
    "Let's take some flowers to Aunt Penelope," June suggested.
4. June suggested ....
    Someone has stolen the Chief Constable's car.
5. The Chief Constable ....
    As he grows older he becomes increasingly cheerful.
6. The older. ....
    He painted his letter-box so that it looked more conspicuous.

5

7. He painted his letter-box red so as. ....
   She asked a policeman the distance to the nearest post office.
8. "How ....
   He went upstairs less quietly than he could have.
9. He went upstairs more...
   Permission for you to use the school library can be taken for granted.
10. It can be taken for granted ....

3 Each of the following pairs of sentences can be combined, while retaining the original meaning, by changing the first sentence so that it can form part of the second sentence. Write the new single sentence in each case.

Example: My friends offered accommodation immediately. This relieved my anxiety.

Answer: My friends' immediate offer of accommodation relieved my anxiety.

a) He failed to complete the course. This spoilt his chances of promotion.
b) He criticised the plan repeatedly. This exasperated everybody.
c) The public received the news enthusiastically. This surprised no one.
d) He signed his father's name on a cheque. This was regarded as forgery.
e) The party tried to seize power by force. This resulted in disaster.
f) The Government devalued the pound a second time. This caused a new monetary crisis.
g) The workers are dissatisfied with the new wage rates. This has led to a strike threat.
h) My friend attacked his previously-held convictions fiercely. This left me speechless.

1
Reading, Vocabulary and Comprehension

The World Invades London

The British may have long been a nation of shopkeepers but they are coming late to the business of tourism. For the past century it has been they who have done the touring while their own hotels have slumbered in atmosphere and inefficiency and even the pubs have closed before eleven. Now, somewhat to their bewilderment, they are having to act as hosts to a vast throng of 5
guests, who, with dollars, francs and marks in their pockets and handbags, are the most successful invaders since the Normans and considerably more welcome. They come to enjoy the antique and traditional but are often less enchanted by the accommodation and catering, which may share the antiquity. At last, even the surprised tourist industry is beginning to open its eyes. Un- 10
fortunately it sees only insoluble problems.

For very many years London has been a business centre with hotel accommodation mainly for visiting businessmen together with other well-to-do travellers and completely inadequate for the swarms of short-stay tourists landing at Heathrow or disembarking at Dover. Some new luxury hotels have 15
soared skywards and a fair number of Victorian houses have been combined to form 'private hotels' of standards from the comfortable to the repellent. Most hotels are expensive—beyond the means of the young teacher or secretary from abroad. The student on holiday fares worst and often finds his accommodation under the unreliable night sky. 20

Every morning the guard is changed at Buckingham Palace with faultless precision and gay military music. The average spectator, squeezed among thousands of others, can glimpse an occasional bearskin and touch of scarlet and at least enjoy the music. Suggestions for a second performance later in the day have been scotched by the guards' acid comment, 'We're doing a 25
job, not acting as performing seals.' It has also been suggested that visitors should be whisked in a given time in groups through Westminster Abbey to relieve the congestion there and the same would apply to the equally-crowded St Paul's and the Tower. A vast football crowd ambles along Oxford Street and surges through the shops there, so that the Londoner leaves the 30
field free for provincials, Americans, Australasians and a babel of exotic tongues.

As a second Westminster Abbey is impracticable and the glamour of (in fact) a slightly seedy Oxford Street remains unrivalled, this problem associated with tourism is indeed insoluble. Tourists are reminded of the charm of 35
the West Country, the romance of Scotland, the historical interest of Stratford, Canterbury and Cambridge but to the once-in-a-lifetime visitor from Kansas City or Adelaide, London will obviously remain the three-day magnet. Other European capitals probably share these problems, and the homeward-

40 bound traveller must revel in swinging his arms, expanding his chest and having time and space to examine and actually enjoy his surroundings.

Notes on the passage

Line

3-4 slumbered in atmosphere and inefficiency

ATMOSPHERE is a usually pleasant feeling of the past derived from one's surroundings.

The hotels are said to have this atmosphere but to have remained too old-fashioned to do satisfactorily their job of looking after visitors.

4 pubs—public houses, places licensed for the sale of alcohol where people can get a drink usually in comfort.

21-22 with faultless precision—moving with perfect control and accuracy

23 a bearskin—a guard's high black fur hat

27 a whisk is a kitchen utensil used for beating mixtures; it is moved quickly—as the visitors would be

28 a vast football crowd—actually a crowd of shoppers, but (apparently) as big as a crowd watching a football match.

31 Australasians—people from Australia and New Zealand.

31 a babel, derived from the Tower of Babel, during the building of which, according to the Bible, everyone started speaking different languages.

Metaphors

The following words are not to be understood literally or exactly but a certain quality or meaning expressed by the word is being referred to. The tourist industry is beginning to open its eyes, which it can hardly do literally. The suggestion is that after a long period of inertia, attention is being paid to what is happening.

Here are some other examples of metaphors in the passage:

their own hotels have *slumbered* (l. 3)
the guards' *acid* comment (l. 25)
a vast *football* crowd (l. 29)
the three-day *magnet* (l. 38)

Comment on the suitability of the metaphor in each case.

Prepositions

Notice the following:

to their bewilderment (surprise, delight, etc.);
act *as* hosts; inadequate *for* the swarms; *on* holiday;
in a given time (but: start *at* a given time);
the same would apply *to* St Paul's; the tourists are reminded *of* the charm;
the traveller must revel *in* swinging his arms.

Word distinctions

What is a comment and what is a commentary?

amble; walk; strut; stride; stroll; saunter; tramp; plod.

The tired farm-worker —— home.
The horse —— slowly.
They —— forty miles in search of work.
The pompous official —— arrogantly.

Couples —— by lazily.
He —— through the town enjoying the sunshine.
He —— out vigorously and angrily.
He —— because the bus had gone.

Expressions to learn and use

beyond the means; — fares worst; — relieve congestion; the same would apply to; — remains unrivalled.

Explaining the meaning of words and phrases

The following words and phrases are explained so as to bring out their meaning as clearly as possible in the context in which they are being used.

a) bewilderment (l. 5)—difficulty in understanding due to surprise
b) invaders (l. 7)—people who force their way in
c) repellent (l. 17)—causing a person to draw back in disgust
d) relieve the congestion (l. 28)—make it easier to move about by reducing the overcrowding
e) amble (l. 29)—move at the slowest pace of a horse
f) seedy (l. 34)—shabby and slightly unpleasant

Explain these words and phrases in the same way:

g) hosts (l. 5); h) traditional (l. 8); i) accommodation (l. 9);
j) insoluble (l. 11); k) swarms (l. 14); l) beyond the means of (l. 18);
m) glimpse (l. 23); n) surges (l. 30); o) provincials (l. 31);
p) impracticable (l. 33); q) revel in (l. 40).

Answers to questions

Short answers of one sentence

The following questions, based on the reading passage, should be answered in complete sentences but not much information is needed. Your answer should however be expressed in your own words and not those of the book. This is important.

1. How has the tourist situation changed in Britain recently?
2. Why are the tourists welcome? (Do *not* begin the answer with 'because'.)
3. Why are the tourists 'less enchanted by the accommodation'?
4. Why is the tourist industry 'surprised'?
5. What is suggested about the shape of the new luxury hotels?

9

6. What difficulties in finding accommodation face many visitors to London?
7. Why do people have difficulty in enjoying the Changing of the Guard?
8. What suggestion has been made about how to reduce overcrowding in Westminster Abbey?
9. Why do Londoners avoid Oxford Street?
10. Why does the homeward-bound traveller revel in 'swinging his arms and extending his chest'?

Longer answers to questions

This exercise is of a similar nature to that in the English Language paper. Each of your answers must be written within the number of words stated. Use only information taken from the passage, but express your answers in your own words as far as possible.

Three essentials

1. Keep within the number of words stated. The maximum may not be exceeded, but this figure also suggests a minimum.
Not more than 70 suggest that 40 or even 50 words would be too few, as not enough material is being included.
2. Use only information taken from the passage.
But make sure you include all the relevant information. Check all through the passage to see that everything is in your answer.
Consider however if all you have extracted is really relevant. This assessment of relevance demands careful reading and thinking.
3. The material from the passage is expressed in your own words.
Do not go to extremes in trying to do this. 'A farmer' need not become 'a cultivator' or 'an earthquake' 'a violent convulsion of the earth'. A single word of this kind may of course be retained when there is no suitable equivalent. But longer word groups do not appear in their original form. Usually they merely become part of a more general idea which is being expressed in some other way.

EXAMPLE
What are suggested as the main reasons for insufficient and inefficient hotels in Britain and London? (Not more than 80 words)

Ideas from the passage

a) Hotels out-of-date because British more accustomed to touring abroad themselves than to using own hotels.
b) Tourism new industry.
c) Very large number of foreign tourists now arriving.
d) London hotels previously catered chiefly for businessmen and rich people. So now too few and expensive for the many poorer tourists.

47 words.
(The fact that their own hotels were not much used by the British is very strongly implied.)

Notice that these notes are already expressed in words different from those of the passage.

The ANSWER is now based on these notes:

British hotels are often out-of-date because British people have been more accustomed to visiting foreign countries than to staying there themselves. The recently-developed tourist industry has been unprepared for the very large number of visitors who are now coming to Britain. Until recently hotels have catered principally for businessmen and rich people so there are not yet enough satisfactory hotels available and the majority of those that exist are too expensive for many potential guests.

75 words.

Further exercises

Use material from the passage only, but this should be expressed in your own words.

1. Besides possible unsatisfactory hotel accommodation, what other difficulties may a visiting tourist experience in London? (Not more than 60 words)
2. In what ways has the tourist industry tried to deal with some of the problems and how far have these been successful? (Not more than 90 words.)

Practice 1

SECTION I GRAMMAR

A. Collective nouns   *Reference material*
                                                page 190
EXERCISES
a) State the living or inanimate things referred to by each of the following collective nouns, e.g. a forest (trees):

. a choir; a gang; a constellation; an archipelago; a staff (several possibilities here); a navy; a fleet (may be the same as navy, but there are other possibilities); a mob; a procession; a congregation; an orchard; a family; a board; a brood; a team; a jury; a cluster; a catalogue; a convoy; a bunch (various possibilities); an anthology; an audience; a swarm; a crew (two different possibilities); a suite (three different possibilities); a herd; a grove; a copse; a bench; a squadron; a bundle (various possibilities); a pack (various possibilities); a flock (two different possibilities).

b) Choose the more suitable one from each of the grouped alternatives in the following sentences:

1. The audience is/are listening to a Beethoven symphony.
2. The class is/are taking notes, its/their pen/pens scribbling quickly over its/their exercise books.
3. The suite of furniture he bought was/were of contemporary design. It/They was/were quite expensive.
4. Can you see that huge flock of birds in the distance? It/They is/are coming this way.

II

5. I think the jury is/are disagreeing over its/their verdict. It/They may have to be dismissed.
6. A pack of cards is/are scattered over the table. It/They was/were opened only a few minutes ago.
7. The Board of Directors is/are shaking its/their head/heads at the Chairman's speech. I think it/they disapproves/disapprove of what he is saying.
8. A panel of distinguished people has/have been chosen to judge this competition. It/They is/are meeting tomorrow.

B. Abstract nouns

Reference material
page 190

EXERCISES

a) What abstract noun has the same root as each of the following words? Explain the meaning in each case.

  1. ambitious; religious; oblivious; cautious; rebellious.
  2. reject; contract; intend; extend.
  3. concentrate; deliberate; emancipate; accommodate; execute.
  4. condemn; resign; prepare; confirm.
  5. repeat; inhibit; extradite.
  6. satisfy; purify; rectify.
  7. extinguish; distinguish.
  8. resolve; revolve; absolve.
  9. accede; concede; recede; proceed.
  10. ambiguous; incongruous; contiguous; assiduous.
  11. generous; pompous; atrocious.
  12. transparent; delinquent; efficient.
  13. visible; audible; legible; eligible; credible.
  14. glorious; luxurious; furious.
  15. honest; modest; difficult.
  16. conform; infirm; extreme; insane.
  17. punctual; equal; legal; stupid.
  18. poor; humble; orthodox.
  19. attain; achieve; content.
  20. accept; persevere; resist; arrogant; extravagant; brilliant.
  21. violent; indifferent; independent.
  22. beautiful; respectful; delightful; conceited; thrifty; charming.
  23. criticise; magnetise; heroic; dogmatic; Catholic; Liberal; Protestant.
  24. boy; knight; priest.
  25. wise; boring; free.
  26. grateful; solitary; apt; inept.
  27. lazy; tidy; pretty; lovely.
  28. gentle; tender; eager; helpless.
  29. angry; hungry.
  30. proud; hate; pathetic; virtuous.

b) In some cases more than one noun may be derived from the same root, each noun having a slightly different meaning. What various nouns are connected with the following words? Give their meanings.

prefer; confer; succeed; pretend; man; attend; admit; remit; tolerant; desperate; friend; apply.

C. A note on possessive forms

What is the difference between:
  (i) 'She is Michael's sister'. 'She is a sister of Michael's'?
  (ii) 'my uncle' and 'an uncle of mine'?
  (iii) 'their cottage' and 'a cottage of theirs'?

Though this is grammatically correct, could we speak of 'a father of mine'?

It is not grammatically possible to say 'a friend of me'. The possessive pronoun must be used in any similar expression.

SECTION II PUNCTUATION

Reference material
page 229

EXERCISES

A. Full Stop

a)   Use each of the following abbreviations in a short sentence in such a way that its meaning becomes clear. There is no need in this exercise to write the abbreviation in full.

(i) c.cs.   (ii) km.   (iii) ft.   (iv) oz.   (v) cwt.   (vi) Ltd.   (vii) B.Sc.
(viii) e.g.   (ix) A.D.   (x) etc.   (xi) M.P.   (xii) J.P.   (xiii) a.m.   (xiv) cf.
(xv) V.I.P.   (xvi) Gdns.   (xvii) R. Avon   (xviii) i.e.   (xix) Ph.D.
(xx) Mt. Snowdon   (xxi) 20°C.   (xxii) V.C.

The following are not true abbreviations but should be used in the same way.
(xxiii) M6   (xxiv) A40   (xxv) MDCLXVI

b)   Rewrite these sentences in such a way that the abbreviation can be avoided altogether.

(i) Soaps, cosmetics, combs, etc., as well as medicines, can be bought in a British chemist's shop.
(ii) A self-employed worker, e.g. a shopkeeper, may contribute to the scheme.
(iii) Close relatives of those on whom degrees will be conferred, i.e. a father, mother, husband or wife, are invited to the ceremony.
(iv) He came to work at 10.30 a.m. and left at 4 p.m.

c)   Explain the abbreviated forms in this advertisement:

FLAT TO LET: S/c. 1st fl. 1 r.r. 1 bedr. k. & b. Balc. All mod. con. c.h. c.h.w. all elec. excel. cg fac. garage av. 20 mins Vict. £20 p.w. incl. Tel 19283 aft. 6.30.

B. Semi-colon and colon

EXERCISE
Insert a colon or a semi-colon where required in the following sentences:

(i) He reached the crest of the hill and paused for breath ahead the road levelled and then rose steeply again.
(ii) The following qualifications are essential for the post an honours degree in English, proficiency in shorthand and typewriting and some experience in journalism.
(iii) Though he is inventive and original, his work is erratic accordingly I cannot recommend him for promotion.
(iv) The meal consisted of a hunk of stale bread, some mouldy cheese and two pickled onions.
(v) Foreigners wonder at the Englishman's concern for animals they say that many English people think more of animals than they do of children.
(vi) The screen is small and the pictures are not sharply defined nevertheless we prefer the set to our neighbour's.
(vii) More and more reports prove the dangers of heavy smoking the risk of contracting certain diseases may be sixty per cent higher for regular smokers.

SECTION III WORD ORDER—A

Reference material
pages 234-5

EXERCISE

Write the following sentences with the word groups arranged in what appears the most suitable order for the meaning expressed.

In some cases the preposition TO or FOR may have to be added.

  (i) his symptoms / his doctor / explained / the patient.
  (ii) good-morning / you must / him / say.
  (iii) the actress / dared to ask / her age / the reporter.
  (iv) she / a lie / I think / him / told.
  (v) the mini-skirt / his grandmother / gave / he.
  (vi) offer / I / a cigar / you / may?
  (vii) some fish / she will bring / the dog / the cat / some bones / and.
  (viii) the way he planned to decorate the room / described / his wife / he.
  (ix) us / expressed / his doubts / the scientist.

Composition

1. WRITING SENTENCES

Two of the most common faults in composition are dealt with here.

a) INCOMPLETE SENTENCES

A fault common to students writing in any language, not least their own, is the creation of incomplete sentences. Great writers often find the incomplete sentence an ideal vehicle for the expression of their ideas, though even in the case of a skilled writer, such practices may produce unfavourable effects: a breathlessness and jerkiness which wearies the reader is one of the commonest. The student writer, however, needs to observe carefully the rules which the experienced craftsman may in special circumstances ignore. Moreover, examiners often have strict ideas about sentence structure and may well deduct marks for failure to conform.

b) INADEQUATELY CONNECTED SENTENCE GROUPS

On the other hand an equally common mistake is the stringing together of a number of complete sentences with commas, or, worse, with no punctuation at all.

Phrases and clauses

Examine this passage:

'That first morning in the Sports' Hotel, he got up earlier than usual and went to the window. Everywhere—snow. Snow driven by the wind against the window panes, piled on the sill, outlining the birch branches in the garden below. Snow thick on the slope to the valley. Snow still tossing and whirling in pirouetting flakes against a slate-grey sky.'

Perhaps in order to emphasise the universality of the snow the writer of this passage has used only one complete sentence, the first. All other full stops terminate PHRASES.

  (i) Consider the word group 'Everywhere—snow',—an adverb and a noun. There is no verb of any kind here.

There are very many PHRASES WITHOUT VERBS. Here are a few:

'of poor quality', 'here and there', 'from time to time'.

Prepositional phrases are common enough: 'in accordance with', 'in front of', 'on account of', 'owing to', 'in the case of'.

One type of phrase can indeed form a whole sentence (though, in fact, a subject and verb are understood). This is the sudden exclamation:

How beautiful!
What a nuisance!

What other word group in the passage about snow is a phrase with no verb form?

(ii) Other phrases in the passage have a verb form.
'Snow driven by the wind . . ., piled on the sill, outlining . . .', 'Snow still tossing and whirling . . .'.

But not one of the verbs is a FINITE form, one which agrees in person and number with a SUBJECT and has a tense, mood and voice. 'Tossing', for example, is a present participle. A finite verb form here would be 'was tossing' with the subject 'Snow'. An imperative form of the verb has the understood pronoun 'You'.

A **phrase**, therefore, is a group of words expressing an idea but not containing a finite verb, that is, a verb in agreement with a subject.

A **clause** is a group of words containing a finite verb.

EXERCISE
Say which of the following groups of words are phrases and which are clauses:
at the end of the day; to be or not to be; time passes; all things considered; with reference to your letter of the 4th May; be quiet; how annoying!; reading between the lines; made to measure; don't speak; please forward; cottage to let; English spoken here; wishing you all the best; contents vacuum sealed; while travelling; while the bus is moving.

Subordinate and main clauses

Supposing you are asked to answer the following questions in complete sentences What is wrong with the answers given?

a) Why is English spelling difficult?
Because English is not a phonetic language.
b) Why was the new telescope installed in the laboratory?
So that the students could study astronomy as an extra subject.

All clauses, subordinate and main clauses, contain finite verbs, but ONLY THE MAIN CLAUSES FORM COMPLETE SENTENCES. Even then, some of these main clauses must include subordinate clauses in order to make sense. A MAIN CLAUSE however exists in its own right, even when its subject or object is itself a subordinate clause. A SUBORDINATE CLAUSE exists only to form part of a main clause or to qualify or modify some part of a main clause (or another subordinate clause). A SUBORDINATE CLAUSE CANNOT THEREFORE EXIST ALONE.

EXERCISE
Extend each of the phrases and clauses in these word groups into a complete sentence using as few words as possible to do so. The sentences need no alteration.

(i) which he brought with him
(ii) having spent all his money
(iii) when you were there?
(iv) when you were there
(v) sit down
(vi) I don't know
(vii) in the event of an earthquake
(viii) who is an old friend of mine
(ix) because he is bad-tempered
(x) what to do next
(xi) so that they could find their way back
(xii) where I put the key
(xiii) when to take it out of the oven
(xiv) in order to hear better

2. WRITING PARAGRAPHS

Study the following paragraph:

Many people who have never been there still believe that London is permanently blanketed by fog. Yet those who spend a winter in London are often disappointed at the non-appearance of this horror. That fogs do form is undeniable. And although a journey through an invisible muffled world may at first seem exciting, this enjoyment is short-lived: smog, that filthy mixture of smoke and fog, brings suffocation to the asthmatic, violent death to the road-user and discomfort to everybody. But fogs of this kind are rare in London. During the average winter, day follows cloudy day without obscuring even the more distant landmarks. It is true that London is often sunless, damp and raw, though the occasional sunny day seems all the more attractive by contrast. With its infinite possibilities for hauntings, terror and sudden death, fog is the novelists' delight and it is they who are mainly responsible for the legend of a city eternally submerged in sulphurous vapour.

Features of paragraph construction

a) The paragraph deals with one topic—in this case, the incidence of fog in London.

b) The idea expressed is developed from one sentence to the next.

Here the theme of the paragraph is introduced in the first sentence which in this instance makes a statement supported by the ideas expressed in the rest of the paragraph.

Fog is believed to be permanent in London yet many long-term visitors have never seen it. It does occur with evil consequences occasionally. But London, though cloudy and damp, is only seldom afflicted by thick fog. It is the novelists who have been mainly responsible for the city's reputation.

Notice that the last sentence acts as a suitable conclusion in this case, explaining the cause of the fallacious criticisms mentioned in the first.

c) The sentences vary in length according to the idea being presented. Longer and shorter sentences in succession provide variety.

d) Sentence openings vary. Many are of the conventional 'subject-verb' opening. Some start with an adverbial phrase or clause. Other possibilities are the subject-verb inversion after a negative adverbial opening or the form in which a subject is separated from its verb by a qualifying adjectival clause. Occasionally a single word, a conjunction or possibly an adverb such as 'moreover' or 'accordingly', helps to link the thought in succeeding sentences.

A comparison of this paragraph with those of the reading passage will show that few paragraphs have all these features: sentence openings in the passage vary only in the first. The main essential of a good paragraph is the careful logical development of a single topic.

EXERCISES

A. Using the ideas grouped below, construct logical and carefully formed paragraphs. The order of the ideas may be changed and material may be added if necessary.

a) Awaiting an important interview

NOTES—shown into small room and asked to sit down—check appearance: hair shoes, etc.—feeling of confidence: how one will control the interview—turn over pages of magazine on table—lack of concentration—gradual loss of confidence—realisation of possibility of appearing brash or stupid—panic—mind a blank—summons to the interview room.

b) The drawbacks of living near a large airport

NOTES—Considerable protest whenever idea of development of airport in district discussed—noise: drowning conversation, preventing sleep, causing nervous exhaustion—possible damage to buildings—fall in value of property (house or flat)—increase of traffic—loss of valuable farmland—early railway development caused furious opposition, but airport construction brings far greater discomfort.

c) Reasons against the introduction of right-hand driving in Britain

NOTES—Most countries have right-hand traffic—irritation of visitors to Britain—expense of converting buses and traffic signs—cars not adapted—vast educational programme for closely-packed population—Britain an island so conformity less important—export cars purpose-built—Sweden with small popula-

16

tion and two land frontiers not a good example—no real justification for expenditure of money and possibly lives involved in change.

d) Sundials

NOTES—Oldest method of telling time possibly circle of stones with central stick casting shadow—development into sundial—traditional sundial: metal plate with figures and pointer on pedestal—usefulness and drawbacks—associations—why some people have sundials in gardens—sundial as characteristic of past serenity and lack of science compared with clock, characteristic of modern bustle and accuracy.

Style of writing

Until you can use English almost as easily as your own language, try to write SIMPLY.

Use only words and expressions that you are really sure about and AVOID COMPLICATED SENTENCES.

ALWAYS THINK IN ENGLISH. NEVER TRANSLATE.

B. PARAGRAPHS BASED ON YOUR OWN IDEAS

a) Explain one way in which the town or district you live in might prove unsatisfactory to tourists from other countries.

b) You are alone at night in a country cottage but find it very difficult to fall asleep because of the many noises around. Describe your efforts to sleep and the disturbances.

c) Your feelings when you were trapped in a very large crowd of people.

d) The qualities of a first-class footballer, or a racing cyclist or a good teacher, secretary or nurse.

PRACTICE PAPER 2

I READING COMPREHENSION

Section A

In this section you must choose the word or phrase which best completes each sentence. Write down each number and beside it the letters **A, B, C, D** and **E**. Then in each case cross through the letter before the word or phrase you choose. Give one answer only to each question.

1. The dog felt very ——— when his owners left the house, dressed for a long walk.

    A disillusioned **B** deceptive **C** disappointed
    D deceived **E** cheated

2. Nobody has been able to explain the ——— of this commonly-used expression.

    A reason **B** beginning **C** starting-point **D** cause
    E origin

3. The bus company apparently ignores the many ——— about unpunctuality and overcrowding of buses.

    A reclamations **B** claims **C** griefs **D** objections
    E complaints

4. The forecast predicted ——— weather with snow, sunshine, wind and thunder and that is just what we have had.

    A variable **B** various **C** differing **D** unsteady
    E fluctuating

5. The prisoner ——— that he had assaulted a policeman.

    A refused **B** rejected **C** contradicted **D** declined
    E denied

6. Most people were no longer listening to his long ——— story.

    A irritable **B** boring **C** tiring **D** annoying
    E weary

7. There is often so much traffic on the main thoroughfares that motorists may be able to travel faster on ——— roads.

    A inferior **B** subordinate **C** minor **D** district
    E local

8. A force of desperate men burst out of the besieged city and ——— the army that had surrounded them.

    A won **B** defeated **C** broke down **D** gained
    E submitted

9. He says he would write an English course book if he could find a(n) ——— to deal with the less interesting parts.

A accomplice   **B** ally   **C** collaborator   **D** confederate
E partner

10. The —— cats that are still found in some remote places are distantly related to our friendly domestic companions.

A savage   **B** cruel   **C** wild   **D** fierce   **E** untamed

II COMPOSITION

Section B

Read the following passage and then answer the questions on it.

Wise compromise is one of the basic principles and virtues of the British.

If a continental greengrocer asks 14 schillings (or crowns, or francs, or pengoes, or dinars or leis or δραχμαί or πεβα, or whatever you like) for a bunch of radishes, and his customer offers 2, and finally they strike a bargain agreeing on 6 schillings, francs, roubles, etc., this is just the low continental 5 habit of bargaining; on the other hand, if the British dock-workers or any other workers claim a rise of 4 shillings per day, and the employers first flatly refuse even a penny, but after a six weeks' strike they agree to a rise of 2 shillings a day—that is yet another proof of the British genius for compromise. Bargaining is a repulsive habit; compromise is one of the highest human virtues 10 —the difference between the two being that the first is practised on the Continent, the latter in Great Britain.

The genius for compromise has another aspect, too. It has a tendency to unite together everything which is bad. English club life, for instance, unites the liabilities of social life with the boredom of solitude. An average English 15 house combines all the curses of civilisation with the vicissitudes of life in the open. It is all right to have windows, but you must not have double windows because double would indeed stop the wind from blowing right into the room, and, after all, you must be fair and give the wind a chance. It is all right to have central heating in an English home, except in the bathroom, because 20 that is the only place where you are naked and wet at the same time, and you must give British germs a fair chance. The open fire is an accepted, indeed a traditional, institution. You sit in front of it and your face is hot whilst your back is cold. It is a fair compromise between two extremes and settles the problem of how to burn and catch cold at the same time. The fact that you 25 may have a drink at five past six P.M., but that it is a criminal offence to have it at five to six is an extremely wise compromise between two things (I do not quite know between what, certainly not between prohibition and licentiousness), achieving the great aim that nobody can get drunk between three o'clock and six o'clock in the afternoon unless he wants to and drinks at 30 home.

English spelling is a compromise between documentary expressions and an elaborate code-system; spending three hours in a queue in front of a cinema is a compromise between entertainment and asceticism; the English weather is a fair compromise between rain and fog; to employ an English charwoman is a 35 compromise between having a dirty house or cleaning it yourself; Yorkshire pudding is a compromise between a pudding and the county of Yorkshire.

'How to Compromise' from *How to be an Alien*, George Mikes

1. Explain what the writer is referring back to with the word 'etc'. in line 5 and why he uses it in this case.

2. From the same paragraph select the expression which is intended to contrast with 'low continental habit of bargaining' in line 5-6. (Write only the expression.)

3. Suggest a) one of the liabilities of social life mentioned in line 15 and b) one of the curses of civilisation found in houses anywhere in the world (line 16)

4. The two sentences following the opening words 'It is all right . . .' (line 17) satirise another supposed British quality which is referred to specifically in two different expressions, the first of four and the other of eight words. Quote these expressions.

5. Rewrite the sentence beginning 'The open fire . . .' (line 22) using very nearly the same words but with the opening phrase 'Not only . . .'

6. With what meanings are the words 'prohibition' (line 28) and 'licentiousness' (line 28) used in this context?

7. How does the author expose the absurdity of closing public houses with the purpose of reducing drunkenness?

8. In what way can English spelling justifiably be described as an elaborate code-system?

9. Express what is implied about the English weather in a short sentence containing the word 'never'.

10. In not more than 25 words explain how the author makes fun of British ideas and customs.

11. Describe the Englishman revealed in this passage in not more than 40 words.

III GENERAL PRACTICE

In the following sentences, four alternative verbs are suggested for completion. Some of these verbs need to be followed by a preposition to make sense. Write down the number of each sentence, followed ONLY by those verbs which need a preposition and giving the preposition.

Example: 13. Many Londoners
criticise
condemn
complain
find fault
their irregular bus services.

Answer: 13. complain about/find fault with

1. Our teacher
apologised
referred
regretted
explained
his absence yesterday.

20

2. I don't think you would
$$\begin{array}{l} \text{succeed} \\ \text{profit} \\ \text{lose} \\ \text{survive} \end{array}$$
doing a hard day's work.

3. He was
$$\begin{array}{l} \text{congratulated} \\ \text{pitied} \\ \text{delighted} \\ \text{envied} \end{array}$$
having eight children.

4. Nobody is
$$\begin{array}{l} \text{objecting} \\ \text{opposing} \\ \text{resisting} \\ \text{interfering} \end{array}$$
the scheme to close down the factory.

5. He tries to
$$\begin{array}{l} \text{assist} \\ \text{contribute} \\ \text{subscribe} \\ \text{support} \end{array}$$
so many good causes that he never has a penny to bless himself with.

6. The man next door is
$$\begin{array}{l} \text{paying} \\ \text{purchasing} \\ \text{disposing} \\ \text{saving up} \end{array}$$
a second-hand car.

7. His collection of records
$$\begin{array}{l} \text{includes} \\ \text{consists} \\ \text{comprises} \\ \text{covers} \end{array}$$
jazz, folk-songs and madrigals.

8. My room-mate
$$\begin{array}{l} \text{insists} \\ \text{disapproves} \\ \text{persists} \\ \text{delights} \end{array}$$
getting up early.

9. He always
$$\begin{array}{l} \text{differs} \\ \text{supports} \\ \text{opposes} \\ \text{disagrees} \end{array}$$
other people's opinions.

10. The Opposition intends to
$$\begin{array}{l} \text{fight} \\ \text{agree} \\ \text{accept} \\ \text{dissent} \end{array}$$
the new proposals.

11. Mary's great-aunt was
$$\begin{array}{l} \text{warned} \\ \text{punished} \\ \text{advised} \\ \text{caught} \end{array}$$
exceeding the speed limit.

12. He
$$\begin{array}{l} \text{depended} \\ \text{confessed} \\ \text{considered} \\ \text{specialised} \end{array}$$
stealing for a living.

IV THE INTERVIEW

Reading Aloud to the Examiner

About ten minutes before a candidate's interview, he is handed an extract from a play and asked to prepare to read aloud what is said by one of the characters. During the interview itself he reads this part while the examiner reads any other parts. According to the syllabus:

'The main emphasis in the assessment will be on pronunciation factors, including stress, intonation and rhythm, and appropriate forms.'

GENERAL ADVICE ABOUT READING ALOUD

1 A student embarking on a Proficiency course should already be able to read and speak clearly and intelligibly enough for there to be no difficulties in understanding him.

2 His SOUNDS (vowels, diphthongs and consonants) may not yet be perfect but he should be aware of those that need extra care and practice and should be working to improve them throughout the course to a standard where the faults are hardly noticeable.

3 He should be familiar with WEAKENINGS, both in individual words (e.g. condition kəndíʃən; particular pətíkjələ; suggestion sədʒéstʃən) and in connected speech:

Peter and Pauline were looking at some notices that had been put up on a board that was near the entrance to the library.

píːtə‿r‿ən póːliːn wə lúkıŋ‿ət səm nóutısız ðət‿əd bın put‿ʌp‿ɔn‿ə bɔːd ðət wəz nıə ði‿éntrəns tə ðə láıbrərı.

4 STRESS will still cause some difficulty (among others to French speakers, who have to escape from their own egalitarian stress system) to some extent in individual words and more especially in word groups and sentences.

5 A more theoretical approach to INTONATION and EMPHASIS, with the closely-linked subject of RHYTHM, may well be new to the student starting a Proficiency course. The following is a very brief summary of some features of this aspect of speech.

a) INTONATION refers to the rise or fall of the voice at the end of a speech unit (a single word, phrase, clause or sentence) to indicate meaning and/or feeling and is an extremely complicated subject. Here are one or two basic principles, but these are open to almost infinite variations.

For convenience here, a falling intonation pattern (When did you come? come ↘) is called Pattern 1 and a rising intonation (Is he? ↗) is called Pattern 2.

(i) STATEMENTS
A plain statement without any implication: *Pattern* 1
I don't like tea. (↘)

(ii) QUESTIONS
A. with a 'yes' or 'no' answer: *Pattern* 2
Are you going to church? (↗)

B. with an unknown answer (unless surprise or a request for repetition is expressed): *Pattern* I
   Why are you going? _⁻
   but: What did you just say?⌡

(iii) EXCLAMATIONS: *Pattern* I
   What a beautiful day! How tired I feel!

b) EMPHASIS can also express meaning and feeling. Say the following sentence with as many different meanings as you can be emphasising different words.

My previous employer is renting a caravan for the whole of July.
Emphasis is indicated by a much wider range of voice tone.

   He (❭) did it, not I (❭).

A person with a good ear for rhythm and pitch normally has few problems with stress and intonation.

Practice Passage

Read the following passage silently first with special attention to the part of Alexander, which is the part you will read aloud later. Then practise in detail the first two long speeches, with the help of the notes at the end. The name Philotas can be pronounced filoúta:s

Alexander: For all that, Philotas, I am still your friend, and determined, if I can, to save you from yourself. You call me a despot. What else can I be? How else can this vast Empire be ruled but by despotism? Like Athens—with a democratic revolution every year? You say I make myself a god. Do you remember Aristotle, my tutor in the old days? You remember what he used to say to us all? The true King is a god among men—bound no more than Zeus by country or law—because he himself is the law? Can you blame me then, if, in the loneliness of my present state, I sometimes think of myself as the kin of God? (He pauses and turns away.) It's a small comfort and seems to me to harm no one.

Philotas: No one but yourself.

Alexander (savagely): What is that to you? I give you the lie, Philotas. What a man is—is nothing. What a man does is everything. I don't know —and don't care—what I am— or what I do to myself with my thoughts and deeds. I do know—and do care—what I've done; and what I've done I shall not allow to be destroyed either by the actions of my enemies or the taunts and jeers of my friends. Which is why, in a few days' time, you—my dear friend—may have to die; (he pauses) for this document will be your death warrant, if I give it to the Council.

Philotas: Then why give it them?

Alexander: I shall burn it if you fulfil one small condition.

Philotas: That I fall down in public and worship you as a god?

Alexander: That you make a speech at your trial, in which you retract every word you've ever said against me; and that you swear to me now, on the most solemn oath you know, that you will never say another as long as you live.

23

Philotas:	(after a pause; quietly): But that's what I just said, Alexander. That I fall down in public and worship you as a god. (He rises, finishes his drink and puts the goblet on the table.) Thank you for the wine, Alexander.

(*He turns.*) Guard.
(*The soldier enters.*)

Take the assassin back to his gaol.

Alexander:	Philotas—I beg of you—think before you do this.
Philotas:	(turning to Alexander): Oh, I've thought, Alexander. I've thought quite long enough. What else do you suppose I do in my cell all day—and all night? I'm tired of thinking.
Alexander:	What I ask of you is not a great thing to ask of a friend.
Philotas:	It's a small thing to ask of an enemy. If you were Darius, I would be a fool not to save my life on such terms. But you're not— you're Alexander—and what you ask is greater than the world we've conquered together.
Alexander:	Do you expect me to have mercy for you?
Philotas:	No. I understand what you must do.
Alexander:	Philotas—have pity on me—if not on yourself.
Philotas:	I have, strange to say. Pity on both of us.

Adventure Story, Terence Rattigan

NOTES ON ALEXANDER'S FIRST TWO SPEECHES

Pattern 1 is a falling intonation; *Pattern* 2 a rising one.

Questions: (a) with an unknown answer (b) with a 'yes' or 'no' answer.

FIRST SPEECH

Sentences

1 A statement: *Pattern* 1
   Emphasis: slight on 'all'; strong on 'still'.
   Remember that 'yourself' is stressed on the second syllable.
2 A statement: *Pattern* 1
   Emphasis: slight: call; stronger: despot.
3 Question (a): *Pattern* 1
   Emphasis: else
4 Question (a): *Pattern* 2
   Emphasis: else   but
   Slight pause—*Pattern* 2—at 'ruled'.
5 There are really two questions here, one ending on 'Athens', both (b) type with *Pattern* 2.
   A slight pause after 'Athens'.
6 A statement: *Pattern* 1
   Some emphasis on 'you'.
7 Question (b): *Pattern* 2——to Aristotle (æristótl—English pronunciation).
   Second half of sentence an echo: also *Pattern* 2.

24

8   Question (b): *Pattern* 2. Emphasise 'he'.
      'say' is the last stressed word with each following word rising.

9   A question, connected in sense with the preceding sentence. Little variation in tone until the second 'is' and the final Pattern 2 on 'law'.

10   Question (b): *Pattern* 2 at the end and also at the pauses on 'then' 'if' and 'state'.
      Emphasise 'kin'.

11   Statement: *Pattern* 2 on 'comfort'; *Pattern* 1 'no one'. Emphasise slightly 'small' and 'no'.

SECOND SPEECH

1   Question (a): *Pattern* 1. Emphasise strongly 'you'.

2   Statement: *Pattern* 1.

3   Statement: *Pattern* 1. Emphasise strongly the first 'is' and 'nothing'.
      A noticeable pause at the dash.

4   A statement, largely an echo of sentence 2: *Pattern* 1. Emphasise strongly 'does' and 'everything'.

5   Statement: *Pattern* 2 'know'; *Pattern* 1 'care' 'am' 'myself' and 'deeds'. Emphasise 'know' 'care' 'am' 'myself'.

6   Statement: *Pattern* 2 'know' second 'done' 'enemies'; *Pattern* 1 'care' first 'done' 'destroyed' friends'.
      Emphasise strongly: 'do (know)' 'do (care)' first 'done' second 'what' 'destroyed' 'actions' 'enemies' 'taunts' 'jeers' 'friends'.

7   Two statements (... die; ... Council): both *Pattern* 1. 'why' 'time' 'warrant': *Pattern* 1.
      'time' 'friend' 'document': *Pattern* 2. Emphasise: 'why' 'you' 'dear friend' 'death'. Emphasise strongly: 'if'.

Practise these two speeches in careful detail. The same method can be applied to a close analysis of Alexander's other speeches.

2
Reading, Vocabulary and Comprehension

A Report

The 'Tawny Lion' Hotel, Northchester

A representative of the Goodfare Travel Agency whose job was to inspect accommodation for the future use and recommendation of the Agency drew up the following report on the 'Tawny Lion' Hotel in Northchester, a small cathedral city.
Here is the report:

THE TAWNY LION HOTEL, NORTHCHESTER 8th November, 19-.

SITUATION	This hotel is situated in the main shopping street of Northchester, three hundred yards from the Cathedral.
5	
ACCOMMODATION	The original building was erected in 1710, but this structure has been largely transformed and extended, the present hotel having been completed in 1910. It is four storeys high with a lift (installed in 1950) serving all floors. The public rooms comprise a dining-room seating fifty people, a lounge and a bar. There are sixteen single and thirty double bedrooms, three of the latter having private bathrooms. Each floor has one bathroom and two separate W.C.'s. All bedrooms are fitted with washbasins with hot and cold water, and a slot-meter controlled radio and gas fire. The courtyard round which the hotel is built provides parking space for ten cars and there is space for twenty more off a side street two hundred yards away. This is quite inadequate.

TERMS Terms are fixed throughout the year and include a three-course breakfast, but not service. Bed and breakfast costs £3.50 and the daily tariff which includes all meals is £5. Reduced rates are available for a stay of more than three nights.

SPECIAL FEATURES The lounge and dining-room are said to have formed part of the original building and they are decorated and furnished in conformity with the style of that period.

COMMENTS The hotel is conveniently situated for sightseeing, business and shopping.

All bedrooms are adequately decorated, furnished

26

and maintained though the furniture is for the most part old-fashioned. The single rooms on the top floor are reasonably big but have the sloping ceiling of an attic. The lounge is equipped with television but is rather dark and has seating for only fifteen people. 35

The dining-room and modern bar are attractive and cheerful.

The service is poor owing to a shortage of staff. Only the head waiter has a London hotel training, the rest of the staff being local or from abroad. All are willing and pleasant but overworked. 40

The food is conventional but well-cooked and adequate in quantity. 45

GENERAL
STATEMENT

The guests appear to be mainly commercial travellers and businessmen. There are some tourists, many of them from America and Australia. This is a reasonably good two to three star hotel, of about the same standard as 'The Wild Rabbit' near the Market Cross. 50 The management is willing to accommodate one coach party at reduced rates at week-ends but not during the week.

General note on the passage

The writing of a report is dealt with later in this chapter. However one important aspect of this kind of composition is noted here.

The writer of a report is doing a practical job. His purpose is to convey information briefly, exactly, clearly and in good English. He is unconcerned with literary excellence.

The side-headings are not essential in a report but serve as an aid to absorbing the contents more rapidly.

In keeping with the plain factual style there are no metaphors here.

Prepositions and Adverbs

Notice the following:

a) IN the main street—a building, people, a car, are IN, not on a street.
b) three hundred yards FROM the Cathedral
c) It is four storeys HIGH.
   He is two metres TALL.
   It is two kilometres LONG.
d) Water consists OF hydrogen and oxygen.
   The cleaning equipment comprises a bucket, a mop, two cloths and a dustpan and brush.
e) fitted WITH washbasins
f) provides parking space FOR ten cars
   provide someone WITH money
   supply someone WITH money

27

g) Reduced rates are available FOR a stay of . . .
   a room available FOR a meeting
h) furnished IN CONFORMITY WITH the style of that period
i) ON (not 'in') the top (first) floor
j) equipped WITH television
k) The service is poor OWING TO a shortage . . .
l) AT reduced rates
m) AT week-ends   DURING the week

Word distinctions

fairly   reasonably   relatively big (but not very big)
rather big (much more definite)

QUITE with two meanings:

It's quite big = It's rather big.
I've quite finished = I've completely finished.

His flat isn't very COMFORTABLE but it's CONVENIENT for getting to his office.

reduce decrease diminish dwindle lessen deteriorate decline

Certain tablets are said to —— a person's weight.
His vitality and creative power are —— with age.
The danger of drowning is —— by swimming instruction.
Owing to the strike, coal supplies are rapidly ——.
I hope that the number of mistakes you make will ——.
Goods will —— if they are not properly stored.
Classes —— as more and more students went back home.

Some of these words are almost interchangeable.

Expressions to learn and use

form part of (ll. 26–7)
for the most part (l. 34)
of about the same standard as (l. 49)

A three-course breakfast   a five-pound note
a ten-mile walk   a four-year-old child
a two-day journey   a three-man team
    a two-star hotel

Notice the singular form of the noun in these hyphenated adjectives.

Explaining the meaning of words and phrases

The following words and phrases are explained so as to bring out their meaning as clearly as possible in the context in which they are being used.

a slot-meter controlled radio (ll. 15–16)—a radio that will operate if money is put into a regulating mechanism
service (l. 40)—attendance from the staff
maintained (l. 33)—kept in good condition

Explain the following words and phrases in a similar way.

a) extended (l. 7); b) a lounge (l. 11); c) a courtyard (l. 16);
d) reduced rates (l. 24); e) conventional (l. 44);
f) commercial travellers (l. 46).

Answers to questions

Short answers of one or two sentences

The following questions, based on the reading passage, should be answered in complete sentences but not much information is needed. Your answers should however be expressed in your own words and not those of the book as far as possible. This is important.

1. How old is this hotel?
2. What arrangements are there for heating bedrooms?
3. What are two things that would form part of the service referred to in connection with the hotel terms?
4. Why in your opinion might a hotel offer reduced rates to guests staying more than three nights?
5. For what reasons might the dining-room and bar be made more attractive than the bedrooms and lounge?
6. What drawbacks might there be to eating in the restaurant?
7. Why should the management refuse to accommodate parties during the week?
8. The hotel is said to be conveniently situated for sightseeing, business and shopping. In what ways is this true?

Longer answers to questions

These questions should be answered within the number of words stated. Use only information taken from the passage, but express your answers in your own words as far as possible.
Remember to include ALL the relevant information. Read right through the passage to make sure.

1. What evidence is there in the passage that the various hotel proprietors have tried to keep up with the times? (not more than 60 words)

NOTES AS AN AID

The interpretation of the words 'keep up with the times' is slightly difficult. One can assume that the following points should be included:

The building was considerably reconstructed early in this century
The addition of a lift
A few private bathrooms available
A radio in each room
Some parking-space for cars
Attractive dining-room and bar
Television in lounge

Remember to use your own words when incorporating these notes in your answer.

2. What features of the hotel might attract an American couple staying there? (not more than 70 words)
3. What things would you yourself find unsatisfactory in this hotel? (not more than 70 words)

Practice

SECTION I GRAMMAR

A. UNCOUNTABLE AND COUNTABLE NOUNS

Reference material
pages 190–5

SUMMARY OF REFERENCE MATERIAL

a) UNCOUNTABLE NOUNS which have only a Singular Form. Those that are most often misused are:

information; advice; furniture; luggage; news.
> I was given several useful pieces of information at the Tourist Office.
> Information for Passengers.
> The news is depressing.

accommodation; traffic; progress; money.
Mathematics is his best subject.
heat; warmth; sunshine.
jewellery; footwear; underwear.
architecture; vegetation.
Gerunds such as: shopping; dancing.
Many commodities including bread.
Uncommon: fruits, fishes.

b) NOUNS WITH UNCOUNTABLE AND COUNTABLE FORMS—RELATED MEANINGS

  (i) Countable forms may indicate 'kinds of', e.g. National foods.
  (ii) Countable forms may indicate separate examples:
    experience an experience;   life a life;
    chocolate a chocolate;   coffee a coffee (a cup of).
  (iii) SPECIAL CASES
    These include
    Space a space;   speech a speech;
    hair a hair (remember: his hair NOT hairs).

c) NOUNS WITH UNCOUNTABLE AND COUNTABLE FORMS—WITH A MEANING CHANGE

Some of these are:

  wood a wood (woods);   tin a tin;   cold a cold;   youth a youth;
  work a work (of art);   damage damages (compensation);
  middle age (adjective = middle-aged) the Middle Ages (adjective = medieval).

d) COUNTABLES THAT HAVE ONLY A PLURAL FORM

Among these are:

  trousers; scissors; (plural) a pair of — (singular);
  goods; cattle; premises.

30

e) UNCOUNTABLE AND COUNTABLE NOUNS—DIFFERENT FORMS FOR
RELATED MEANINGS

EXAMPLES: work   a job;   the police (plural)   a policeman;
clothes, clothing   a garment.

f) ADJECTIVES OF QUALITY USED AS NOUNS—PLURAL MEANING

Example: The poor need help.

EXERCISES
Use should be made of the *Reference material* on pages 190–5.

I. Whenever this is possible change singular to plural forms in the following
sentences. Many forms being already plural or having no plural cannot be changed.
  a) His poetry describes the mountain and its surroundings, rain and wild weather,
     a remote countryside of austere but magnificent scenery.
  b) The resident made little progress in discovering any information about the
     strange machinery dumped in front of his house. As the protruding rod might
     cause damage to traffic he decided to seek the advice of the police.
  c) Business is improving but much more hard work and common sense will be
     called for before any substantial profit can be realised.
  d) She has brought home the week's shopping. Now she has leisure for her
     correspondence.
  e) Yesterday my aunt bought some new furniture for her flat at the seaside. She
     paid for it with some of the money she had saved for her old age.
  f) Sir Albert Alban gave his daughter some jewellery which was designed to off-
     set her dark hair.
  g) The youth makes a practice of using bad language to his parent's friend. Such
     behaviour probably gives him pleasure but it creates gossip locally and causes
     sorrow to his parent.
  h) The news is bad. All food is to cost more, especially fish and fruit.
  i) That shop sells bread and serves afternoon tea. Can I get a drink there
     now?

2. Whenever possible change the words in these sentences into the singular,
leaving unaltered those that cannot be changed. In one or two cases, the singular
form may be a quite different word.
  a) They were wearing strange clothes, far too big for them.
  b) Their earnings come to £20 a week and they have accommodation on the
     premises.
  c) All their belongings, together with the remains of torn-up newspapers and the
     contents of the waste paper baskets, lay scattered over the carpets.
  d) There have been long negotiations at the headquarters of the firms con-
     cerned, but the odds are against any agreements being reached about changes
     in the goods being manufactured.
  e) They were lost in the wilds of the lonely marsh country. It seemed that the
     cattle on the sides of the dykes were the only living creatures in these desolate
     surroundings.
  f) Their business prospered and they became people of means. Yet, despite their
     great riches, they gave no alms to the needy and no thanks to the benefactors
     whose savings had contributed to their welfare.

3. Explain the meaning of each of the following expressions:
  a) There was an air of expectancy in the classroom.
  b) To behave in character, out of character.
  c) He is in practice in Nottingham.
     In practice it is unsatisfactory.
     He is out of practice.
  d) It's in the paper.
     paper work; a paper-chase; a paperback.
  e) to be in irons; iron rations; cast iron; a flat iron; ironwork; ironworks.
  f) by force; in force; come into force.

g) in power; out of power.
   a power station; nuclear power
   power politics.
   He has lost his power of speech.
   at the height of his power.
h) overweight; underweight.
   to gain (put on) weight; to lose weight.
   excess weight.
   a weights and measures inspector.
   a weight-lifter; a heavyweight.
i) a charity performance.
j) space research; space heating; to space out one's visits.
   Don't leave a space at the end of the page.
k) a relief bus; a relief fund; a relief map.
l) a sense of danger; a sixth sense; to make sense.
   In a sense you are right.
   to come to one's senses.
m) He has his wits about him.
   quick wits.
   He is a well-known wit.
n) take something on trust.
   hold something in trust.
   cartels and trusts.
o) mass production; over-production.
p) to pay duty; to do one's duty.
q) Customs' formalities.
r) divided loyalties.
s) by law; a brother-in-law; to take up the law; law and order; against the
   law.
t) the art of making friends; arts and crafts; artistic; artificial; artful.
u) on fire; under fire; a fire brigade; a fire extinguisher; fire insurance.
v) to exceed the speed limit; a speedway; a speed-boat; a speedometer.
w) reinforced concrete; a concrete proposal.
x) a parking meter; a parking offence.
y) a correspondence college.
z) at leisure; leisure-time activities.

4. In each of the following sentences the indefinite article has been inserted in
brackets. This changes the uncountable noun which follows into a countable noun
(with possible plural). Explain the difference in meaning the inclusion of the article
makes.
   a) The businessman attributed his failure to (a) depression.
   b) The young doctor wants to have (a) considerable practice so that he can
      widen his experience.
   c) (A) Wit is usually appreciated.
   d) (An) Iron is heavy.
   e) (A) Speech demands careful attention.
   f) The clergyman would like (a) living in Yorkshire.
   g) Do you consider that (a) strict order is necessary? (Three possible meanings
      here.)
   h) They have established (a) trust which should prove a great asset to their
      business.
   i) The shop assistant has lost (a) weight.
   j) They are preparing (a) gas in the laboratory.
   k) He has recently received (a) royalty.
   l) Is that (a) coloured marble?
   m) (An) Experience can teach us a useful lesson.
   n) Is (a) light invisible?

32

B. THE FORM AND USE OF THE PASSIVE   *Reference material*
page 195

There are many examples of the use of the passive in the reading passage. Here are some of these:

The original building *was erected* in 1710
The present structure *has been* largely *transformed* and *extended,*
the present hotel *having been completed* in 1910
The lounge and dining-room *are said* to have formed part of . . .

In each case it is the existing fact that is important. The DOER of the action is unknown.

This use of the passive is common in reports and practical descriptions. Notice the other use, where the verb, then BY and then the doer, establishes a kind of climax and so may EMPHASISE the importance of the DOER.

EXERCISES
1. Convert the following sentences into the Passive Voice throughout.
In most cases the agent need not be stated. Keep to the corresponding tense.

a) They have installed an extra large refrigerator so that they can keep fresh the additional supplies of food they will need now.

b) Only by the use of the beauty soap we are now introducing, can you ensure the flawless complexion that everyone admires.

c) By early September farmers will have completed the harvest and stored the corn in barns so that they can thresh it.

d) When the residents realised that the authorities were constructing a new motorway through the housing estate, they sent a petition against it to the Ministry of Transport.

e) They have so designed the safe that a person can open it only if someone has already pressed a concealed electric switch.

f) After they have towed the ship into the dock, they will overhaul her thoroughly, redecorate her state-rooms and cabins and install new navigational equipment on the bridge.

g) They did not take anyone in. In fact no one took any notice of what they said.

h) They have decided on a final date by which they expect that everyone will have taken advantage of the council's offer and have installed the necessary equipment in his house.

i) Throughout the week-end gales had lashed the countryside. They had flattened corn in the fields, blown down trees and ripped off roofs, and stories were circulating of ships that the gales had driven aground and wrecked.

j) Everyone hated him. Not only did he force them to work throughout the long hours of daylight and even summon them at nightfall to his castle when he needed extra servants for the banquets that he gave, but he even decided for them whom they should marry, and controlled every part of their lives.

2. Convert the following passage to the Passive Voice. In certain cases where the Active Voice is more suitable than the Passive the former should be retained.

'The Press has reported that people have committed a series of unusual thefts in the West of England. They have cut down and taken away a large number of trees over a wide area. The local inhabitants have discovered what has been happening only recently as they do not often visit the woods in winter, but they think that the thefts may have covered a considerable period as they have affected several districts. The thieves have cut down the trees in remote localities where no one could have heard any noise of sawing or transport by lorries. No one can explain why people have taken the trees or what they will do with them. One can extract alcohol from certain types of wood but one can hardly take seriously the possible existence of a wood-alcohol distillery. Are these secret marauders constructing a hidden village sanctuary in the hills with wooden houses provided with tables, benches and cupboards? Are they surreptitiously selling blocks of wood to the local country people, who, like their German counterparts, are now

33

secretly devoting their time to the construction of cuckoo clocks? Or have the ghosts of the early charcoal-burners, unaware of the existence of coal, petrol and atoms, resumed their ancient activities in these aged woods? People say that the police, gamekeepers and forest wardens are keeping watch so presumably sooner or later someone will explain unromantically the odd and unprecedented mystery of the disappearing trees.'

3. Write an account of each of the following processes, using only the passive voice.

    a) How an egg is fried in a frying pan.
       Begin: A frying pan is placed over heat and a small piece of fat is melted in it
    b) How to light a fire in the open air.
    c) How to use a public telephone in your own country.
    d) How to make coffee.
    e) How to cover a book with brown paper.

4. Change the verbs in the following sentences into the Active Voice. Changes in word order will have to be made and the new subject may have to be suggested. Use the corresponding tense in each case.

    a) A message has been broadcast by the B.B.C. in which a certain Mr Green, who, it is thought, is on holiday in Scotland, has been asked to go to the Overhill Hospital where his wife is being treated after a severe stroke.
    b) If sufficient time and attention have been given by the students to their work, passages can be taken down in shorthand at 60 words a minute and letters can be typed quickly, neatly and accurately. Some knowledge of book-keeping and office practice will have been acquired and the students' command of English should have been increased considerably.
    c) Christmas was being celebrated in every town. Christmas trees, which had been decorated earlier by busy mothers, were being admired by delighted children. The branches were adorned with tinsel while parcels had been placed by each member of the family beneath the tree. Outside, the roofs were festooned with icicles and the ground was covered thickly by the snow while flurries of whirling flakes were still being tossed by the wind.

SECTION II PUNCTUATION

THE APOSTROPHE

Reference material
page 230

EXERCISE

Copy the following word groups, inserting an apostrophe where this is needed.

hell be here soon;   at four oclock;   the fishermans rod; you maynt stay; childrens games;   buy it at the booksellers; shes away; peoples homes; teachers representatives; theyd be pleased to go; the actresss daughter; the bank managers umbrella; theyre away; John Davis horse; ten years work

SECTION III

WORD ORDER B

Reference material
pages 235-6

EXERCISE

Arrange the phrases grouped together, in their correct sentence order. The number over the first one in each case indicates its position in the sentence.

            1
    a) I wonder (the driver of that car) (along the wrong side of the road) (he is doing) (thinks) (what) (now racing).

            3
    b) He fell (a little drunk) (headlong) (coming home late last night) (into the ditch).

34

6

c) The small girl (the furry caterpillar) (along the leaf) (in terror) (as) (slowly) (crawled) (screamed).

1
d) Why (tell) (this morning) (the cook) (me) (did) (that) (not)?

1
e) Some students (in gloomy cafés) (very much) (with one another) (excitedly) (enjoy) (arguing).

1
f) He (had arrived) (told) (at Victoria) (at exactly four minutes past four) (to London) (1944) (me) (on his first visit) (he) (on the 4th April) (that).

3
g) He (during his holiday) (to his mother) (by registered post) (some embroidered linen handkerchiefs) (in Ireland) (sent).

3
h) Her husband (always) (very quietly) (the rest of the family) (still) (at six o'clock) (left) (upstairs) (were) (when he had to go to work) (soundly) (the house) (so as not to disturb) (who) (sleeping).

1
i) The Duchess (choosing vegetables) (has) (in the market) (often) (early in the morning) (carefully) (been seen).

Composition

I WRITING SENTENCES

Kinds of sentence

Many sentences have more than one main clause and each of the following types of sentence is classified according to the clauses of which it consists.

THE SIMPLE SENTENCE
One main clause.

'Owing to the inability of the newly-arrived student to make himself understood in any language but his own, he *decided* not to venture far from home during the first few days of his stay in this country.'

THE COMPLEX SENTENCE
One main clause. Any number of subordinate clauses.

'If I had realised that she would repeat the story that I had told her confidentially, *I should have changed the names of the people* who were involved so that even though the facts became public no one would have known to whom they applied.'

How many subordinate clauses are there here?

THE DOUBLE SENTENCE
Two main clauses. Any number of subordinate clauses.

'*He tasted the wine* which the waiter had poured for him and *then he shook his head.*'

THE MULTIPLE SENTENCE
Three or more main clauses. Any number of subordinate clauses.

'*She tried on one of the shoes* which the assistant had brought but *it was uncomfortably tight* so *she removed it quickly* and (she) *handed it back with the remark* that she had no intention of hobbling between her car and her front doorstep.'

Joining sentences

I. TWO OR MORE MAIN CLAUSES MAY APPEAR IN THE SAME SENTENCE provided that:

  (i) they are separated by a colon or semi-colon (sometimes more effective than a conjunction).
  (ii) they are joined by a co-ordinating conjunction: and; but; so; for; or; (whereas).

Remember that though certain of the following words are sometimes used as though they were conjunctions, they are really adverbs, and appear awkward and ineffective when used as conjunctions:

then; therefore; however; moreover; also; nevertheless; besides; in addition; accordingly.
'He paused at a wayside snack bar for a cup of tea (and) then he settled down to a further long stretch of continuous driving.'

Subordinate clauses can also be linked with each other by means of co-ordinating conjunctions:

'I once met a man who earned his living as an artist and worked as a waiter as a hobby.'

When the conjunction 'and' is used and the subject of the following verb is identical with the subject of the verb just used, the second subject is often though not always omitted. This omission is less common when the conjunction is 'but'.
'That dog growls at the milkman and snarls at the postman but he wags his tail when the butcher boy comes.'

EXERCISE
Join the following groups of sentences using a semi-colon, a colon or a co-ordinating conjunction. In several cases, various words can be omitted.

  a) The Board of Directors discussed the idea for two hours. They came to no conclusion.
  b) Not a leaf stirred in the silent forest. Not a bird sang in the gathering darkness.
  c) Life offered no hope to him. He decided to leave home.
  d) The firm raised the men's wages. Working hours were reduced. Even then the men were not contented.
  e) A new underground railway was constructed. Streets were widened wherever possible. The central area of the city was still extremely congested.
  f) You can travel by train to Newcastle. Then you take a boat to Oslo from there. You can travel overland via the Hague and Copenhagen. In either case you may have to spend two nights travelling.
  g) This correspondence is now closed. Accordingly no further letters will be published at present. The author of the original article will be dealing with further aspects of this subject in a month's time.
  h) You can call at the office to claim your lost property. You can send in a written description. You cannot telephone about it. We have not the staff available to deal with calls.
  i) A critic's job is to assess the value of a work. Many modern critics make their review a vehicle for exhibiting their own personalities.
  j) He claims to be tolerant and detached. He condemns sweepingly all opinions not identical with his own. He rarely examines the implications of what he advocates.

SUBORDINATING CONJUNCTIONS
These conjunctions serve to join a subordinate word group to a clause—a phrase to a subordinate clause, a subordinate to a main clause.

These are some of the commonest:

that; if; unless; although (though); even if; so that; in order that; when; where; how; why; provided that; on condition that; as;

because; since; while (whilst); until; immediately; as soon as; after; before; assuming that.

Subordinating conjunctions precede the subordinate clause in whatever position it appears in the sentence. Many of them may therefore start a sentence. Co-ordinating conjunctions stand between the word groups they join. If they start a sentence, they have the effect of linking the thought expressed in the following sentence with what has gone before.

RELATIVE PRONOUNS as, for example:

who; whom; whose; which; that; what; whoever; whichever; whatever; as;

may also link subordinate to main or other subordinate clauses.

EXERCISE

Join the following groups of sentences using appropriate subordinating conjunctions or relative pronouns. Show where there is more than one way of doing so. The main clause is underlined in each case. Some words may have to be omitted or changed slightly but the ideas introduced must appear in full.

a) He had a sore throat. He had spoken for three hours.
b) My wife was using the vacuum cleaner. I was trying to listen to a broadcast play.
c) He came out of the Conference Room. Reporters surrounded him.
d) He ate too little and worked too hard for weeks on end. He became ill.
e) His mother waited up. He came home.
f) You promise to behave yourself. You shall not go to the party this afternoon.
g) The weather keeps fine. I see no reason why the village fête should not be a success.
h) We shall pay you a thousand pounds. We have the sole publishing rights.

II WRITING REPORTS

Reports can be of many different kinds, from the laconic 'Some improvement shown' on a school terminal report intended for parents to a two-hundred-page Government blue book giving information about betting and gambling, parks and open spaces or civil aviation. They may be written for the Government, newspapers or learned journals, the police authorities, employers, research councils or the general public; they may provide information gathered on the spot about single incidents, about meetings, people, progress in some undertaking; they may be based on statistics, graphs or diagrams. Facts are always set out; conclusions and recommendations are often appended.

Look again at the reading passage. This is an example of the SIMPLE EXACT style of INFORMATIVE writing. Another example is the reading passage of Chapter 3

Characteristics

1. Accuracy of the material.
2. A logical development of facts.
3. A new paragraph for each subject or stage.
4. A plain but efficient style.
   Words chosen for their exactness.
   Sentences of simple construction.

Arrangement

Decide on the subjects or stages of the report before beginning to write.
It is a good idea to list these as a PLAN.
In the reading passage the plan appears as side headings.

Practice topics for reports

Here are a few different types of situation which might lead to the making of a report. Ideas for paragraphing are included in some cases.

REPORTS BASED ON INCIDENTS

1.   A bus passenger refuses to pay his fare as he says he has had to wait forty minutes for the bus. The bus conductor eventually has to find a policeman to eject him. Write the report of the incident handed in by the conductor on his return to the bus depot.
>   a) Details of bus service, route, direction, date, time.
>   b) Where passenger boarded, refusal and reasons.
>   c) Action taken, passenger's name and address given to policeman. Signed by the conductor.

2.   Policemen in a patrol car passing a school at night notice the light of a moving torch inside. They investigate from round the back and catch a man climbing out of a window. He is carrying a suitcase containing silver sports cups. The man is taken to the station and charged.
(Invent names of people and places and also times. Remember this is a police report, not a crime story.)

3.   A report written by a London travel courier after accompanying a party of English tourists from Lucerne to London by special train. During the journey passengers reported that a man from their compartment had gone to get a drink at Bâle Station and not returned. Another passenger claimed he had been cheated in the restaurant car, but this was reported only after the car had already been detached at Chaumont. At Folkestone, only one London train was available for eight hundred passengers landing, necessitating a wait of forty minutes before another train materialised. Write this report.
>   a) Route, date, time.
>   b) Passenger left behind.
>   c) Complaint of cheating.
>   d) Folkestone.
>   e) General comments, e.g. no other incidents or complaints, train and boat punctuality, etc.

NEWSPAPER REPORTS

4.   Write the 200 word article which follows these headlines:
TEENAGE BATTLE IN YOBLEY
RIVAL GANGS TERRORISE LOCAL RESIDENTS

5.   Write a report of about 250 words with these headlines:
AN EXTRA YEAR AT SCHOOL?
DISAGREEMENT BETWEEN TEACHERS IN CONFERENCE

6.   A report of about 250 words with these headlines:
MORE PREHISTORIC CAVE PAINTINGS UNEARTHED
DOG LEADS TO FANTASTIC DISCOVERY

7.   The Duke of Cosmos has opened a foreign student hostel in London. Write a newspaper report of about 250 words on the occurrence, supplying suitable headlines.

8.   Write a newspaper article which might have been written to give preliminary summarised information about some great scientific or engineering discovery or achievement of the past.

9.   The following telegram is received in a London newspaper office from a reporter on the spot. Using some (imaginary) information about the small state of Mutabilia, write a 200–250 word article about the incident for the next edition of the paper. Supply suitable headlines.

38

Hotel Conspiracion, Effervador, Mutabilia

Rebellion in capital. Army Group, leader, General Coodeita in control. Seized airport, police and radio headquarters last night. President disappeared. Many Government leaders arrested. No rioting, soldiers cleared streets. Radio warning population keep calm. Coodeita broadcasting 8 p.m. tonight. Highly organised anti-militaristic workers' units reported gathering outside capital. Anticipate hostilities. Embassy preparing evacuate British women, children.

Jeremy Ferret

REPORTS SUPPLYING PRACTICAL INFORMATION

The facts in such reports are required for utilisation. A future course of action will be decided in accordance with the details given. Usually your own conclusions and in some cases your suggestions will be expected.

10. Your firm wishes to open a small office in a nearby town. You are sent to inspect premises consisting of three or four rooms which are available there and to ascertain whether they are suitable. Write a report on the premises, together with your recommendations.

Here is a suggested plan:

1) Suitability of location of premises.
2) Type of building (height, age, state of repair, etc.) and position of rooms in the building.
3) Number, size, arrangement of rooms.
4) Heating, lighting, state of repair and decoration, etc.
5) Recommendations.

11. You have been sent to make a preliminary examination of a piece of land being considered for development as a holiday camp site. (A more detailed survey prior to actual construction will be made later.) Make a report on the situation of the land and its suitability for development so far as non-technical details are concerned.

12. An educational advisory agency in your own country has asked you to make a report on the courses, organisation and efficiency of a small (imaginary) private language school.

13. You have been asked by the editor of a publication providing information about careers to prepare a short report on your job, including details of salary, hours of work, holidays, duties, qualifications, prospects of promotion, surroundings and other conditions in which you work, advantages and drawbacks of the job and the type of person you would consider best suited for the work.

REPORTS BASED ON DIAGRAMS

14. The following diagram shows the fatal and serious casualties of all road users in Great Britain according to age during a certain year. It is based on information provided by the Royal Society for the Prevention of Accidents.

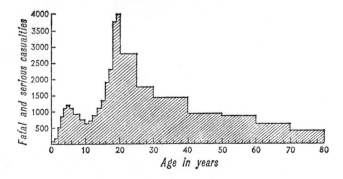

Study the diagram and then prepare a report suitable for a newspaper or magazine. Besides summarising the facts shown, the report should suggest reasons for the variations, and make one or two recommendations for reducing the number of accidents affecting certain age groups.

Here is a suggested paragraph scheme:

a) Introduction: Purpose of the report.
b) An account of the facts shown.
   (Avoid giving too much detail. The years 30 to 80 may be summarised as follows: a gradual decline from just below fifteen hundred at the age of thirty to approximately four hundred at eighty.)
c) Reasons for children's accidents.
d) Reasons for the peak period 15–30.
e) Reasons for the gradual decline.
f) Recommendations.

15.   These diagrams relate to an accident in which a man on a pedestrian crossing was knocked down by a motor cyclist appearing from behind a lorry. Write a report of the accident, as given by the policeman. The time is 3.30 p.m. on the 22nd June.

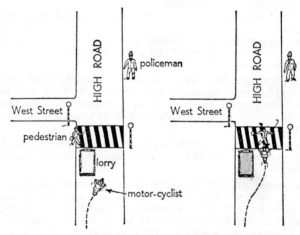

PRACTICE PAPER 3

I READING COMPREHENSION

Section A

In this section you must choose the word or phrase which best completes each sentence. Write down each number and beside it the letters **A, B, C, D** and **E**. Then in each case cross through the letter before the word or phrase you choose. Give one answer only to each question.

1. I should like to rent a house, modern, comfortable and —— in a quiet position.

   A before all   **B** above all   **C** over all   **D** first of all
   E after all

2. I have had a —— of misfortunes.

   A success   **B** continuation   **C** repetition   **D** succession
   E continuity

3. He had an —— habit of emptying ash trays out of his upstairs window on to our doorstep.

   A objectionable   **B** offensive   **C** uneducated
   D uncultivated   **E** offending

4. The music aroused an —— feeling of homesickness in him.

   A intense   **B** intentional   **C** intensive   **D** intending
   E intended

5. The jury —— him o having committed the robbery and he was then sentenced to five years' imprisonment.

   A convinced   **B** accused   **C** charged   **D** convicted
   E acquitted

6. Bitterly cold grey weather together with the after-effects of influenza made him feel very ——.

   A deprived   **B** depressed   **C** bored   **D** disgusted
   E worried

7. The book proved to be very unreliable and so was quite —— to him in his research.

   A invaluable   **B** unimportant   **C** useless   **D** negligible
   E unusable

8. The train was —— by a heavy snowfall.

   A protracted   **B** postponed   **C** cancelled   **D** delayed
   E adjourned

9. The bully tried to take away the younger boy's violin but the youngster —— him with considerable courage.

   A disobeyed   **B** challenged   **C** defied   **D** rebelled
   E dared

10. He is a clever mimic who can take —— most of the lecturers in his college.

    A over   **B** down   **C** off   **D** for   **E** up

II USE OF ENGLISH

Section B

Read the following passage and then answer the questions which follow it.

A great textbook on tidiness remains to be written, with chapters on theory and practice, with footnotes, bibliography, appendices and index. It would be shown, from historical example, that tidiness is easier where space is sufficient, with attics and cupboards, with outbuildings and cellars. It would
5 be proved from case-histories and depth interviews that the best workmen cannot even begin work before they have brushed the floor and laid out their tools in their accustomed sequence. It could be argued, on the other hand, that the most precise order has its origin in the more confined space. Where men live under canvas or at sea they are often compelled by their surroundings
10 to keep everything, literally, ship-shape. Whatever may be needed, from a rope to a rifle, can be found in pitch darkness within a matter of seconds. Tidiness can thus be made to seem an aspect of efficiency. But is it? For some work is always performed under conditions of squalor. Backstage at the theatre is always chaos and so are the working parts of a television studio. What is
15 true, moreover, of an English cabinet-maker or research scientist is quite untrue of the Chinese woodcarver or joiner. The most intricate patterns are carved by Chinese workmen on the sidewalk of busy streets amid a confusion of hawkers and children and poultry and dogs. Nor is the tidiness of a British warship repeated faithfully on the deck of a Cantonese junk, which
20 nevertheless earns its living and makes its landfall. The truth is that tidiness is not so much practically necessary as it is aesthetically and psychologically satisfying.

Tidiness means keeping things out of sight and yet available when wanted. It implies that there is a place for everything and that each thing used finds
25 its way back to its place by a continuous process, not by a spasmodic effort. The process depends, however, upon the drawer, cupboard and storage space being provided, for lack of which some things may literally have no place to go. Like the perambulator and trolley, the luggage and the golfclubs may be homeless. The same may be true of the deck-chairs and the bulkier plastic
30 toys. As there is no place for them, it is no good telling people to put them away. The architect who thus economises on storage space is apt to claim that a good-sized sitting-room is the result. What advantage is there in that, however when half the living-room has to be used for storage? The aesthetic order depends, in turn, upon storage space. While it may be true that no
35 house ever had cupboards enough, there are some houses which have practically no cupboards at all. In these our choice must lie between chronic untidiness and ruthless destruction. That is not to say, however, that cupboard

space will itself create tidiness. Some people are happier, it would seem, in chaos. There is the question, furthermore, whether the cupboards themselves are tidy. That everything has been swept out of sight is no proof, in itself, that anything can be found. 40

From: C. Northcote Parkinson, *Mrs. Parkinson's Law*, Murray.

1. What basic contradiction in types of conditions conducive to tidiness is suggested here?
2. What two things have the working conditions of Western mass entertainment and of an Eastern carpenter in common?
3. In what two ways might it be claimed that a house-owner may benefit from lack of storage space?
4. Explain what may still make a tidy house unlikely even where there are plenty of places to put things.
5. What details about the type of family the author has in mind can we learn from the kinds of things for which storage space must be found?
6. Quote the part of a sentence used to satirise the research carried out in preparing some of the present-day sociological text books. What field of knowledge do the words apply to?
7. Rewrite more simply the expression 'in their natural sequence' so that it is clear how the workmen have laid their tools.
8. What is suggested about the origin in meaning of the word 'shipshape'?
9. 'What is true, moreover, of the English cabinet-maker or research scientist . . .'. What 'truth' is being referred to here?
10. 'it finds its way back to its place by a continuous process, not by a spasmodic effort'. In what way does this statement draw a distinction between a genuinely tidy and a less tidy person?
11. Rewrite the sentence beginning with the words 'The same . . .' (line 29) so as to make clear the meaning of the first two words without actually using them.
12. Explain why the untidiness referred to in lines 36–37 must be 'chronic' and the destruction 'ruthless'.
13. What kind of false tidiness does the author mention?
14. Explain in fewer than 40 words the relationship between tidiness and efficiency suggested in the passage.
15. Write a paragraph of not more than 100 words explaining the factors that may encourage the maintenance of tidiness as the author defines it.

III   USE OF ENGLISH

Section A

1   Fill each of the numbered blanks with one suitable word or expression.

Example: I shall buy some of that new soap powder when I .... my
          shopping next week.
Answer: do.

1. As he started at his present firm when he was fourteen and he is now nearly sixty he .... there for almost forty-six years.
2. I shall expect you to dinner next Tuesday .... I hear anything to the contrary.
3. I can't help .... that I made a mistake in buying that orange hat.
4. Most of this coastline is unspoilt; just north of here, ..., an extensive caravan site has been established.
5. I have definitely decided that this is the last time I .... my holiday camping.
6. The grass should .... before it got so long.
7. I shall probably oversleep as I am not used .... so early.
8. The children were making .... that we couldn't hear ourselves speak.
9. The cake would .... and been quite uneatable if it had been left in the oven five minutes longer.
10. The birds were already awake when I got up and I could hear .... cheerfully.

2 For each of the sentences below, write a new sentence **as similar as possible in meaning to the original sentence,** but using a form of the word given in capital letters.

Example: It was his wish that his daughter should marry a doctor.
WANT
Answer: He wanted his daughter to marry a doctor.

1. I didn't see the carnival procession this year.
MISS
2. It would have been better if he had worn thicker clothes.
SHOULD
3. He gave me permission to publish his memoirs.
AGREE
4. He advised me to return home as soon as possible.
SUGGEST
5. They both said hello when they met.
GREET
6. I shall not travel to Paris before next Monday.
POSTPONE
7. Perhaps he didn't hear what you said.
MIGHT
8. He works in his garden most of the day.
SPEND
9. He described his flat to me.
LIKE
10. I was going to answer his question when there was a knock at the door.
PREVENT

44

IV GENERAL PRACTICE

1. The items in Column *B* suggest short responses (affirmative or negative) to the questions or statements in Column *A*. The verb is shown in brackets and in some cases the short answer must be completed by one other word. Write out in full the responses in Column *B* together with the number of the sentence.

Example: (xiii) Will your daughter go to University? Yes, I (hope).
    (xiii) Yes, I hope so.

	A		*B*
(i)	What do you think of this dress?		I (LIKE)
(ii)	Will the work be difficult?		Yes, I'm (AFRAID)
(iii)	Will you be going to Italy this year?		Well, I (WANT)
(iv)	Is there a cathedral in York?		Yes, I (THINK)
(v)	You must arrange them like this. Is that clear?		Yes, I (SEE)
(vi)	Do they own that enormous house?		Yes, I (BELIEVE)
(vii)	Will you lose your job?		No, I (HOPE)
(viii)	Will all your relatives be there?		Yes, I (SUPPOSE)
(ix)	Are you sorry you left home?		Yes, I (REGRET)
(x)	Your handwriting is almost illegible		Yes, I (KNOW)
(xi)	Is Athens bigger than Paris?		No, I (THINK)
(xii)	Do you think she will really marry him?		Well, I (WONDER)

2. Change each of the phrases and clauses below into a compound adjective and use the word you have formed in a sentence.
Example: which has long hair
Answer: My sister has a long-haired cat.

(i) having brown eyes
(ii) with keen sight
(iii) sure of himself
(iv) having four sides
(v) with the power of sixty watts
(vi) who is ten years old
(vii) which has good lighting
(viii) in which people serve themselves
(ix) which saves labour
(x) which has been lost for a long time

3. Each of the three sentences in the example expresses the same meaning but in a slightly different form. Make similar sentence groups based on the pattern provided and write out all the sentences. Do not change more than is necessary to express the exact meaning.

Example: a) He spoke with utter conviction.
      b) He spoke utterly convincingly.
      c) His words were utterly convincing.

1. a) He struggled with remarkable courage.
2. a) He moved with unexpected speed.

45

3. a) The boxer punched with extraordinary strength.
4. b) The expert predicted amazingly accurately.
5. b) The surveyor measured very carefully.
6. c) His behaviour was absurdly formal.

V USE OF ENGLISH

Section C

The figures below are records of the average attendances of students who enrolled for French courses in the Whitehampton Evening Institute throughout one session.

The organiser of the courses has to prepare a report based on these figures for the Principal of the Institute. Besides summarising the facts, he suggests reasons for the main variations in the figures and makes whatever recommendations seem useful to improve attendances during the coming year.
Write the report he prepares using between 190 and 225 words.

(Some help in this type of exercise can be obtained from a similar report based on a graph which is explained on pages 39–40)

THE WHITEHAMPTON EVENING INSTITUTE
ATTENDANCE AT COURSES

FRENCH COURSES: ADVANCED   MON.   WED.   6.30–7.30
(External examination class)
INTERMEDIATE   MON.   WED.   7.30–8.30
ELEMENTARY   MON.   WED.   8.30–9.30

M. Pierre Blancheville is the teacher at all three levels.

AVERAGE CLASS ATTENDANCES

	ELEMENTARY	INTERMEDIATE	ADVANCED
September	42	20	20
October	44	19	21
November	37	16	19
December (till 22nd)	26	12	18
January	28	15	16
February	20	12	16
March	16	12	16
April	14	12	16
May	12	11	16
June	9	9	10

46

VI INTERVIEW

Section B

The candidate is given three topics on a printed sheet fifteen minutes before the Interview and he has to speak for about two minutes on one of them. He is allowed to make a few notes but not to write his speech out.

SOME ADVICE ON DEALING WITH A TOPIC

This speech will resemble a short essay in that the ideas should be organised and dealt with in a logical order. It will be different insofar as the language will be more relaxed and colloquial.

Here is an example. The candidate might prepare the notes shown and his actual speech might then be on the lines of the account below.

TOPIC

The value of spending a year or two in a foreign country.

NOTES

Most common reasons for doing this:
1) learning a language or other study
2) a job (training or better pay)
Other reasons:
3) the interest of seeing new places
4) broadening knowledge of life and people
5) seeing one's own country from outside
6) independence.

SPEECH

A child may have to spend time living in another country with his parents but this topic probably refers to an adult who goes there alone.

A fair number of young people in my country do in fact spend at least a year abroad. In most cases they go for study in their special subject or to learn and get more practice in the language of that country because they need this in their future job and you can't speak a foreign language really well without having lived in the country where it's spoken. Others go to work there, either as part of their training (hotel employees are an example) or because they can get better pay.

A lot of people are satisfied with just learning or working: they go to classes or earn money and that's enough. They get to know very little about the country itself: its interesting places, its scenery and its history, what sort of ideas the people have and how they live. If I went abroad, I'd travel around the country as much as I could and try to get to know as many people as possible, not only to practise the language on but to have discussions with and I'd hope to make some real friends.

It's a good thing too to spend some time seeing your own country from the outside: it helps you to get a sense of proportion and become more tolerant and less narrow-minded. Sometimes living at home is like being in a small room with only a window to look at the world through, and going to another country is like opening the door and stepping out.

Finally you learn to stand on your own feet. Some young people abroad lose their heads and get into trouble but perhaps they learn something even from this. Others gain self-confidence and are able to make much more out of their lives.

SOME OTHER POSSIBLE TOPICS

1. What might be the main problem the world will be facing in the year 2000?
2. How I should like my children to be educated.
3. Should a woman work after marriage?
4. Some of the ways in which Nature is being threatened by Man.
5. If you could choose a house at a reasonable price to bring up a family in, what features would you hope to find in it?
6. What are your views on the upbringing of children?
7. Do you think sport is too much commercialised nowadays?
8. Some of the problems facing a young couple without much money who intend to get married.
9. What social services should be made available by the State for every citizen?
10. If you were involved in the establishment of a youth club in your town, what activities would you suggest should form part of the programme?
11. If someone offered you a job which you were qualified for, what information would you want to have about it before accepting it?
12. Describe the type of person you most admire.
13. A school or college club is formed of young people who wish to carry out some kind of social service for the community. What are some of the ways in which groups of young people could help other less fortunate people who could benefit from their help?
14. What are some of the reasons for the increase in violent crime nowadays?
15. To what extent do you consider it important to be completely honest?

Reading, Vocabulary and Comprehension

Science report

Pollution: Warning of new ice age

If pollution continues to increase at the present rate, formation of aerosols in the atmosphere will cause the onset of an ice age in about fifty years' time. This conclusion, reached by Dr S. I. Rasool and Dr S. H. Schneider, of the United States Goddard space flight centre, answers the apparently conflicting questions of whether an increase in the carbon dioxide content of the atmosphere will cause the Earth to warm up or increasing the aerosol content will cause it to cool down. The Americans have shown conclusively that the aerosol question is dominant.

Two spectres haunting conservationists have been the prospect that meddling with the environment might lead to the planet's becoming unbearably hot or cold. One of these ghosts has now been laid, because it seems that even an increase in the amount of carbon dioxide in the atmosphere to eight times its present value will produce an increase in temperature of only 2°C, which would take place over several thousand years. But the other problem, now looms larger than ever.

Aerosols are collections of small liquid or solid particles dispersed in air or some other medium. The particles are all so tiny that each is composed of only a few hundred atoms. Because of this they can float in the air for a very long time. Perhaps the most commonly experienced aerosol is industrial smog of the kind that plagued London in the 1950s and is an even greater problem in Los Angeles today. These collections of aerosols reflect the Sun's heat and thereby cause the Earth to cool.

Dr Rasool and Dr Schneider have calculated the exact effect of a dust aerosol layer just above the Earth's surface on the temperature of the planet. As the layer builds up, the present delicate balance between the amount of heat absorbed from the Sun and the amount radiated from the Earth is disturbed. The aerosol layer not only reflects much of the Sun's light but also transmits the infrared radiation from below almost unimpeded. So, while the heat input to the surface drops, the loss of heat remains high until the planet cools to a new balanced state.

Within fifty years, if no steps are taken to curb the spread of aerosols in the atmosphere, a cooling of the Earth by as much as 3½°C seems inevitable. If that lasts for only a few years it would start another ice age, and because the growing ice caps at each pole would themselves reflect much of the Sun's radiation it would probably continue to develop even if the aerosol layer were destroyed.

The only bright spot in this gloomy forecast lies in the hope expressed by Dr Rasool and Dr Schneider that nuclear power may replace fossil fuels in time to prevent the aerosol content of the atmosphere from becoming critical.

By Nature-Times News Service
Source: Science, July 9 (173, 138: 1971)
© **Nature-Times News Service, 1971**

The Times, Saturday, July 24, 1971

Notes on the passage (Line numbers are followed by column ref. i.e. left, right, centre, shown as (l), (r), (c).)

Line

1–4   Notice this 'shock' opening sentence. This would be unusual in a report circulating only among scientists, but is common enough in reports appearing in newspapers or periodicals. The rest of the report provides evidence of this assertion.

22   —— might lead to the planet's becoming ——
Here 'planet' is followed by the gerund 'becoming', which serves as a noun. 'Planet' has therefore a possessive form.

30   'Which would take place over several thousand years.'
The other half of this condition is not stated. What would it be?

31(c) INPUT.
'Output' is in common speech, e.g. the output of a factory
'Input' is still rare, though its meaning here of 'putting heat in' is obvious

8(r)　What is being referred to by the words 'that', 'it' and (later again) 'it' in this sentence?

14(r)　'even if the aerosol layer *were* destroyed'.
The past subjunctive of the verb 'to be' used in a condition

Metaphors

Metaphors are not common in scientific or other reports. Their use here could indicate the slightly more dramatic approach of an article of interest to the public.

The first, of 'two spectres haunting convervationists', is continued later with 'one of these ghosts has now been laid'.

How far do you think the metaphor applies in this case?

Would the fact that the future is being referred to make the metaphors less applicable?

'Looms' 1 (c) and 'plagued' 13(c) are two others. Discuss their suitability.

Prepositions

Notice the following:

at the present rate; (at a certain speed);
an increase in the carbon dioxide content; an increase of only 2°C;
meddling with (interfering with); over several thousand years (extending over); 'over two thousand years' could also mean 'more than two thousand years'; 'composed of atoms; consisting of atoms; comprising atoms; float in the air; the effect on the temperature; within fifty years; lies in the hope; in time to prevent the aerosol content from becoming.

Word distinctions

Line

24(l)　'One of these ghosts has now been laid'
One of the commonest mistakes in English is caused by the confusion of intransitive LIE (LAY LAIN—IS LYING WILL LIE—NO PASSIVE) and transitive LAY (LAY LAID—IS LAYING WILL LAY—WITH A PASSIVE FORM, as here

　　Examples:　LIE It is lying on the table;
　　　　　　　　The town lay silent in the moonlight.
　　　　　　　　He was lying on the beach all yesterday.
　　　　　　　　The dog has lain there for an hour.
　　　　　　LAY The men are laying bricks.
　　　　　　　　The Mayor laid the foundation stone.
　　　　　　　　She was laying a carpet.
　　　　　　　　The hen had laid an egg.
　　　　　　　　Conditions were laid down relating to the size of boats taking part in the race.

12(c)　industrial: industrial development. but: industrious students (more usual: hard-working students—diligent is not commonly used nowadays)

50

19(c) effect: noun—the effect of extreme cold
            verb: effect changes, improvements, reforms (produce)
        affect: verb—Strikes have affected output. (made a difference to; influenced)

29(c) convey; transmit; transport, carry; transfer.
        to —— to another course;   to —— wireless messages;
        to —— a handbag;   to —— someone's greetings.
        to —— goods by lorry (two possi-
        bilities).

17(r) gloomy; squalid; dreary; drab; dowdy; sordid; dismal; shabby.
        Her life was not tragic, only monotonous and ——.
        The old house was clean but with little light and colour it seemed ——.
        His mournful eyes and hollow cheeks gave him a —— expression.
        The poorest people shared their —— homes with pigs and chickens.
        Some novelists concentrate on the ugly —— aspects of life.
        He wore a —— old coat of a —— colour.
        Her clothes are expensive but ——.

22(r) critical: After the poor harvest the food situation is critical.
                (related to 'crisis')
                But—His critical remarks were not appreciated by his employers.

Expressions to learn and use

at the present rate: At your present rate of working, you won't finish before midnight.
reach a conclusion: Finally I reached the conclusion that it would be best to sell the car.
lead to: Overwork led to a deterioration in his health.
thereby: Factories are being built in the area thereby creating many more jobs.

Explaining the meaning of words and expressions

The following words and expressions are explained in such a way as to bring out their meaning as clearly as possible.

a) at the present rate 2(l)—to the same extent as it is happening now
b) apparently conflicting 10(l)—giving an impression of disagreement
c) conclusively 16 (l)—without any doubt

Explain these words and word groups in the same way:

d) that the aerosol question is dominant 17(l);   e) conservationists 19(l);
f) prospect 20(l);   g) meddling with 21(l);   h) dispersed 5(c);
i) builds up 22(c);   j) the present delicate balance 23(c);
k) unimpeded 31(c);   l) curb 5 (r).

Answers to questions

Short answers of one or two sentences

The following exercises, based on the reading passage, should be dealt with in complete sentences. In most cases only one piece of information is required, so one or at most two sentences are called for. Your answers should however be expressed in your own words and not those of the book.

1. What kind of pollution is being referred to in this article?
2. Why should the two scientists be in a position to make this prediction?
3. Suggest one way in which present-day industry is 'meddling with the environment'.
4. Explain in a few words why the two scientists believe that the danger of a warming up of the earth's atmosphere is less urgent.
5. How is it that large collections of aerosols in the atmosphere decrease heat received from the sun?
6. How does the earth maintain a balanced temperature under normal conditions?
7. In what two ways will heat be lost in the presence of a layer of aerosols?
8. How would the increasing area of ice itself lower temperatures?
9. What might avert the danger of the building up of a high concentration of aerosols?

Longer answers
These answers should be expressed within the number of words stated. Use only information taken from the passage, but express your answers in your own words as far as possible.

Remember to include ALL the relevant information. Read right through the passage to make sure.

1) Explain the two dangers to the future temperature of the earth which are being created by increased industrial development. (not more than 50 words)
2) Explain how an increase in concentration of the aerosol in the atmosphere could result in a loss of heat by the earth. (not more than 100 words)

Practice

SECTION I GRAMMAR

DEFINITE AND INDEFINITE ARTICLES   *Reference material*
pages 195-201

EXERCISES
1. The dashes in the following sentences may indicate definite or indefinite articles but in some cases neither article is needed.
Give each sentence as it should be written.

a) —— Doctor Rodney now has —— practice in —— suburbs of Milsby, which is —— county town of —— Milshire.
b) What —— miserable weather we had on —— holiday! We hardly saw —— sun and —— rain came down nearly every day. In —— country, —— enjoyment of —— holiday depends on —— weather.

52

c) I want —— drink. Is —— café on —— corner open or must we go to —— one at —— back of —— Town Hall.
d) —— children were curious about —— men who came into —— classroom. They said they had come to —— school to make —— film of —— children at —— work.
e) —— Thames rises in —— Cotswolds and flows into —— North Sea.
f) —— statesman, who is —— expert on —— foreign affairs, often reads '—— Times' and '—— Economist' in —— library of —— House of Commons. He makes —— note of —— important news of —— day as he must have all —— latest information about —— international situation at his fingertips.
g) —— man is busy exploring —— space but he still knows —— little about —— mystery —— human life.
h) Go to —— solicitor for —— advice and —— information but avoid going to —— law if possible. Tell him —— truth about —— dispute and ask him to write —— letter to —— people who are causing you —— trouble.
i) I saw —— accident involving two cars on —— Great North Road —— other day. One was —— sports model; —— other —— saloon. One passenger was seriously injured; —— other was bruised and suffering from —— shock and —— others escaped unhurt.
j) —— Christmas came on —— Thursday —— last year. —— Boxing Day, —— twenty-sixth of —— December, is also —— national holiday. —— most people look forward to —— eating and —— drinking —— lot and having —— enjoyable time. There is seldom —— snow but —— weather can be quite cold.
k) He moved from —— Isle of Man to —— Anglesey, which is also —— island in —— Irish Sea.

2. Explain the difference that the inclusion of the article in brackets makes to the meaning of each of the following sentences:

a) The reporter sent (the) news about the hurricane damage.
b) (The) Luggage was stolen from the van.
c) (The) Washing will take (a) little time.
d) Was it (a) (the) Doctor Sykes whom you consulted? (three possibilities here).
e) That is (the) (a) most important fact.
f) James Jones, { (the) head postmaster, / (a) head postmaster, / Head Postmaster, } announced the new collection times.
g) It was (the) last week that the notice was printed.
h) The lawyer is now in (the) prison.
i) (The) Dinner was excellent.
j) He is resting to-day. Can you come back in (a) week?
(the) week?
k) Percy Littleman is now in (the) office.
l) I shall elucidate that problem on (the) board.
m) In (answer) (the answer) to your letter of the 1st May, we have dealt with your (an answer) complaint.
n) He works in (a)/(the) factory near (a)/(the) lake.
o) The old sailor now works on (the) land.

3. Explain the difference between these alternatives:

a) The whole family lives in (a)/(one) caravan.
b) He is having (the)/(his) chest examined.
c) Bring me (blackcurrant jam, please)./(some blackcurrant jam, please).
d) Did you both go to the cinema?
Are you both interested in the cinema?

e) She always buys a pint of shrimps.
   She always buys shrimps by the pint.
f) The workman was given (a) change.
   (cake).
g) He has asked for (some cake).
   (a cake).
h) He studies (Nature).
   (human nature).

4. Write the following definitions in the form of complete, properly constructed sentences, inserting as required 'the', 'a', 'some', 'any' and any verbs necessary.

a) COAL—dark, hard mineral, formed originally from decayed vegetable matter, used as fuel.
   COAL-MINE—deep pit often containing underground passages from which coal excavated.
   COAL-MINER—worker in coal mine.
   COAL-FIELD—area where coal mined.
   COAL-MERCHANT—tradesman who supplies coal to consumer.
b) INFORMATION—knowledge about certain subject supplied by apparent authority on subject.
c) FINE—money paid as form of punishment for minor offence against law or regulations governing community.
d) CHARGE (noun)— (i) energetic forward movement of attacker against opponent.
   (ii) sum of money required for goods or service.
   (iii) amount of explosive material to fire gun or blast rock.
   (iv) task, duty, responsibility.
   (v) accusation against possible offender.

SECTION II PUNCTUATION

CAPITAL LETTERS

Reference material
page 230

EXERCISE
Rewrite the following sentences replacing small letters with capitals where this is necessary.

1. he lives in beech street facing the river ash not far from oakchester station.
2. as a clerk in the swiss tourist office he has to speak french, italian, german and english, though he has never crossed the english channel.
3. he has a b. sc. degree in economics from a scottish university but he is now only a counter clerk in marketham post office.
4. on the first tuesday in february he started reading a book called the history of civilisation and now at christmas he has just finished reading it.
5. the member of parliament for elmers bank said, "if more people read the times and listened attentively to the b.b.c. news broadcasts i should feel more assured of the success of our educational system."

SECTION III

WORD ORDER—C

Reference material
pages 236-7

EXERCISES
1. Rewrite these sentences with the negative or other relevant adverbial phrase at the beginning of the appropriate sentence. Make any other changes necessary.

a) He had never in his life worked so hard.
b) Mr Littlejohn was hardly inside the office door before his boss summoned him.

54

c) She didn't realise her good fortune until then.
d) Fishermen have to be very patient. Their wives do too.
e) We rarely have such a stormy summer.
f) Most politicians think about fulfilling their earlier promises only in an election year.
g) He realised the danger he had been in only after he had read the newspaper the following morning.

2. Rewrite the following sentences so as to make the meaning less ambiguous.

a) He has ordered a dictionary to improve his spelling.
b) The aspidistra near the window which keeps out the light annoys me.
c) The guide was showing the prehistoric carvings to the tourists with their grotesque faces and staring eyes.
d) He only speaks his own language.
e) I bought some fish in the market place which smells atrocious.
f) The flowers will be examined by the judges in clusters of three or four.
g) He hardly eats anything.
h) Several moons have been detected by astronomers circling round the planet Jupiter.
i) It is always interesting to read about the new fashions in newspapers.
j) The director said he barely earned enough to pay his chauffeur.
k) He assured me that a ghostly horse had been seen by a tramp without a head.
l) Your prize can either be a washing machine or a refrigerator.

3. Explain the significance of the word order in the following sentences in expressing a certain shade of meaning.

a) The postman came yesterday at seven o'clock in the evening.
b) He speaks politely occasionally.
c) Only after he had consulted his solicitor, would he answer their questions.
d) She walked through the High Street quickly.
e) The news will be published soon.
f) Why did he give the job to you?
g) He will come next week without fail.
h) Never had he seen such chaos.
i) I enjoy a cigarette sometimes.

SECTION IV CHOICE OF EXPRESSION

COMMON GRAMMATICAL AND STRUCTURAL FAULTS

*Reference material
pages* 238–9

EXERCISES
Rewrite the following sentences, correcting any of the faults dealt with in the reference material.

a) One is advised to buy your ticket in advance as one may find that all seats have been taken and you will have to stand.
b) Living in a remote country village, many forms of entertainment are inaccessible to us.
c) The mist was thickening as darkness fell. Being only a five-minute walk to the village, there was no reason to feel afraid, she picked up her shopping basket therefore and left the house. Only a few yards and the mist swallows her up. She feels her way along the fence, a twig lashes her face, then she hears heavy footsteps moving behind her. She stops and they stop, she hurries forward and they pursue. A panic feeling of helplessness and blindness in a lost suffocating world.
d) Edinburgh is a fascinating city, it has witnessed many dramatic and romantic events: Mary, Queen of Scots, had her home in Holyrood Palace, Bonny Prince Charlie enchanted the Edinburgh ladies during his brief stay there.

e) Many people like to entertain their friends in small restaurants especially when they are cheerful and friendly and they can enjoy a good meal in pleasant surroundings.

f) The next day they went to inspect their newly-inherited property. A huge rambling derelict house. Standing in a large garden which had been utterly neglected. Approaching the unpainted door it was only too clear that it would take a fortune to renovate it.

g) He left a message for his deputy that he'll spend the following day in York.

h) Several textile firms had to close down, therefore there was widespread unemployment in these areas. Also there was redundancy in some of the light engineering works.

i) It is not pleasant to awaken at midnight in an ice-cold cellar.

j) It is said that he enjoys letter-writing very much.

k) He likes very much a glass of wine.

Composition

I WRITING SENTENCES

EXERCISE
Below unlinked groups of sentences, clauses and phrases are assembled. Join the parts of each group to form a satisfactory sentence using the sentence above each as a main clause. The order of the parts can be changed and words can be omitted where desirable but all the ideas should be included.

EXAMPLE: Only a self-conscious gourmet could deny.
The meals served in British restaurants are often dreary. It is true. Well-cooked traditional English fare can be appetising, nourishing and very enjoyable. This is served in many homes. The housewife in these homes is a good cook.

ANSWER: Although it is true that the meals served in British restaurants are often dreary, only a self-conscious gourmet could deny that the well-cooked traditional English fare served in many homes where the housewife is a good cook can be appetising, nourishing and very enjoyable.

(This example is more difficult than the following exercises.)

1. I came across a shaded pool.
I was exploring the garden. Water-lilies floated upon it. Gold and black fish moved sinuously in the clear dark water.

2. It must be admitted.
The English weather is exceedingly changeable. People usually have to take an umbrella with them. This variable weather has one advantage. It provides an infallible method of opening a conversation.

3. In the sixteenth and seventeenth centuries music of a high standard was being written and performed in England.
It is difficult to understand. There were so few talented native composers in the next two centuries. British music of the twentieth century is more highly esteemed. It is generally accepted.

4. It narrowly escaped being run over.
It was six o'clock in the evening. A dog ran straight in front of a car. The driver braked sharply.

5. The clerk has lost his job.
You saw him last week. He was lazy and inefficient. The clerk was often late arriving. Mr Cooper will be able to help you instead.

6. You may be taken to the circus.
   If you are a good boy. They will be much cleverer than those in the Zoo. If we are able to get tickets at such short notice. You will see performing seals and elephants.

II WRITING PRACTICAL DESCRIPTIONS

The reading passage at the beginning of this chapter, like the report in Chapter 2, is an example of writing for a practical purpose. The material in the scientific explanation is far more complex than that of the hotel report but it is equally clear, matter-of-fact and skilfully arranged so that every essential is included in a strictly logical order.

The following examples of practical description may help in achieving a similar exactness, clarity, economy and logical arrangement of facts.

The PRACTICAL description is utilitarian in purpose. Facts are presented plainly, clearly and without emotional colouring. The emphasis is on LOGICAL ARRANGE-MENT, ACCURACY and a degree of COMPLETENESS which will be related to the complexity of the subject and the purpose for which the description is required. (A report may in some cases be a form of description.)

a) **Description of objects**

Study this description of a coat-hanger.

As its name denotes, a coat-hanger serves to hold coats, dresses, jackets and similar garments in such a way that they hang vertically.

A simple coat-hanger consists of two parts: a bar and a hook. The flat bar made of wood, plastic or metal, is usually approximately an inch wide and about sixteen inches long. It is made in the form of a slight regular curve so as to resemble the shape of the human shoulders and thus fit conveniently into the top of a coat. The metal or plastic hook is screwed into the middle of the outer edge of the bar. Vertical for about two inches, it is then rounded to form a segment of a circle which can be fitted over a rail.

The bar of the hanger is fitted into the shoulders of the garment to be supported and the rounded crook is placed over a metal rail or hook.

Among the many varieties of coat hangers are those with a straight bar to hold skirts fixed underneath the curved outer bar and the folding hanger whose bar is hinged in the middle so that the two sections can be folded over each other when not in use.

Four paragraphs are needed:

(1) Uses (2) Structure (3) How it is used (4) Varying types. The second paragraph is usually the most complicated and is dealt with as follows:
   (i) List the main parts.
   (ii) Describe each part thoroughly: size, shape, material.
   (iii) Show the relationship between the parts.

The amount of detail given in this second paragraph must depend on the complexity of the object being described. Obviously a complicated object such as a bicycle or, even more so, a car, will call for careful selection. The main parts of a bicycle will be the frame, wheels, handlebars, brakes, saddle, chain and pedals and only the essential features of each can be described.

In the case of a bicycle or any other working object, *an additional paragraph explaining how the object works* will be necessary.

Only a few of the most striking variations are described in the fourth paragraph, with their one essential distinguishing feature named.

This is an exercise in clear thinking and it demands the ability to seize essentials and express them concisely and exactly.

57

Describe one or more of the following objects. Useful words which may be unknown to you are given in some cases.

a toothbrush (tufts, bristles)
a bicycle pump (shaft, piston, washer, connector)
a ladder (shaft, rung)
a postage stamp (perforated, adhesive)
a thermometer (graduation, mercury, bulb)
a child's scooter
your passport
a torch (battery, bulb, spring, switch)
a sewing needle (taper, eye)
a knitting needle.

b) **Description of places**

The qualities of logical arrangement, exactness and selection of essentials are just as important when a place is being described.

In most cases it is wisest to go from the general, to outline the place as a whole, before fitting in the smaller details.

Here is a description of a supermarket:

PLAN

(i) Walls, windows, floor space.
(ii) Shelf units and contents. Baskets.
(iii) Cash counters.

Most supermarkets need a very spacious floor area, sometimes at least ten times as big as that of an ordinary shop. There are usually two doors, one as an entrance, the other an exit. The rest of the side facing the street is largely of plate glass, with goods or advertising material displayed. The other three walls are normally tiled or decorated in light colours, giving an impression of cleanliness and brightness. Most supermarkets are on one floor only, goods being stored in rooms at the back or upstairs.

At right-angles to the window stretch long structures about six feet high with a number of shelves on each side. Similar shelf units or frozen or chilled food containers extend round the walls. Broad aisles between the shelf units and ample space between them and the window and also the far wall allow room for the circulation of many people. Individual commodities, in tins, bags, boxes or other containers, are stacked in groups on the shelves, and each group is labelled with a price ticket. Metal baskets near the entrance are taken by the shoppers who collect in them the goods they select from the shelves. Assistants replenish stocks when necessary.

Between shelf units and window in one half of the shop are a number of small counters about three feet high and at right-angles to the window. Beside each sits a cashier, who operates a machine for totalling the cost of each customer's purchases. The customer places the basket at one end of the counter so that it can be emptied by the cashier who records the price of the commodities one by one, before putting each on a moving section of the counter top. The goods are collected and packed into the customer's bag by another assistant at the end of the counter. The cashier finally hands a printed slip recording all prices to the customer, who pays the total, collects the bag and departs through the exit.

In each case show the paragraph plan.

1. Describe a garage for a single car.
2. Describe the interior of a lift.
3. Describe the platform of an underground railway station.
4. Describe a canal lock.

5. The following diagram shows the ground floor of a house. Describe this floor.

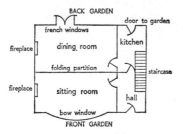

6. This is a plan of the small village of Frithville. Describe the village.

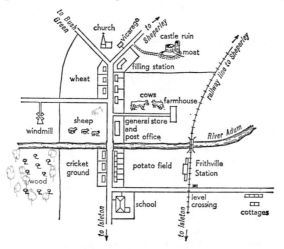

7. Design a children's playground, with a diagram and written explanation.
8. Design a small garden with a diagram and written explanation.
9. Describe the booking hall of a small railway station with which you are familiar.

c) **Description of people**

The conductor of a bus waiting at traffic lights sees a man rush out of a jeweller's shop, pause a moment and then dash across the road just as the lights change. He is followed by the shopkeeper who is shouting at him but is hindered by the now-moving traffic. The man disappears down a side street.

The bus conductor is later interviewed by the police. This is all he remembers of the man:

'Well, he was fairly tall but not very and he hadn't a hat on—he might have had dark hair. Any age—though youngish I should say. Had a raincoat on—can't remember the colour.'

A retired police detective had been sitting in the bus, and his description was far more detailed.

'Height five foot ten. Slim build but broad-shouldered. Wearing a dirty fawn raincoat with no belt and one button missing, grey flannel trousers and black shoes with pointed toes. No gloves. He was carrying a cheap-looking briefcase with one side undone. Clean shaven. Pale complexion, large mouth with thick lips. Small dark eyes with heavy dark eyebrows meeting over his nose. Short dark hair receding at the temples. Age uncertain—possibly between 30 and 35.'

59

The detective had been trained in careful detailed observation but even he made two mistakes. Previous police records stated that the man had blue eyes and was only twenty-eight. His name was Samuel Snatcher.

Notice, however, that in this kind of practical description, only certain *facts* are given. Impressions such as 'shifty cunning eyes', 'a sensual mouth', 'a brutal face' are opinions, not facts, acceptable in imaginative description but not in this kind of exercise.

The above description could be arranged in connected prose.

PLAN

(i) Name, age, reason for search.
(ii) Physical characteristics.
(iii) Clothes and what he was carrying.

Samuel Snatcher, aged twenty-eight, is wanted by the police in connection with yesterday's robbery (3rd May) from Trinket's, the Jeweller, in Parkhurst High Street.

Snatcher, five foot ten in height, is slimly built but broad-shouldered. He is clean-shaven and has a pale complexion and dark hair receding at the temples. He is blue-eyed with heavy dark eyebrows meeting above his nose. His mouth is large and full-lipped.

When last seen he was wearing a dirty fawn raincoat, unbelted and with one button missing, and grey flannel trousers. His shoes were black with pointed toes. He had no gloves or hat.

EXERCISES

Write a similar description of one or more of the following.

a) A child is missing from home. The parents have no recent photograph. A full description is published in the newspapers.
b) You are arriving in London Airport and will be greeted by an unknown hostess. Write a full description of your appearance and what you will be wearing and carrying.
c) A film company wishes to find an actor to take the part of some famous person (dead or living). State who the person is and give the description circulated to the agencies.
d) A missing woman of thirty, possibly suffering from loss of memory. Add details of speech, mannerisms and movement.

How do you see the following:

e) A typical English policeman.
f) A man of sixty who has been a farm labourer all his life.
g) Yourself in thirty years' time.
h) A very studious University lecturer.
i) Hamlet.

d) Description of processes

Here is an account of how a motorist in England carries out a three-point turn in his car.

'The car is positioned on the left-hand side of the road in neutral gear and with the handbrake on though the engine is running.

The driver depresses the clutch and engages first gear. He presses the accelerator pedal slightly, releases the handbrake, and, having looked left and right for other traffic, with careful control of the clutch, allows the car to move forward slowly, while he turns the steering-wheel rapidly to the right and holds it at full lock until the car has turned in an angle of at least seventy degrees. At this point he starts to turn the wheel in the opposite direction while allowing the car to continue its forward movement, still controlled by the clutch. He brakes before the front wheels of the car touch the kerb. The handbrake is applied and neutral gear engaged.

He is now ready to engage reverse gear, again depressing the accelerator slightly but releasing the handbrake as for a hill start, after looking left and right for approaching traffic. As soon as the car is moving, he continues turning the steering-wheel to the left, beginning to reverse this direction only when the car is in a position to be driven forward without difficulty in the opposite direction to that in which it was originally parked. Speed is again controlled by the clutch pedal and the rear wheels may not touch the kerb. The handbrake is applied and once again neutral gear is engaged.

The car can now be driven in the new direction. Observation is made for traffic in either direction before a hill start is made in first gear and the steering-wheel is turned sufficiently to the right for the car to move forward on the left-hand side of the road.

Before and during each stage of the operation it is essential to ensure that the road is clear both by using the mirror and by looking round to right or left.'

Verb form used

In the above example two forms are used: the active voice with a noun or pronoun subject ('the driver', 'he') and the passive voice.

In other cases a direct command may be given. This form is commonly used in instructions on a package or container which explain how to open it or use the contents.

The passive voice is common when a process is being described as if it were taking place before the reader's eyes.

The use of 'you' or 'one' may lead to complications and is best avoided.

EXERCISES
1. Describe the job of washing-up after a dinner for four people (passive voice).
2. Describe the cleaning and polishing of a pair of muddy shoes (passive voice).
3. Instructions on the care of some domestic pet or of a horse.
4. Describe how to cover a book for protection.
5. Advice on catching a certain kind of fresh water fish.
6. Describe how to make a simple apron for a lady.
7. Instructions on mending a puncture in a bicycle tyre.
8. How to make a child's swing.
9. How to pitch a simple tent.

PRACTICE PAPER 4

I. READING COMPREHENSION

Section A

In this section you must choose the word or phrase which best completes each sentence. Write down each number and beside it the letters **A, B, C, D** and **E**. Then in each case cross through the letter before the word or phrase you choose. Give one answer only to each question.

1. His authority and —— make him an excellent leader.

   A self-consciousness   **B** self-confidence   **C** self-centredness
   D self-regard   **E** self-satisfaction

2. Being both spoilt and lazy he —— everyone else for his lack of success.

   A accused   **B** charged   **C** criticised   **D** condemned
   E blamed

3. When I learned that I had passed the examination I felt —— and relaxed.

   A careless   **B** troublefree   **C** negligent   **D** carefree
   E triumphal

4. After the collision he examined the considerable —— to his car.

   A destruction   **B** damages   **C** injuries   **D** deterioration
   E damage

5. A very large cat was watching us intently from the top of a —— car.

   A moveless   **B** immovable   **C** stationery   **D** motionless
   E stationary

6. This is the —— piano on which the composer created some of his greatest works.

   A actual   **B** real   **C** genuine   **D** original
   E contemporary

7. Your usual teacher has lost his voice and —— I am taking his place today.

   A besides   **B** nevertheless   **C** however   **D** moreover
   E accordingly

8. He was tried for forgery in a law court but was lucky enough to ——.

   A get off   **B** get on   **C** get through   **D** get by
   E get away

9. A —— woman is needed to take care of two small children.

   A confident   **B** reliable   **C** confidential   **D** dependent
   E faithful

10. He went to Somerset House —— looking up the terms of his grandfather's will.

    A in the event of   **B** on account of   **C** in case of
    D with the purpose of   **E** with reference to

II COMPOSITION

Section B

Read the following passage and then answer the questions which follow it.

How is it that, when we put our hand in our pocket to dispense the bright matchless currency of our language, we bring out such a disproportionate sediment of fluff? Why, if asked a question, do we practically always begin our answer by saying, "Well"? Why, apart from the constant interpolation of "sort of", are we so loath to use an adjective without putting "rather" or 5 "quite" in front of it or tacking "-ish" on to the end? Whence comes our insensate addiction to almost meaningless phrases like "on the whole" and "by and large"? Why do we all, all the time, say "er"?

Supposing you asked a thousand, or if you like a million, adult Britons to express viva voce their opinion of some non-controversial measure—say a 10 reduction in the Entertainment Duty—of which they might all be expected to approve, in which of the two following ways do you suppose the majority would express their approval:

(a) "I think it is a good scheme";
(b) "Well, er, I think it's rather a good sort of scheme, on the whole"? 15

I have no doubt myself that the longer of these two formulae would show, particularly in the South of England, a great preponderance over the shorter.

It surprises me that no inquiry has been made—either by some learned booby or by a Government-appointed working party or commission—into the loss of productivity caused by "er". It must, when you come to think of it, 20 run into astronomical figures. Take education alone. What proportion of the school year is devoured by "er"? If all the teachers and all the pupils stopped saying "er", I estimate that between 10 and 20 per cent more learning could be imparted in the course of a term.

Think, too, of its effect on commerce and industry, and perhaps above all 25 on the civil service. Ask any stenographer, or any secretary who has to keep the minutes of a conference, how much of their working day is sterilised by "er". People are always proving, in time-and-motion studies, that vast sums of money can be saved by paring away from any activity the small, unnecessary exertions which slow it down, and progressive farmers who 30 adopt these methods find that they can milk forty cows in the time it once took them to milk thirty. Yet speech—the bottle-neck through which all decisions are arrived at in a democracy—remains unpruned and overgrown, nor only with circumlocutions and needless qualifications, but with small, ugly, pointless grunts. In Parliament, in the law courts, indeed almost every- 35 where except on the parade-ground and on the stage, the nation's business is being eroded by "er".

I am sure that I am not speaking only for myself when I say that, by and large, some sort of change in this really rather unsatisfactory state of affairs is, not to put too fine a point on it, just about overdue: if you see what I 40 mean.

From: Peter Fleming, *The Gower Street Poltergeist*

a) In the first sentence the writer carries through a metaphor of a simple everyday action. Describe what happens in the action referred to. Then apply the 'currency' and the 'sediment of fluff' to what is said about everyday use of language in the rest of the passage.

b) Suggest a typical English sentence which begins with 'Well' and has the expressions 'sort of', 'rather' and an adjective with '-ish' on the end.

c) Suggest the main use of 'er' in English speech.

d) Suggest an example of some other non-controversial measure besides a reduction in the Entertainments Duty.

e) How could this statement taken from the passage be expressed more simply: 'the longer ... would show ... a great preponderance over the latter' (lines 16–17)

f) What impression is given of the type of individual who makes inquiries?

g) What would be an 'astronomical figure' (line 21) and why is the expression used here?

h) In deploring the time wasted in school, the writer probably has his tongue in his cheek. How can these last six words be said in another way?

i) In what way is speech a 'bottleneck through which all decisions are arrived at in democracy'?

j) What is usually pruned and what does pruning entail? What is the meaning of 'pruned' here?

k) Why should the parade-ground be an exception?

l) Why does the last sentence make a very appropriate ending to the passage?

III   THE INTERVIEW

Section A

A CONVERSATION BASED ON A PHOTOGRAPH

The candidate is given a photograph to examine for a few minutes and will then be asked questions directly or indirectly related to it. The first ones will be about the photograph itself but others will involve more general topics in some way connected with it.

The main purpose of this part of the examination is to assess the candidate's ability to speak fluently, correctly and with a sure command of construction and vocabulary. He should be able to describe scenes and people, to express his opinion on personal and general matters and to maintain a conversation with the examiner on these matters.

One of the main aims of the Proficiency examination is to assess whether a candidate has the ability to understand an English-medium University-level course and to express himself usefully and fluently in a discussion or seminar at this level.

Advice

1. Listen very carefully to the question so that you understand clearly exactly what type of answer you are expected to give. If you fail to understand, do not hesitate to ask for a repetition or rephrasing, perhaps in this way:

"I didn't completely understand the question. Would it be possible for you to explain the last few words in another way?"

2. Take a short time to sort out your ideas. In answering make the most of your language knowledge: it is not sufficient at Proficiency level to restrict yourself to the extreme simplicity of a second-year learner. On the other hand, avoid translation from your own language.
3. It is obviously unnecessary to speak at too great a length, but at Proficiency level you should be able to express yourself freely and fluently.
4. Bear in mind the qualities of clear pronunciation and suitable intonation, stress and rhythm, even though these are less easy to remember in conversation than when reading aloud.

Pre-examination Preparation

Your standard can be raised very considerably by practising this type of exercise beforehand. You will probably do this in class but you can also ask yourself questions about pictures you see and think out possible answers which take advantage of your knowledge of English.

Practice

The photograph on page 66 shows a queue waiting to see the Treasures of Tutankhamun on the last day they were on show at the British Museum.

A1. What is your usual attitude towards queueing for a long time?
Possible answer: While I admit that it's better to queue than to push and fight for something, I always avoid queues if I possibly can, especially in the cold weather. If I know I'll have to join a queue, I usually go prepared with a book to read so as to pass the time as pleasantly as possible, but even then, if I have to wait a long time, I get bored and impatient.

2. Would you give a general description of the people standing in this queue?

Advice: At Proficiency level, avoid picking out one or two examples and describing the appearance of these. You should at this stage be able to generalise—and it is in fact a generalised description you have been asked for.

Possible answer: The most appropriate word I'd use to describe these people is 'ordinary', or perhaps 'average'—in age, clothes, expression and general appearance. While there are some children, there are almost no elderly people and I'd assess most of their ages as between twenty and fifty. They're warmly dressed, most of them wearing coats, though very many are bare-headed. They all look surprisingly patient and relaxed, as if resigned to a very long wait: in fact, few of them have any noticeable expression on their faces. Several are reading or chatting and two are buying cups of tea. I can't see anyone who looks striking or exceptional in any way. Well-meaning and, I repeat, ordinary: the inconspicuous, reasonably contented people, who never attract attention but would represent the average twentieth-century man or woman who has at least a passing interest in beautiful and historical things.

3. Describe the building you can see.

It's a very large building, with a large courtyard in front of it. The architect seems to have been imitating some kind of Ancient Greek building, though on a very large scale, as it's surrounded by very solid pillars. A flight of steps leads up to the entrance. Some of the pillars look black, probably from soot and other forms of air pollution.

B1. What do you regard as the main value of a museum?

Possible answer: Even a small town may be proud of its museum because it may house a record of the past life of the town and give an idea of the local wild life and countryside. Large museums may have much more valuable collections of the past achievements of humanity: carvings, pottery, embroidery, jewellery and statues. Some of the exhibits are very beautiful and all tell us something about the creative power of the human race. We can learn, derive enjoyment and even get new ideas from museums.

2. Describe a museum you've visited.

3. It's sometimes said that human beings appear at their worst in large crowds. How far do you agree with this statement?

4. What's your opinion of the style of architecture shown in this picture?

2. These questions are related to the photograph on page 68, which was taken at London Airport. Express your ideas as fluently as you can.

A1. What various aspects of the photograph would make you fairly sure that it was taken in the hall of a large airport?

2. What details suggest that the hall is normally used by a large number of passengers and various of their needs were taken into consideration when designing the building?

3. What are some of the other provisions for the needs of passengers at a large airport or large railway station that are not visible in the photograph?

B1. What are some of the attractions and some of the drawbacks of either a pilot's or an air hostess's job?

2. What are a few of the effects that the development of air travel has had on modern life and world events?

3. When the Government suggests building a new airport there are usually very strong protests from many people living in the surroundings of the proposed site. What various objections might they have?

4
Reading, Vocabulary and Comprehension

My Views on Gambling

Most of life is a gamble. Very many of the things we do involve taking some risk in order to achieve a satisfactory result. We undertake a new job with no idea of the more indirect consequences of our action. Marriage is certainly a gamble and so is the bringing into existence of children, who could prove sad liabilities. A journey, a business transaction, even a chance 5 remark may result immediately or ultimately in tragedy. Perpetually we gamble—against life, destiny, chance, the unknown—call the invisible opponent what we will. Human survival and progress indicate that usually we win.

So the gambling instinct must be an elemental one. Taking risks to achieve 10 something is a characteristic of all forms of life, including humanity. As soon as man acquired property, the challenge he habitually issued to destiny found an additional expression in a human contest. Early man may well have staked his flint axe, his bearskin, his wife, in the hope of adding to his possessions. The acquirement of desirable but non-essential commodities, must 15 have increased his scope enormously, while the risk of complete disaster lessened.

So long as man was gambling against destiny, the odds were usually in his favour, especially when he used commonsense. But as the methods of gambling multiplied, the chances of success decreased. A wager against one 20 person offered on average even chances and no third party profited by the transaction. But as soon as commercialised city life developed, mass gambling became common. Thousands of people now compete for large prizes, but with only minute chances of success, while the organisers of gambling concerns enjoy big profits with, in some cases, no risk at all. Few clients of the betting 25 shops, football pools, state lotteries, bingo sessions, even charity raffles, realise fully the flimsiness of their chances and the fact that without fantastic luck they are certain to lose more than they gain.

Little irreparable harm results for the normal individual. That big business profits from the satisfaction of a human instinct is a common enough pheno- 30 menon. The average wage-earner, who leads a colourless existence, devotes a small percentage of his earnings to keeping alive with extraordinary constancy the dream of achieving some magic change in his life. Gambling is in most cases a non-toxic drug against boredom and apathy and may well preserve good temper, patience and optimism in dreary circumstances. A 35 sudden windfall may unbalance a weaker, less intelligent person and even ruin his life. And the lure of something for nothing as an ideal evokes criticism from the more rigidly upright representatives of the community. But

few of us have the right to condemn as few of us can say we never gamble—
40 even if it is only investing a shilling a week in the firm's football sweep or the
church bazaar 'lucky dip'.

Trouble develops, however, when any human instinct or appetite becomes
overdeveloped. Moderate drinking produces few harmful effects but drunkenness and alcoholism can have terrible consequences. With an unlucky com-
45 bination of temperament and circumstances, gambling can become an obsession, almost a form of insanity, resulting in the loss not only of a man's
property but of his self-respect and his conscience. Far worse are the sufferings
of his dependants, deprived of material comfort and condemned to watching
his deterioration and helplessness. They share none of his feverish excitement
50 or the exhilaration of his rare successes. The fact that he does not wish to be
cured makes psychological treatment of the gambling addict almost impossible.
He will use any means, including stealing, to enable him to carry on. It might
be possible to pay what salary he can earn to his wife for the family maintenance but this is clearly no solution. Nothing—education, home environment,
55 other interests, wise discouragement—is likely to restrain the obsessed
gambler and even when it is he alone who suffers the consequences, his
disease is a cruel one, resulting in a wasted, unhappy life.

Even in the case of the more physically harmful of human indulgences,
repressive legislation often merely increases the damage by causing more
60 vicious activities designed to perpetuate the indulgence in secret. On the
whole, though negative, gambling is no vice within reasonable limits. It
would still exist in an ideal society. The most we can hope for is control over
exaggerated profits resulting from its business exploitation, far more attention
and research devoted to the unhappy gambling addict and the type of educa-
65 tion which will encourage an interest in so many other constructive activities
that gambling itself will lose its fascination as an opiate to a dreary existence.
It could be regarded as an occasional mildly exciting game, never to be taken
very seriously.

Notes on the passage

Line
18 the odds
This is an expression commonly used in betting to suggest the chances in
one's favour. 'The odds are four to one' suggests that the chances of one's
winning are four to one. Remember that in telling the time one says 'four
minutes to one'. The word minutes can be omitted only with multiples of
five: 'five to one'; 'twenty past one', etc.
26 Bingo
A form of mild gambling involving numbers, which is very popular
with a large section of the public. Numbered tickets are sold and then a
number or numbers are 'drawn' to determine the prizewinners. Profits
go to charity.
40 a sweep or sweepstake
Often organised in firms. The participants pay a quite small sum each
week, and each is given the name of a football team (or a horse). The
team getting a certain number of goals first may determine the winner.

70

There are usually no profits, all the money being shared. As most people usually win sooner or later, this might be regarded as a form of investment.

47 far worse are the sufferings
Notice this inversion of subject and verb which gives emphasis to the adjective. It is not common and probably best left alone by the student writing.

Metaphors

Suggest why the adjective 'colourless' can be used to describe the average wage-earner's existence. (l. 31)

Comment in a similar way on the use of the following metaphorical terms: dream (l. 33); a non-toxic drug (l. 34); unbalance (l. 36); feverish (l. 49).

Prepositions

Notice the following:
result IN tragedy (FOR someone) (His illness resulted FROM overwork)
It found expression IN a human contest
in the hope OF adding to his possessions
compete AGAINST other people FOR a prize
devote part of his earnings TO keeping alive ——
invest a shilling a week IN a football sweep
deprived OF material comfort; condemned TO watching his deterioration;
the most we can hope FOR; regarded AS a mildly exciting game.

Word distinctions

1. destiny (l. 7) is another word for 'fate'. What does 'destination' mean?
2. desire, want; long for; crave (for); yearn (for):
   to —— a drug;   to —— happiness;
   to —— affection;   to —— some money;
   to —— one's home and family.
3. In what way does the adjective 'minute' (l. 24) differ from the noun 'minute'?
4. Few clients of the betting shops realise the flimsiness of their chances.
   A few clients of the betting shops realise the flimsiness of their chances.
   What is the difference in meaning between these two statements?
5. How does a client differ from a customer?
6. A DEPENDANT (noun—l. 48) is a person who is DEPENDENT (adjective) on another person for the necessities of life.
7. steal rob plunder loot burgle
   to —— someone's watch.
   to —— a house.
   to —— a bank.
   The raiders —— the countryside.
   The mob —— the town shops.

71

Spellings

Each of these letter groups is a skeleton of a word in the passage. Complete each, paying careful attention to the spelling.

1. im—ly
2. a—irement
3. ir—ble
4. phe—n
5. ob—ion
6. cons—ce
7. det—ion;
8. ex—ion
9. p—gical
10. main—nce
11. exag—ted.

Expressions to learn and use

Early man MAY WELL HAVE staked (It is quite likely that he did)
He may well have got lost.
Your behaviour may EVOKE CRITICISM.
HAVE you THE RIGHT TO drive his car? No, I'VE NO RIGHT TO do so.
He NOT ONLY entered my room BUT ALSO (BUT EVEN) read my letters.
He wrote NOT ONLY novels BUT ALSO poetry, history and plays.
Did you have a good holiday? ON THE WHOLE, though the weather wasn't too good.
This may be a reunion party but keep the noise WITHIN REASONABLE LIMITS.
She has DEVOTED a lot of ATTENTION TO child welfare.
There were warnings of the possibility of flooding but nobody TOOK THEM SERIOUSLY.

Explaining the meaning of words and expressions

Explain the following words and word groups in such a way as to bring out their meaning clearly.

a) indirect consequences (l. 3); b) increased his scope enormously (l. 16);
c) the odds were in his favour (l. 18); d) flimsiness (l.27);
e) a sudden windfall may unbalance a weaker---person (l. 36);
f) repressive legislation (l. 59); g) an opiate to a dreary existence (l.66).

Short answers of one or two sentences

The following exercises, based on the reading passage, should be dealt with in complete sentences. Only a little information is required in each. Your answers should as far as possible be expressed in your own words.

1. Suggest one action not mentioned in the first paragraph which is in fact a gamble against destiny.
2. What fact indicates that most gambles against destiny are successful?
3. What difference to the gambling habits of primitive man did the acquirement of possessions make?
4. What possible benefit apart from actually winning anything may gambling have for ordinary people?
5. What is one of the main criticisms directed against gambling as such apart from its connection with big business?
6. What pleasure does the gambling addict derive from his obsession?

7. In what way might his family be assured of money?
8. Why might it be inadvisable to forbid organised gambling by law?
9. To what extent can legislation mitigate this problem?

Longer answers

These answers should be expressed within the number of words stated.
Use only information taken from the passage, but express your answers in your own words as far as possible.
Remember to include all the relevant information. Read right through the passage to make sure.

1. Explain the difference between early forms of gambling among individuals and large-scale commercial gambling. (not more than 60 words).
2. Why is obsessive gambling so terrible a disease? (not more than 80 words)
3. What remedies are suggested which might help to mitigate the undesirable aspects of gambling? (not more than 70 words)

Practice

SECTION I GRAMMAR

A. PRONOUNS   *Reference material*
                                               pages 201–12

EXERCISES

1. In the following sentences pronouns are used carelessly, and in such a way as to cause ambiguity. Rewrite the sentences so that their exact meaning is made quite clear. In some cases you will have to decide for yourself the meaning intended.

   a) The clerk told his friend that in spite of his inefficiency his boss was always referring to his lack of qualifications. He wondered why he had been appointed.
   b) A man carrying a red flag preceded the train along the quayside street. It was crowded with holiday-makers.
   c) He has rented a caravan near a farm. He says he can buy most of his food from it.
   d) I put a pie to warm in the oven, which was already very hot. After ten minutes I was able to eat it.
   e) The clock on the mantelpiece, which has to be wound up twice a day, is very old.
   f) B.B.C. interviewers often question people in the streets. They are sometimes indignant.
   g) The rose bowl in the centre of the table, which she had just filled with fresh water, had come from Italy.

2. The following examples, which are considerably longer than the preceding ones, also contain ambiguities. Various kinds of changes, including the substitution of nouns for pronouns or of the passive for the active voice and also the omission of a few words, may be necessary. The rewritten example should be quite clear but should include all the ideas of the example being corrected.

   a) On a fine summer Bank Holiday, seaside places are so crammed with people and cars that they can hardly find space to sit down which is why those people who hate crowds keep away from them.

73

b) Many British farmers rear turkeys for the Christmas festivities. They usually get good prices for them, though sometimes, when there is a surplus of them, they fall considerably, and some even remain unsold. In this case, much of their trouble and the food which they have had to buy, are wasted.

c) The children watched the ripples spreading over the lake surface. They were caused by the stones they were throwing. They lifted momentarily the floating dead leaves, which gave the impression of a miniature ocean. They were like tiny waves rocking minute and fragile boats.

d) The intonation with which one expresses what he wants to say may alter your meaning completely. One is sometimes unaware that one seems abrupt which may offend people. This is not because of the words he is using but because the rise and fall of your voice conveys its own special meaning. One is advised to accustom his ear to detecting the varying shades of meaning that you can give to any one phrase merely by a change in intonation.

e) Owing to the shortage of milk supplies, which is essential for children, it must be imported, which is regrettable as it will necessitate the organisation of a special transport service, which will be very difficult, as it can be obtained in sufficient quantities only from countries a considerable way off.

3. Rewrite the following sentences, supplying a suitable antecedent for the relative pronoun.

a) They have rounded up the ponies in the forest and are counting them, which happens only once a year.

b) The ship ran aground in the fog, which could have been disastrous.

c) A body has been discovered near the sea, which the police are investigating.

d) William fought the Battle of Hastings in 1066, which everybody remembers.

4. From the alternatives given in the following sentences, select and underline the form correctly used in written English. If two are correct, underline twice the more suitable. Indicate where the form could be omitted altogether.

a) In these roughly-cobbled streets he   long(s) to examine the beautifully-carved
           one
           you
façades of the houses to one's left and right, but he   must watch his   feet
           his   you   your
           your   one   one's
carefully the whole time.

b) The missing journalist, who/whom the newspapers had denounced as a spy who/whom had left the country with official secrets, was discovered quietly fishing from the end of Southend Pier.

c) The children all say that their mother needs a holiday more than them / they / they do / they need

d) All that/which I said was true.

e) The Mayor of Biggleswig, whom/who the police arrested yesterday by mistake, is threatening to sue the latter/that for assault.

f) One says/It is said that a momentous battle was once fought here.

g) They are driving the pig back into its/it's sty.

h) He is one of those irritating people who has/have to force his/their opinions on other people.

i) They have not lived in this neighbourhood as long as we have. us./we.

74

j) The cowboy   whose horse   ———,

j) The cowboy of whom the horse the cattle thieves had stolen ——,
       of whom   the horse,
was stranded on the vast empty prairie.

5.   Rewrite each of the following sentences using the correct one of the alternative forms and punctuating the sentence as required. In some cases more than one form will be suitable. Indicate sentences in which a preposition may appear also in a different position, and also where forms may be omitted.

a) The character of Hamlet $\frac{\text{which}}{\text{that}}$ can be interpreted in many ways has fascinated actors of most nationalities.

b) The ship's captain $\frac{\text{who}}{\text{whom}}$ we expected to find on the bridge was having tea
                           that
with the ship's owner in the latter's cabin.

c) I should like a word with the student $\frac{\text{who}}{\text{that}}$ drew that picture of me on the
                                  whom
blackboard

d) Where did you put the recipe $\frac{\text{that}}{\text{which}}$ Aunt Matilda gave me?

e) Shropshire $\frac{\text{which}}{\text{that}}$ A. E. Housman commemorates in his poems is a wild and beautiful county.

f) That is the most $\frac{\text{which}}{\text{that}}$ I can do for you.

g) The car $\frac{\text{which}}{\text{that}}$ they are travelling in can be used as a camping coach.

h) The wild flowers of the countryside $\frac{\text{which}}{\text{that}}$ few people heed are as lovely as any
$\frac{\text{which}}{\text{that}}$ grow in the garden.

i) His grandmother $\frac{\text{who}}{\text{whom that}}$ he often sends money to exists otherwise on a small
pension.

j) This is the mouse $\frac{\text{which}}{\text{that}}$ lived in the house $\frac{\text{which}}{\text{that}}$ Jack built.

k) The girl $\frac{\text{who}}{\text{whom that}}$ they have chosen as the Carnival Queen has since received ten
offers of marriage.

l) This satirical theatrical revue $\frac{\text{of which the author}}{\text{whose author}}$ insists on remaining anonymous makes fun of the contemporary drama.

B.   PRONOUNS AND ADJECTIVES

1.   Explain the difference in meaning between the sentences grouped together.

a) He is willing to undertake some job that will provide useful experience.
He is willing to undertake any job that will provide useful experience.
b) She is looking for a maid; someone who is quiet and tidy.
She is looking for a maid; anyone who is quiet and tidy.
c) Somewhere in these hills you will find wild orchids.
Anywhere in these hills you will find wild orchids.
d) Would you like some brandy with that?
Would you like any brandy with that?

e) He had got his clothes on somehow.
   He had got his clothes on anyhow.
f) Do some of your relations live locally?
   Do any of your relations live locally?
g) I asked him what fruit he had eaten.
   I asked him which fruit he had eaten.
h) The invalid has eaten a little.
   The invalid has eaten little.
i) The television company has shown few films of the British countryside.
   The television company has shown a few films of the British countryside.
j) The Duchess would hardly entertain anybody.
   The Duchess would entertain hardly anybody.
k) Dumb people cannot talk to themselves.
   Dumb people cannot talk to each other.

What two possible meanings has each of the following?

l) John, George and Henry often exchange cars. Over long distances John always drives the fastest.
m) They wouldn't employ anybody.
n) He has done some work on that subject.

2. Rewrite the following sentences using the more acceptable of the alternatives given.

a) Will everyone who $\frac{\text{wants his}}{\text{wants their}}$ exercises marked, please see that $\frac{\text{they hand their}}{\text{he hands his}}$ books to me now.

b) Neither of the contesting groups $\frac{\text{intends}}{\text{intend}}$ to abandon $\frac{\text{its}}{\text{their}}$ claims.

c) None of our efforts $\frac{\text{was}}{\text{were}}$ wasted.

d) The police have asked every resident whether $\frac{\text{he has}}{\text{they have}}$ seen the lost child.

e) Not $\frac{\text{all have}}{\text{everybody has}}$ a sense of humour.

f) I have forgotten $\frac{\text{all.}}{\text{everything.}}$

3. Correct the following sentences:

a) He went salmon-fishing today and caught several large.
b) Our detergent will give you so white washing.
c) There is always much noise in the West End of London.
d) Two of the four kittens are fluffy; others are short-haired.
e) Poor girl! She has a few influential friends.
f) Those kind of aeroplanes are obsolete.
g) How he is handsome!

4. Complete the following sentences with one of these words:
whoever, whatever, whichever, whenever, wherever, however.

a) You have made no progress ——
b) —— they went, they encountered the same hostility.
c) I couldn't thread that needle —— hard I tried.
d) —— you thought you saw at the bingo session, it wasn't my wife.
e) That ring will be too tight for you, —— finger you wear it on.
f) —— I start to sing, my dog starts to howl.

C. ADJECTIVES

1. Form adjectives corresponding to the words given. Do not use participles.
traitor; courage; fire; appear; reverse; Parliament; Government; consult; revolution; humour; intermission; impulse; monotony; enthusiasm; adventure; planet;

science; sympathise; elude; circle; apology; energy; apathy; decoration; experiment; title; muscle; angle; mountain; water; winter; book; oblige; geometry; accept; invent; ingenuity; infant; idiot; absorb; dictator.

2. Write sentences to show the difference in meaning between the adjectives assembled in the following groups.
earthy, earthly, earthen; brass, brassy, brazen; childish, childlike; young, youthful; graceful, gracious; old, elderly, olden; human, humane; wood, wooden, wooded; gold, golden; sunny, solar; glass, glassy, glazed; hearty, heartfelt.

3. Use each of the following words in two sentences, in the first case as a noun, in the second as an adjective. The form should be the same: the meaning may be different.
light; fit; cold; chief; principal; common; square; top (two noun meanings); fat; stout.

4. By using it in a sentence show how each of the following nouns can do the work of an adjective:
prize; correspondence; Brussels; garden; stamp; evening; bargain; toy; china; tape.

5. One adjective corresponding to each of the following words is different in form from the words given. State the related adjective. In some cases the meaning is slightly modified and in these instances indicate the change.
surface; moon; night; island; mind; nose; eye; ear; hand; back; tooth; mouth; time; wall; sea; thought; law.

6. Each of the following words has at least two adjectives (not participles) with different meanings corresponding to it. Give the adjectives and their meanings.
tolerate; trust; confide; select; appreciate; night; power; nerve; gas; pity; event; effect; depend; comprehend; flower; luxury; brother; father; mother; continue; force; nebulae; star; hand; law; picture;

7. Before each of the hyphens shown, supply an adverb which will modify suitably the given participle. The adverbs should all be positive in implication:
a -read newspaper; a -esteemed statesman; a -planned campaign; a -organised society; a -lit room; a -criticised report; a -made suit; a -needed reform; a -coloured poster; a -awaited change.
Present participles are less commonly modified. Here are a few examples:
a hard-working student; rapidly-rising costs; fast-moving traffic.

8. Explain the difference in meaning made in the following sentences by the use of the present or of the corresponding past participle.

a) Tribesmen gathering / gathered from all parts of the country were being organised in combat groups.

b) Watched / Watching intently, the prisoner stood motionless in the dock.

c) The man following / followed was obviously in a hurry.

d) Fruit ripening / ripened in the sun could be seen in every orchard.

e) The cows sheltering / sheltered from the rain under the trees continued peacefully to chew the cud.

f) The men discussing / discussed in the public house did not seem to be popular.

g) The race just starting / started is one of the preliminary heats.

h) The holy man worshipping / worshipped at the shrine was gaunt and fiery-eyed.

i) The writer now criticising / criticised in the review is well known for his sarcasm.

10. Complete the following comparisons:

   a) Teenagers are not —— conservative —— their elders.
   b) English people are usually —— reserved —— Italians.
   c) A lorry is —— powerful —— a car.
   d) Housework is —— tiring —— office work.
   e) Eve is said to have been —— —— woman on earth.
   f) Lead is —— —— aluminium.
   g) Wasps are not —— —— —— bees.
   h) Swans are —— —— —— ducks.
   i) A gold sovereign is —— —— —— a pound note.
   j) It takes nearly —— —— to reach London Airport by coach from the terminal —— it does to fly from the Airport to Paris.
   k) Many people consider Einstein —— —— —— twentieth century scientist.

11. Rewrite the following sentences in such a way as to avoid the unrelated participle or adjective:

   a) When depressed, a new hat will make a woman feel happier.
   b) Loaded with a Christmas tree, parcels and a bulging shopping bag, a taxi was a welcome sight.
   c) Speaking as a married man, my five-year-old son is far more advanced than I was at his age.
   d) Carried away by his enthusiasm, every obstacle in his path disappeared.
   e) Having been deserted by his guide, there seemed little hope that the explorer would find his way through the jungle.
   f) Racing along the quiet road at sixty miles an hour, an old man suddenly started to cross in front of him.

SECTION II   PUNCTUATION

COMMAS   *Reference material*
                                                  pages 230–1

EXERCISE

Copy out the following sentences, inserting commas where these are required.

   1. Still puzzling over the matter he said 'But I know I couldn't have dropped it' and added 'I've never seen anything like it before.'
   2. What you say upsets all our calculations and if it's true we'll have to start all over again.
   3. The rain which had been falling since early morning now began to ease off a little.
   4. Have you eaten the sweets that I left on the mantelpiece you bad boy?
   5. A policeman asked the youths what they were doing in the deserted building and as they could give no satisfactory answer told them to come to the police station.
   6. How you behave suggests what kind of person you are.
   7. Sandra have you seen my wallet? Yes, it's on the draining-board in the kitchen together with a box of matches a pipe three letters a diary and a cheque book all of which you dumped there before you went out.

SECTION IV   CHOICE OF EXPRESSION

WRITTEN AS DISTINCT FROM SPOKEN FORMS
                                                  Reference material
                                                  pages 239–40

EXERCISE

Rewrite the following sentences, correcting any of the faults mentioned in the reference material.

   a) George I and George II, the first two Hanoverian kings of Great Britain, couldn't speak much English.

b) John Keats wrote lots of lovely poetry.
c) Rather a lot of people are often unemployed in the shipbuilding industry.
d) Not many families in Great Britain own 2 cars yet, but a large number have one car and many other luxuries, e.g. a television, a washing machine, a refrigerator, a vacuum cleaner, electric blankets, etc.
e) An ear-splitting shriek startled the hushed universe. It gave me quite a turn.
f) When he was on shift work he started at ten o'clock p.m. and finished at six o'clock a.m.
g) Many au pair girls work under considerable disadvantages such as for example too little free time, not enough opportunity to speak English, spoilt impertinent children to manage, etc.
h) There was a proper menagerie in her house and garden: 5 dogs, 3 cats, 2 canaries, 5 rabbits and 5 adopted children. It was very decent of her to let herself in for so much responsibility, but we did rather feel she had taken on too much.
(This remark is quite acceptable in its present obviously spoken form but practise converting it to a more formal style.)

SECTION V

SPELLING AIDS—A

Reference material
page 245

EXERCISE
Complete each of the words in the list below with the endings on the same line, doubling final consonants where necessary.

label	-ed	-ing		
wrap	-ed	-ing	-er	
disappear	-ed	-ing	-ance	
sad	-er	-est	-en	
ship	-ed	-ing	-ment	
remit	-ed	-ing	-ance	
slim	-er	-est	-ing	
instal	-ed	-ing	-ation	-ment
stop	-ed	-ing	-er	
conceal	-ed	-ing	-ment	
transfer	-ed	-ing	-ence	
benefit	-ed	-ing		
knit	-ed	-ing	-er	
common	-er	-est		
prefer	-ed	-ing	-ment	-ence
in	-er	-most	-ward	
happen	-ed	-ing		
quarrel	-ed	-ing	-some	
defer	-ed	-ing	-ment	-ential

Composition

I WRITING SENTENCES

Loose, periodic and mixed sentences

This classification of sentences is related to the development of the thought they express.

LOOSE SENTENCES

In speech, especially, we tend to string ideas together loosely. The sentence may grow longer but in fact it can be terminated at the end of any one of its succeeding clauses and still be complete and have meaning.

Here is an example of such a sentence in written style:

A transistor radio is fairly cheap/and very easily carried about/and therefore appeals to many people/who want entertainment at all times,/in the street, on trains, in the countryside or on the beach,/even if they ruin other people's enjoyment/of the relatively peaceful surroundings/the latter had experienced before the transistor's arrival.

This sentence could conveniently end at any of the points indicated by vertical lines.

PERIODIC SENTENCES

A more literary, and sometimes more structurally satisfying, kind of sentence, the Periodic, builds up phrase by phrase and clause by clause to an awaited end which usually comes as a climax to the thought.

In this small, half-ruined farmhouse, ten miles from the nearest town, surrounded by moorland inhabited only by sheep, isolated by snow from the world in winter, bleak and wind-swept even in summer, the man whose acting had enthralled millions of filmgoers lived now in poverty and self-imposed isolation.

MIXED SENTENCES

A sentence may combine the characteristics of the Loose and the Periodic structures. The following sentence builds up to its main thought in the middle, then adds related ideas in loosely grouped clauses. (The main thought is underlined.)

Although the day had been very still and purple-grey clouds had been quietly massing and swelling to cast chill shadows over the vivid green fields, the heat had seemed so much less oppressive than that of the previous day that I was unprepared when a jagged streak of lightning followed by an immediate crash of thunder shocked the silence and within a minute heavy rain splashed the windows while blinding flashes and titanic roars suggested the fury of combat between angry gods.

Even a short sentence may belong to one of these categories:

LOOSE   He walks six miles a day when the weather is suitable as he needs more exercise.

PERIODIC As he needs more exercise, when the weather is suitable he walks six miles a day.

MIXED   As he needs more exercise, he walks six miles a day when the weather is suitable.

For longer sentences the Loose structure is the commonest and most natural.

On the other hand, certain effects of suspense, climax or shapeliness can be achieved by the Periodic sentence.

EXERCISES

1. Write sentences of thirty to forty words beginning with each of the following word groups and assembled according to the Loose pattern already illustrated.

a) The actress posed for photographers with her tame cheetah—
b) Certain remote areas of the country are losing their already small populations—
c) The English passion for family pets has often been criticised—
d) Abstract art may never appeal to some types of people—
e) A minority group of young people in very many countries are causing considerable anxiety—

2. Write sentences of thirty to fifty words ending with each of the following word groups and assembled according to the Periodic pattern already illustrated.

a) — — — many writers are better-known abroad than in their own country.
b) — — — he at last found a home with a kindly old lady.

c) — — — he disappeared over the edge of the cliff.
d) — — — he found a parking summons attached to the windscreen of his car.
e) — — — the house was suddenly plunged into darkness.

3. Write sentences of thirty to fifty words in which each of the following word groups, representing the main thought, appears approximately in the middle.

a) — — — that he had been trapped by the tide — — —
b) — — — he discovered that he was completely lost — — —
c) — — — that the use of the printing press made possible the widespread dissemination of learning — — —
d) — — — they at last sighted land — — —
e) — — — the conductor threw down his baton — — —

II ESSAY WRITING

An essay is a piece of written work in which the writer expresses his own ideas on a subject instead of merely assembling facts. It should therefore manifest individuality and independent thinking although facts will certainly be needed both in supporting an opinion and in helping to create a certain impression.

The literary form of the essay which is the work of a professional writer has its own character. The author has read widely, is a master of his craft and has qualities of curiosity, originality, tolerance, urbanity and, often, humour. His essay does not deal with a subject: it explores a thought gently and casually, allowing time for all kinds of apparent irrelevancies and deviations. Often the author may seem to be indulging in a reverie, a free association of ideas, and at the end he has only brushed lightly over the subject of his title. Yet the reader has had the opportunity of sharing some of the riches of the writer's mind; his curiosity has been awakened and this apparently undisciplined rambling has its own pleasing design, the more satisfying in that the form is not imposed from without but is one with the often very subtle pattern of associative thought.

Some essays do indeed contain far more substantial subject matter, especially many of those on specific artistic, political or philosophical topics. Even in these, however, the apparently subsidiary ideas may be just as significant and illuminating as those which relate directly to the writer's main theme.

THE EXAMINATION ESSAY must, however, differ from the type of essay just described.

a) Time and therefore length are limited.
   An essay which has to be completed in not more than two hours cannot extend to many more than 600–700 words.
   Accordingly it becomes important to concentrate on the points to be made.
b) A well-constructed plan is important.
   One of the reasons for the essay is that it provides a means of assessing the student's ability to deal with subject matter logically, relevantly and in due proportion. Another is to see whether the candidate can construct a complete form of expression with a beginning, middle and end, all together forming a competent design.
c) All this still allows the candidate to use his creative independence, to express his own views provided that he can justify them, to use his imagination, to enrich a description with his own vision, feelings and fancy. An essay becomes an expression of ordered individuality, ideas, thoughts and feelings freely conceived but presented in conventional sentences and paragraphs.

One of the most valuable results of essay-writing is that the author is forced to start thinking deeply about the subject, to probe deep into his conscious, even into his subconscious mind for impressions and judgments he had never previously realised he had formed. Practice develops this ability.

A first-class essay writer produces original ideas or presents old ideas in a new way. Not everyone can do this, or at least, not without a wide background of reading and discussion. An essay which restates known facts and conventional ideas in an interesting way can satisfy the examiner provided it is competently arranged and expressed. Obviously, however, originality and depth combined with competent expression result in a far better essay.

Preparation and planning of an essay

This stage is usually considerably more difficult in the writing of an essay than of a composition. The writer has to decide just how he is going to treat his theme, his main interest and emphasis. It is at this stage that he has to be most independently creative.

Having decided his approach to the subject, he has then to determine what form of construction will be most effective. In a 500–600 word essay, there may be about six related aspects of the subject he wishes to deal with. He must decide what arrangements are most natural and also suitable topics for introductory and concluding paragraphs.

Treatment of an essay topic—various examples

Here are four examples of different treatments of the same subject. Each group of ideas suggests an individual approach. The notes could later be extended into full essays.
The title: The Seashore.

Theme A—remote beauty combined with danger.

    (i) Introduction. To child seashore may seem a friendly, delightful place—sand castles, paddling, ice creams, deck chairs, etc.

    (ii) Even then, sea a destructive force, sweeping away sand castles. Advancing tide causes beach parties and children to retreat. Loud noise of waves on shingle. Loneliness of beach at night, etc.

    (iii) Shore in a storm. Fury of waves which invade promenade. (Other details of power of stormy sea.)

    (iv) Dangers even in calm: bathers swept away in currents, sometimes sharks, quicksands, caught by the tide, etc.

    (v) Yet danger linked with strange beauty—the sea garden—rock pools and inhabitants—shells—underwater world of fish and seaweed can be explored—effects of light below water—pebbles and rocks—mythical sirens and mermaids.

    (vi) Beauty of sea surface—colours and lights—sunset, moonlight—white horses in storm—ridged sand.

    (vii) Sea the end of land—to earliest man the end of the earth—empty horizon where earth meets sky—lure to discover what lies beyond.

    (viii) Part of fascination of seashore to child is that it is so changeable, sea so immense and different from everyday life. Even the danger can allure the adventurous.

Theme B—the extraordinary variety of the seashore.

    (i) An English child's picture of typical seashore—yellow sands, blue-green sea—would not apply in many parts of world. Sand, if existing, can be of any colour. Sea can be grey or yellow.

    (ii) Conventional English seaside-resort—dry sand or pebbles leading to wet rippled sand—tides, rocks, cliffs, possibly caves. Promenade, hotels, gardens, piers.

    (iii) Even in England many variations. Pebble, rock and mud beaches. Dykes keeping sea back. Black, grey, red or sand-coloured cliffs. Bays, inlets, capes, estuaries, etc. Marshes.
    (Beware of making this paragraph a list.)

    (iv) The Englishman's dream beach—tropical island, cloudless blue sky, deep blue sea, lines of surf, palm trees, guitars and sweet music. Yet often sharks, stinging fish, risk of typhoons, tidal waves, etc.

(v) Scandinavian seas—often mountains or granite-based forests washed by sea—many islands. In Baltic, sea and lake often almost indistinguishable. Polar seashores.

(vi) Where seashores have virtually disappeared—ports with quays and wharves, harbours, etc.

(vii) Conclusion: Not only do seashores vary all over the world but the sea itself may be changing the form of one part as it advances and covers or retreats and reveals.

Other themes could be:

C—The Enjoyment and Interest of the Seashore.

D—The Uses of the Seashore (e.g. relaxation, sport, health, fishing, defence and attack, study of marine biology, crystal and unusual stones, seaweed, etc.).

So far as subject matter is concerned Theme D could be classified as practical description. This would really depend on whether the subject was treated concisely and factually or whether the treatment was more leisurely and reflective.

Beginnings and endings

However difficult essay writing may seem, the ability to start and finish effectively demands even more ingenuity than the actual writing. Once the essay is under way, ideas develop by association, each suggesting the following one by natural sequence or by contrast. But the essay starts in a vacuum and the final idea must imply firmly that there is no following thought, that the work is whole, rounded, complete, that the essay exists intact as a unified literary form.

Beginnings are difficult therefore because of the absence of a link of association. They are difficult also because in many cases they demand a special touch of originality from the writer. Except in the case of specialised essays designed to present and comment on information, the aim of the introduction is to arouse the interest of the reader. If the first paragraph is stimulating, unusual, apt—the reader will want to find out more about the opinions of this independent writer: if humorous, provocative, anecdotal, it may arouse the reader's curiosity.

The concluding paragraph must indeed round off the essay. It should also leave the reader with the impression of having made contact with an interesting and original personality. Accordingly the effective last paragraph will not only reflect skilfully the thought of the whole essay but will also convey some dominant impression: of humour, wit, profundity, challenge, speculation, immediacy or merely of satisfying finality.

Below are suggestions of themes for opening or concluding paragraphs. One's choice will depend partly on the subject and one's approach to it and partly on one's own personality.

Suggestions for opening paragraphs

1. Definition of the subject to be dealt with—in an essay on a specialised topic, e.g. scientific, philosophical, etc.
2. The concrete example from which certain general conclusions will be drawn in the rest of the essay.
3. A general statement to be illustrated by examples and types in the rest of the essay.
4. Historical, geographical or other background.
5. An anecdote or quotation introducing the theme.
6. A personal experience from which the main theme develops.
7. A startling, unexpected, provocative statement.
8. A topic which will serve as a contrast or exception to what follows.
9. A special questioning reference to some word or idea in the title.
10. A reference to a matter of topical interest.

Suggestions for concluding paragraphs

1. The essay on a specialised subject may have various endings including a summary of the thought which has been expressed, conclusions drawn from this, suggestions for future developments.
2. A challenge to the future.
3. Suggesting a theme for further thought by the reader or discussion.
4. A suggestion of other cases or fields to which the subject of the essay is related.
5. A reference to far wider abstract or philosophical implications of the subject.
6. A topic which is nearly related to that of the introduction, bringing the essay, so to speak, full circle.
7. A 'twist' to what has preceded, suggesting (usually humorously) a possible complete reversal of all that has been stated.
8. A neglected aspect of the main theme or a comment on it dealt with lightly and humorously.
9. Anecdote, personal experience or quotation.

Examples of opening and concluding paragraphs

BRIDGES

1) *Introduction* (dealing with bridges in the literal sense of the word. The introduction shown suggests the origin of the idea expressed in the title).

'A rotted tree was uprooted by the wind and fell across a stream or a floating log wedged firmly between the banks, and sure-footed man found he could cross the water without wading or swimming. Later he learned to place his log bridge just where he wanted it, and very much later, to cement stones to form a flattened arch. Those old hump-backed stone bridges which still survive here and there, already represented in terms of inventive genius, a halfway stage in the development of the ferro-concrete wonders of today.'

2) The reasons for the development of early bridges.
3) Greater demands on bridges—for armies, herds of animals and vehicles to cross by.
4) The drawbridge. Bridges to be defended.
5) The development of industry—rail and river—purpose and characteristics.
6) Emergency bridges.
7) Modern bridge building achievements.
8) *Conclusion* (an abstract interpretation of the subject and reference to the future).

'Bridges will doubtless span wider gulfs as new materials and methods of construction are devised. In a symbolical sense too, man is trying to create new links. His main contemporary ambition seems to be to bridge the gap between his own planet and the rest of the universe, not by a continuous track, but at least by a rocket-propelled space-ship linking satellite stations. On whether he is willing to devote an even greater share of his energies and ingenuity to building a metaphorical bridge between the conflicting aims and beliefs of his own and other nations, his future existence depends.'

(The subject could be dealt with in various other ways. Bridges could be equated with links between people. The essay would then deal in part with actual bridges and then explore the attempts to bridge national and social differences. The first and final paragraphs would be adapted accordingly.)

CAFÉ LIFE

1) *Introduction.* (The Englishman's attitude to café life. This paragraph serves as a contrast to what follows.)

'The ordinary Englishman may feel comfortably at home in his pub, but confronted with a table, a waiter, the women of his family and the aroma of coffee mingled with the smell of beer, he is completely out of his element. One has only to watch the English tourists glumly staring at each other in the cafés of Ostend to understand why for all but young people, the café as half of Europe enjoys it, has little future in Britain. Now that television brings entertainment into the home, it is the exceptional Englishman who, apart from an occasional visit to the pub, does not prefer to relax in his armchair and watch the "telly", free from the claims of intelligent conversation.'

2) The climate and natural characteristics of the countries where cafés flourish.
3) The essentials and atmosphere of a typical café anywhere.
4) The café clientele.
5) The attractions of café life—special reference to artists and students.
6) Substitutes for café life in other countries.
7) *Conclusion* (a topic related to the idea of the introductory paragraph).

'Dr. Johnson and his circle of eighteenth-century intellectuals were typical café habitués. But their coffee houses developed into exclusive clubs where silence is more highly prized than the most brilliant conversation. Throughout the nineteenth century British people were becoming increasingly reserved, diffident and introverted. Café life is not for the introvert, for the individual who selects his acquaintances with care and in any case prefers pottering in his garden or tinkering in his workshop to sociable chat. Working men's clubs and many public houses have something of the free and easy atmosphere of the café but the average Englishman together with his North European Germanic and Scandinavian relatives, prefers to escape the grey skies and bleak winds, smoking his pipe and thinking his silent thoughts in the non-controversial atmosphere of his home.'

EXERCISES
Prepare a plan of paragraph topics for any of the following subjects. Then write appropriate introductory and concluding paragraphs.

I. Carpets.
2. The Beauty of Glass.
3. The Olympic Games.
4. The Moon.
5. A Factory Canteen.
6. The Influence of Geography on Building Design.
7. Describe what you would consider an ideal small provincial museum.
8. Describe a journey along a very spectacular railway track.

The complete essay

AN EXPRESSION OF OPINION
Essays of this type fall into two categories.

a) Those that deal with the two contrasting sides of a question or with two different subjects and present some kind of conclusion.

Such essays may have a title which clearly indicates their nature.

'The Advantages and Drawbacks of Being Young.'
'Compare the Values of a Town and a Country Childhood.'

Dealing with such subjects involves careful planning. Never try to list all the points on one side and then follow them with all the contrasting arguments. The essay would be quite unmanageable.

Decide first the topics which can be considered from both points of view, and devote a paragraph to each. Here is a plan for the first of the above subjects.

I. Poetry, sentiment and advertising all favour youth. Yet the more mature are often happier than the young.
2. Youth the time of physical strength—energy, beauty, emotion, idealism. Yet this very forcefulness can lead to more intense unhappiness. Maturity learns to make full use of its powers and to accept disappointment.
3. Youth a time of eagerness but also sometimes of rebellion, disillusion, cynicism.

85

4. Youth a time of creative energy and of confidence in achievement. Yet because much is still to be learnt, a time of uncertainty, exaggeration, lack of control.
5. Youth may feel intensely but usually soon forgets. An older person may feel less keenly but has fewer consolations and less to hope for.
6. The outstanding advantage of youth is that most of life still lies ahead. Yet, even here, if permanent tragedy does happen, its effect will be deeper, last longer.
7. An attempt to assess at what age (if at any) there is an ideal blend of youthful vigour and mature wisdom.

b) Other essays apparently require only one aspect of the subject to be dealt with. Yet remember that, in the case of a possible controversial subject, both sides have to be taken into account. No subject has been dealt with adequately so long as doubts or questions remain in the mind of the reader.

An answer to a question on Literature or History may well be an example of this type of essay when expressions of taste or opinion are required.
e.g. 'What in your view are the main faults of Charles Dickens as a novelist?'
'Estimate the permanent achievements of Napoleon.'
Other examples might be a review of a book, play, film, or other work of art, an assessment of a political party or the work of a statesman, an interpretation of present events or a prediction of events to come.
Many subjects which may suggest a descriptive treatment could be dealt with controversially. The title 'Birthday Celebrations' for example would normally suggest a description. But this could be a matter on which to express an opinion: perhaps a criticism of this custom, its formality and expense, the reminder of the passage of time.

The essential characteristics of this type of essay

1. A background of supporting evidence based on relevant facts and the ability to use such evidence effectively.
2. The ability to plan the work intelligently and logically so that the line of reasoning and argument is quite clear.
3. Possible reference to accepted authorities, analogies, illustrations, humour where this may help to convince (or irony if this will be rightly interpreted), quotations, etc.
4. A firm, simple direct style which carries conviction and is never obscure.
This is the plan on which the reading passage was based.

My Views on Gambling

PLAN
1. Introduction: Life as a gamble.
2. Gambling a deep-rooted instinct.
3. Commercialised gambling.
4. Gambling and the normal individual.
5. Gambling as an obsession.
6. Conclusion—Remedies for Evils.

Simplicity of style

Use only English you know is correct. DO NOT TRANSLATE.
At first your style will be simple, both in vocabulary and sentence construction.
With practice you will find that you are using many expressions that you have assimilated (taken into your mind) in your English reading. This must however be a gradual and natural progress. Never make an effort to produce a literary style.
AVOID the long complicated sentence except on very rare occasions, especially if you have a tendency to write such sentences in your own language.
With the feeling for English that can develop from experience in writing it, you may find an occasional need for a longer sentence.
86

On the whole simplicity of sentence construction is a characteristic of good English style.

The use of a dictionary

A dictionary could assist in the writing of essays under the following conditions:

a) It is a large, detailed, reliable one.
b) A check that the right word has been selected is made, preferably in an English dictionary; if not, in the other half of the dictionary.
c) The essay is composed without it. The dictionary is used only for the very occasional isolated word or phrase.

A dictionary is not allowed in the examination.

Practice essay topics—expressing an opinion

Write an essay on one or more of the following topics, using about 600 words.

1. My views on international athletics contests.
2. The importance of sport in education.
3. The commercialisation of the teenager.
4. Strikes as an industrial weapon.
5. Fortune-telling.
6. What is charm?
7. The joy of music.
8. Moving with the times.
9. Keeping up with the Joneses.
10. The advantages and drawbacks of boarding-school education.
11. My views on learning a classical language at school.
12. The teaching of history in school.
13. The privileges and penalties of fame.
14. The nature of success.
15. Superstition.
16. The qualities of leadership.
17. The evils of modern advertising.
18. The special contribution that the cinema can make as a form of art.
19. The responsibilities of the ordinary citizen.
20. 'No man is an island.' What is meant by this statement?

PRACTICE PAPER 5

I READING COMPREHENSION

Section A

In this section you must choose the word or phrase which best completes each sentence. Write down each number and beside it the letters **A, B, C, D** and **E**. Then in each case cross through the letter before the word or phrase you choose Give one answer only to each question.

1. His speech was careful and —— but his words seemed to make no sense.

   A distinguished **B** distinct **C** distinctive
   D distinguishable **E** distinguishing

2. The choir stood in four rows according to their —— heights.

   A respectable **B** respectful **C** respective **D** respected
   E retrospective

3. The campers —— their tent in a sheltered valley.

   A established **B** installed **C** pitched **D** fixed
   E grounded

4. Far more should be done to —— the sufferings of unwanted domestic pets.

   A alleviate **B** improve **C** help **D** remove
   E remedy

5. As a result of the strike, the Government is urging people to be —— with electricity.

   A economic **B** thrifty **C** improvident **D** economical
   E extravagant

6. An almost —— line of traffic was moving at a snail's pace through the town.

   A continuous **B** constant **C** solid **D** continual
   E stopping

7. I shall —— the loss of my reading-glasses in the newspaper, with a reward for the finder.

   A announce **B** publish **C** advertise **D** make known
   E inform

8. He waited in the —— for the front door to open.

   A perch **B** threshold **C** inlet **D** porch **E** crypt

9. I suddenly —— that it was past ten o'clock.

   A understood **B** recognised **C** knew **D** realised
   E resolved

10. The kitchen was small and —— so that the disabled woman could reach everything without difficulty.

    A complete   **B** complex   **C** composite   **D** compact
    E contained

II READING COMPREHENSION

Section B

In this section you will find after the passage a number of questions or unfinished statements about it, each with four suggested ways of answering or finishing it. You must choose the one which you think fits best. Write the numbers 1–10 and beside each the letters **A, B, C** and **D**. Then in each case, cross through the letter you choose. Give one answer only in each case. Read the passage right through before choosing your answers.

The Antler Riddle: Has Lambourne of the Yard been called in 5,000 years too late?

"Scotland Yard's top fingerprint expert, Detective Chief Superintendent Gerald Lambourne had a request from the British Museum's Prehistoric Department to focus his magnifying glass on a mystery "somewhat outside   5 my usual beat".

This was not a question of Whodunit, but Who Was It. The blunt instruments he pored over were the antlers of red deer, dated by radio-carbon examination as being up to 5,000 years old. They were used as mining picks by Neolithic man to hack flints and chalk, and the fingerprints he was looking   10 for were of our remote ancestors who had last wielded them.

The antlers were unearthed in July during the British Museum's five-year-long excavation at Grime's Graves, near Thetford, Norfolk, a 93-acre site containing more than 600 vertical shafts in the chalk some 40 feet deep. From artefacts found in many parts of Britain it is evident that flint was extensively   15 used by Neolithic man as he slowly learned how to farm land in the period from 3,000 to 1,500 B.C.

Flint was especially used for axeheads to clear forests for agriculture, and the quality of the flint on the Norfolk site suggests that the miners there were kept busy with many orders.   20

What excited Mr G. de G. Sieveking, the museum's deputy director of the excavations, was the dried mud still sticking to some of them. "Our deduction is that the miners coated the base of the antlers with mud so that they could get a better grip," he says. "The exciting possibility was that fingerprints left in this mud might at last identify as individuals a people   25 who have left few relics, who could not read or write, but who may have had much more intelligence than has been supposed in the past."

Chief Superintendent Lambourne, who four years ago had "assisted" the British Museum by taking the fingerprints of a 4,000-year-old Egyptian mummy, spent two hours last week examining about 50 antlers. On some he   30 found minute marks indicating a human grip in the mud. Then on one he found the full imprint of the "ridge structure" of a human hand—that part of the hand just below the fingers where most pressure would be brought to bear in wielding a pick.

35 After 25 years' specialisation in the Yard's fingerprints department, Chief Superintendent Lambourne knows all about ridge structures—technically known as the "tri-radiate section".

It was his identification of that part of the hand that helped to incriminate some of the Great Train Robbers. In 1955 he discovered similar handprints 40 on a bloodstained tee-marker on a golf-course where a woman had been brutally murdered. They eventually led to the killer, after 4,065 handprints had been taken.

Chief Superintendent Lambourne has agreed to visit the Norfolk site during further excavations next summer, when it is hoped that further hand-45 marked antlers will come to light. But he is cautious about the historic significance of his findings.

"Fingerprints and handprints are unique to each individual but they can tell us nothing about the age, physical characteristics, even sex of the person who left them," he says. "Even the fingerprints of a gorilla could be mistaken 50 for those of a man. But if a number of imprinted antlers are recovered from given shafts on this site I could at least determine which antlers were handled by the same man, and from there might be deduced the number of miners employed in a team.

"As an indication of intelligence I might determine which way up the 55 miners held the antlers and how they wielded them."

To Mr Sieveking and his museum colleagues any such findings will be added to their dossier of what might appear to the layman as trivial and unrelated facts but from which might emerge one day an impressive new image of our remote ancestors.

1. Mr Lambourne is said to have regarded the examination of the antlers as a task
   A rather more difficult than his usual duties
   B different in nature from routine investigations
   C causing him to leave his usual headquarters
   D involving a different technique from the one in which he was qualified

2. What was the aim of the investigation referred to in the passage?
   A to provide some kind of identification of a few Neolithic men
   B to find out more about the period when the antlers were used
   C to discover more about the purpose of the antlers
   D to learn more about the type of men who used them

3. What had been the principal use of the antlers?
   A to obtain the material for useful tools
   B to prepare the fields for cultivation
   C to help in removing trees and bushes so that land could be cultivated
   D to make many objects useful in everyday life

4. How do archaeologists know that Neolithic men relied considerably on flint?
   A they have found holes that were dug with it

B they have discovered many objects made of it

C they have found many fingerprints on tools made of flint

D it was useful in agriculture

5. The idea that mud was applied to the antlers deliberately was

    A the result of an inspired guess

    B a possibility based on reasoning from facts

    C an obvious conclusion

    D a conclusion based on other similar cases

6. The Museum's deputy director is very interested in the prints because

    A useful facts about this remote period can be learned from them

    B they are valuable records of intelligent but illiterate people

    C very few objects of this remote period have been found

    D the antlers serve as a link with actual people who lived at that time

7. Lambourne's main discovery was related to the prints made when

    A seizing the antler

    B using it as a weapon

    C grasping it in preparation for use

    D using it as a tool

8. What does the term "tri-radiate section" refer to?

    A a print of the hand used in classifying individuals

    B the upper part of the palm of the hand

    C the hand-print left on objects which have been held

    D that part of the hand from which lines strike out in three directions

9. Why is Lambourne cautious about the value of his work to archaeology?

    A It gives no information about the individual to whom the prints belong

    B The prints may not even belong to human beings

    C Any information derived from a print can apply only to the individual who made it

    D The prints are useless in the assessment of a person's ability

10. What is the ultimate value of Lambourne's work?

    A It has no value as so little of importance can be deduced

    B It will provide information about the organisation of work

    C It throws light on an interesting facet of early man's methods of work

    D It can assist in filling in an increasingly detailed picture

III USE OF ENGLISH

Section A

Fill each of the numbered blanks in the passage with one or two suitable words.

    We are now so accustomed —— (1) almost every week newspaper reports about new discoveries being made —— (2) man —— (3) we tend —— (4) the progress and benefit of scientific research for granted. We assume —— (5) science must continue to achieve its many miracles which become merely commonplace as soon as they are replaced by greater ones. Astronauts have made journeys through —— (6), a phenomenon that once —— (7) a time would have been considered —— (8) unbelievable. Yet there —— (9) few people today who feel anything —— (10) a mild interest —— (11) the discoveries that are being —— (12) by scientists. Industrialists and engineers are busy —— (13) advantage of the mineral deposits available, regardless of the fact that this ruthless exploitation —— (14). Nature is depriving their descendants altogether —— (15) those resources which we so carelessly squander on providing ourselves —— (16) luxuries and not merely the necessities —— (17) life. We fail to realise that we are responsible —— (18) generations —— (19) ourselves, and even those who are aware of this rarely —— (20) these responsibilities seriously enough.

IV GENERAL PRACTICE

1. Each of the following sentences is followed by four possible interpretations of its meaning. Write the number of each sentence followed by the letter preceding the most suitable interpretation.

   (i) You may have left your umbrella in a café.
     A This is possible
     B This is likely
     C This is unlikely
     D This is my definite opinion
  (ii) You are said to be broad-minded.
     A But this is untrue
     B But I don't yet know if this is true
     C Everybody thinks so
     D But I don't believe it
 (iii) I was to have made a speech.
     A It was ordered
     B But it did not happen
     C It was interrupted by something else
     D It happened regularly
  (iv) You might have offended him.
     A That would have been a good idea
     B It is possible but unlikely
     C This explanation was suggested by someone
     D It is quite possible
   (v) You should have helped him.
     A But you did not do this
     B You ought to do this
     C Probably you did this
     D So do it now
  (vi) You are to write that letter now.
     A This is arranged
     B This is ordered
     C This is happening
     D This is your duty
 (vii) The new Technical College is to be opened on Thursday.
     A This is arranged
     B This is ordered

C This is necessary
D This should happen
(viii) There is going to be a revolution before long.
    A This is absolutely certain
    B This is predicted
    C This is ordered
    D This is not impossible
(ix) You need not have taken so long.
    A And you didn't take long
    B This was not your duty
    C This wasn't a good idea
    D It wasn't necessary but you did
(x) I didn't need to buy a ticket.
    A And I didn't buy one
    B It wasn't my duty to buy one
    C I wasn't ordered to
    D But I did

V USE OF ENGLISH

Section C

The following article might have been taken from a popular newspaper and has many of the characteristics of reports appearing in this type of newspaper. It deals with the inadequate number of homes and purpose-built flats for old people many of whom at present have to end their days in uncomfortable houses or bed-sitting-rooms without any help or companionship from friends or relatives.

This is the first time you have become aware of this problem, and as a young person with a strong sense of responsibility for others in need, you write a letter to a Radio 'Postbox' programme, hoping that your ideas will be given publicity on the air.

Your letter, which will be written in a more formal and conventional style than that of the article, will sum up the ideas expressed there and will include your reactions to these and suggestions about some things that might be done.

The beginning of the letter has been written for you. Write another 125–175 words.

Dear Sir,

A recent article in the 'Human Echo' has made a deep impression on me as a young person. I should like to refer to the article first before trying to express my own feelings about it. . . .

IT'S NO FUN BEING OLD

Most of us have got at least one elderly relative—mother, father, great-aunt granny even, still alert and cheerful, with a snug warm home, plenty of helpful neighbours and ourselves to drop in now and then.

But how about the other old folks? Those whose children have moved

93

elsewhere, or don't care? Perhaps a nobody's Mum, who's lived alone for years in a dreary old house or a bed-sitter, skimping on the butter and the electric fire, with neighbours who've never even realised she's there, and too tottery and terrified to go out alone.

All right. The local Council do what they can: a cooked dinner brought on weekdays, a home help on two mornings to clear up and do the shopping, a district nurse calling now and then. But most of the time loneliness, depression, a slow decline into doddering helplessness.

"Put her in an Old People's Home. They'll look after her."

They would if they could. With a garden, a lounge with the telly, good meals, someone to see she's all right, and, above all, company. There are some very cosy Council Old People's Homes around.

And the flats for the more active, with central heating, a communal restaurant if they don't feel like cooking for themselves, a lounge to get together in, a warden to give an eye. And—company.

Just what the old folks need—if they can get in. In our town there are two homes taking sixty people together and flats for about a hundred and fifty. And a waiting list of more than a thousand.

It may seem unlikely now but it's on the cards you'll be old one day. Maybe one of the lucky ones with a family to live with or decent neighbours and friends. And maybe alone, cold, even bedridden. With nobody at all to keep you company.

So won't it be yourselves you'll be helping if you start moving heaven and earth and your local Council to do something more for those who've done their bit for society and now just aren't wanted?

More old people's flats for the active: more homes where the nobody's Mum's can find a bit of comfort and friendship in their last but why unhappy years.

Some advice

1. Your letter referring to this article should be more formal in style and far less emotional. Your ideas should be expressed in conventional English and properly-constructed sentences.

2. Between a third and a half of your reply will be concerned with an objective and clear summary of the contents of the article. The rest should explain your reactions (you might be in sympathy with the ideas expressed in the article or disagree with them) and your suggestions for dealing with the problem of the lonely aged. Your style should be reasonable, practical and matter-of-fact, though your indignation, regret or disapproval may show through.

3. One of the main difficulties will be to express facts, opinions and ideas in the 125 to 175 words suggested.

VI INTERVIEW

Section C Reading aloud: A Dialogue

Robert de Baudricourt (boudricúə) *is furious with his steward as the hens have stopped laying, and because Robert is something of a bully, he apparently regards this as the steward's fault.*

(Prepare to read the part of Robert.)

STEWARD: Yes, sir: to a great man like you I must seem like that.
ROBERT: My fault, I suppose. Eh?
STEWARD: Oh, sir: you always give my most innocent words such a turn!
ROBERT: I will give your neck a turn if you dare tell me when I ask you how many eggs there are that you cannot lay any.
STEWARD: Oh, sir, oh sir . . .
ROBERT: No: not oh sir, oh sir, but no sir, no sir. My three Barbary hens and the black are the best layers in Champagne. And you come and tell me that there are no eggs! Who stole them? Tell me that, before I kick you out through the castle gate for a liar and a seller of my goods to thieves. The milk was short yesterday, too: do not forget that.
STEWARD: I know, sir. I know only too well. There is no milk: there are no eggs: tomorrow there will be nothing.
ROBERT: Nothing! You will steal the lot: eh?
STEWARD: No, sir: nobody will steal anything. But there is a spell on us: we are bewitched.
ROBERT: That story is not good enough for me. Robert de Baudricourt burns witches and hangs thieves. Go. Bring me four dozen eggs and two gallons of milk here in this room before noon, or Heaven have mercy on your bones! I will teach you to make a fool of me.
STEWARD: Sir: I tell you there are no eggs. There will be none—not if you were to kill me for it—as long as The Maid is at the door.
ROBERT: The Maid! What maid? What are you talking about?
STEWARD: The girl from Lorraine, sir. From Domrémy.
ROBERT: (*rising in fearful wrath*) Thirty thousand thunders! Fifty thousand devils! Do you mean to say that that girl, who had the impudence to ask to see me two days ago, and whom I told you to send back to her father with my orders that he was to give her a good hiding, is still here?
STEWARD: I have told her to go, sir. She won't.
ROBERT: I did not tell you to tell her to go: I told you to throw her out. You have fifty men-at-arms and a dozen lumps of able-bodied servants to carry out my orders. Are they afraid of her?
STEWARD: She is so positive, sir.
ROBERT: (*seizing him by the scruff of the neck*) Positive! Now see here. I am going to throw you downstairs.
STEWARD: No, sir. Please.
ROBERT: Well, stop me by being positive. It's quite easy: any slut of a girl can do it.

George Bernard Shaw, *St. Joan*

5
Reading, Vocabulary and Comprehension

A Descriptive Essay

My Favourite Season

Theme—Autumn—a time of serene rich lovely maturity (as contrasted with youthful, restless emotional spring).

PLAN

1. Introduction—Contrast between spring and autumn.
2. The serenity and yet the exhilaration of autumn.
3. Autumn colour.
4. The moods of autumn.
5. Evenings indoors.
6. The winter death of nature promising the ideal spring.

It may be that I am a pessimist. For spring it is, not autumn, that makes me sad. Spring has always rightly been identified with youth, and the sorrows of youth are poignant and bitter. The daffodils which challenge so proudly and splendidly the boisterous March winds are soon shrivelled and defeated,
5 limply wrinkling to remind us of the inevitable ravages of time. The world is urgent with bursting life, with the wild exciting beauty of youth, but it is an impetuous beauty of the senses racing impatiently into the florid and sur- feited luxury of summer. Here is no comfort and fulfilment, only passionate creation of transitory delight.
10   Autumn in contrast imposes serenity. The heat and dryness of summer have been transformed to a warm contented loveliness. Even the uncertain summer of England, so often a succession of damp and chilly days, may mellow into a golden September. Mornings have a tang of exhilaration and the evening sun sets redly as a smoke-grey mist softens the outlines of trees
15. and houses. The early chill currents of approaching winter mingle with the lingering warmth of summer so that on dry days the air becomes alive, with the freshness of a sun-dried garden after a summer shower. Living becomes glorious.
    And the world soaks in colour. Not the primary colours of spring, brittle
20 or delicate, the reds, yellows and blues of audacious or self-effacing flowers. Autumn takes all the colours of spring and blends and softens them richly to intense shades of purple, crimson, bronze, amber and mahogany, displayed either tapestry-wise, side by side, or merged in rich new tones. The trees are resplendent in copper and gold, while corn-stacks crouching above the stubble
25 gleam deep yellow in sunlight. Green oblongs defined by hedges flecked with scarlet berries contrast with neatly-furrowed ploughlands. And moorland is spread with a royal massed embroidery of purple heather banked among radiant gorse.

96

Spring displays the noisy, often shallow moods of adolescence. Autumn moods are those of maturity, deeper and more intense. A grave mist-softened 30 morning of reflection is followed within hours by a Valkyrie world of screaming twilight when elemental winds tear withered leaves from branches, rock and strip the shivering forest and raise rolling mountains on dark seas. The wind passes and the billowing clouds condense into rain, which falls with quiet persistence, filling the hardened cart-ruts in country lanes, flooding 35 streams over sodden meadows and emulsifying the fallen leaves. Blue patches widen between the ṣun-lined clouds and soon the glossy bare twigs are brilliant in rain-washed sunshine.

Indoors, as the evenings draw in, lamps are lit and the fire crackles more brightly as early frosts clear the skies and brittle silver sword-points of stars 40 pierce the night-velvet of the sky. There is hot buttered toast for tea and then records for the quiet evening: a Scarlatti sonata, a Sibelius symphony, a Beethoven violin concerto, or books that carry their readers farther than any summer journey. Sleep and contented dreams come easily in autumn. Freed from the demands and excitements of spring, we have time to hear and feel. 45

When the intricate patterns of branches again thread the sky and the winds veer to east and north, we are deeply aware that the death of Nature is close at hand. The birds will huddle in ruffled feathers, shelterless in icy gales and many will die unprotected; countless animals and insects will freeze or starve while we relax in comfortable homes. Yet these deaths are a necessary part of 50 Nature's self-renewal and the spring that glimmers on the far side of the dreary night of winter has the enchantment of hope. Hope is delusive, and the new spring will not live up to expectations: it will bring cold, wind and rain, and the sickly tiredness that accompanies the end of winter. Autumn promises the ideal spring. 55

Notes on the passage—General.

The standard of an essay depends not on the nature of its subject but on the way this subject is presented. An essay on a favourite season, animal, book, could be written by a child or by an outstanding thinker. The impression it gives derives from the material, arrangement and expression.

More is said about the descriptive essay in the last section of this chapter. Suggestions about writing practical descriptions were given in Chapter 3. Notice here however the far greater FREEDOM of the writer to use his own ideas and imagination, the SELECTION of DETAIL to CREATE a POWERFUL IMPRESSION, and the CHOICE OF WORDS for their MEANING, ASSOCIATION and SOUND.

A note on the style of the passage

In the above essay there are various examples of slightly unusual word order. The purpose may be to create a certain rhythm or to give emphasis. Here are two examples:

For spring it is, not autumn, that makes me sad. (ll. 1–2)
which challenge so proudly and splendidly the boisterous March winds (ll. 3–4)
What others can you find?

Special points

Line
1 I am **a** pessimist

Remember this use of the indefinite article before a noun following the verb 'to be'

2 *Abstract Nouns:*

Youth—no article

The (A) youth—the (a) boy between about sixteen and twenty

Time—Time waits for no man.

      Do you remember the time before you first went to school?

Life—Life can sometimes be difficult.

      He is studying the life of Julius Caesar.

Nature—Nature may seem to be very cruel.

      He has a strange, unpredictable nature.

      I don't understand the nature of your difficulty.

4 MARCH winds APRIL showers—months used adjectivally.

7 You have no SENSE at all.

A sense of time. A sense of proportion.

Are you out of your SENSES?

An appeal to the senses, not to the mind.

40 BRITTLE usually means: hard but easily broken.

Explain how the meaning it has here is associated with the above meaning.

24 Why are the cornstacks said to be CROUCHING?

35 Why are the cart-ruts HARDENED?

37 Why are the bare twigs GLOSSY?

Metaphors

Explain the significance of the following metaphors:

the world SOAKS in colour (l.19)

a ROYAL massed EMBROIDERY (l. 27)

a VALKYRIE world (l. 31)

winds . . . RAISE ROLLING MOUNTAINS on dark seas (l. 33)

  (This is in fact a mixed metaphor—mountains do not roll)

BRITTLE SILVER SWORD-POINTS of stars PIERCE the NIGHT-VELVET of the sky (ll. 40-41)

the intricate patterns of branches again THREAD the sky (l. 46)

the spring that GLIMMERS on the far side of the dreary NIGHT of winter (ll. 51-52)

Prepositions

identified WITH—William James, the psychologist, must not be identified with Henry James, the novelist, though they were related.

remind OF—His walk reminds me of the way his father used to walk.

mingle WITH—During the carnival he mingled with the excited crowds.

spread WITH—The table was spread with meat, fish, fruit and cheese.

Word distinctions

Suggest short sentences which make clear the difference in meaning between the following paired words:

poignant and bitter
burst and break
florid and floral
surfeited and satisfied
success and succession
chilly and cool
current and currant
purple and crimson (be careful)
mood and temper
a strip and a stripe
delusive and illusory

Are 'audacious' and 'self-effacing' true opposites? (l. 20)
How are the two meanings of 'condense' connected? (l. 34)
All these words suggest a very large number:
    countless uncountable numberless innumerable

Words associated with certain ideas

List all the words you can find in the same paragraph which assist in creating the following impressions:

a) the association of youth with vigour
   (here are two: challenge, proudly)
b) the association of autumn
    (i) with richness
    (ii) with quietness
    (iii) with violence

Spellings

Notice these:
              poignant surfeited exhilaration adolescence
WR-
Find words with the given meanings and beginning with the letters shown.

wra-   anger covering a ghost
wre-   small bird struggle with opponent miserable
          flowers woven together twist sharply destroy
wri-   twist and fidget twist and squeeze twist as in pain
          fold of skin part of arm
wro-   made treat unjustly

Pronunciation

Practise these words:

poignant ('poiŋant) ravages ('rævidʒiz) surfeited ('sə:fitid)
serenity (si'reniti) exhilaration (igzilə'reiʃən) delicate ('delikit)
comfortable ('kʌmftəbl)

Explaining the meaning of words and phrases

Explain the following words and phrases in such a way as to bring out their meaning clearly.

a) boisterous (l. 4)   b) shrivelled (l. 4)   c) the florid and surfeited
luxury of summer (ll. 7–8)   d) mellow (l. 13)   e) soaks in colour (l. 19)
f) a grave mist-softened morning of reflection (ll. 30–31)   g) billowing
(l. 34)   h) huddle in ruffled feathers (l. 48)   i) live up to expectations
(l. 53).

Short answers to questions

The following exercises, based on the reading passage, should be dealt with in complete sentences. Only a little information is needed in each. Your answers should as far as possible be expressed in your own words.

1. Explain in one sentence why the author claims to be a pessimist.
2. In what way do the daffodils 'challenge' the boisterous March winds?
3. What explanation is offered for the feeling of freshness and exhilaration in Autumn?
4. Explain simply the essence of the contrast between spring and autumn colours.
5. What various kinds of country landscape are alluded to in the third paragraph?
6. Explain in simple words what is happening in the last sentence of the fourth paragraph.
7. In what various ways does the fifth paragraph convey an impression of quiet contentment?
8. What justification is suggested for the deaths in the animal world in winter?
9. How does the envisaged spring contrast with the real one?

Longer answers

These answers should be expressed within the number of words stated. Use only information found in the passage but express your answers in your own words as far as possible.
Remember to include all the relevant information. Read right through the passage to make sure.

1. Explain in simple and unmetaphorical language the general impression of spring that is given in the passage. (not more than 50 words)
2. Describe the various kinds of weather that may be experienced in autumn. (not more than 80 words)
3. From the material in the passage, to what extent is the author justified in identifying autumn with serenity? (not more than 80 words)

Practice

A. PRESENT AND PAST TENSES

Reference material pages 212–16

1. Present forms: active and passive

EXERCISES
   (i) Answer the following questions, using complete sentences introducing the appropriate verb tense.
   (ii) Explain why that tense is used in each case.

a) How many weeks' annual holiday do most people in your own country usually have?
b) How do most people spend their holiday?
c) When does your own next holiday start?
d) What are you doing this evening?
e) What are some of the places you have visited during.your holidays?
f) How long have you been studying English?
g) What do you usually do on your free day each week?
h) Why are you learning English?
i) What books have you read lately?
j) What have you been doing for the past half hour?
k) How long have you been living in your present house?
l) What does your best friend do for a living?
m) Why are some young people always changing their jobs?
n) What international questions have your fellow countrymen been discussing recently?
o) When is the next General Election being held in your country?
p) How is coffee made in your country?
q) What important subjects have been dealt with in the newspapers this week?
r) What new fashions have been introduced recently?

2. Past and present forms

Explain the differences in meaning between the sentences grouped together.

a) He went to New Zealand.
   He has been to New Zealand.
b) As he ate his lunch, he read a book.
   As he had eaten his lunch, he read a book.
c) She stood up and he sat down.
   She was standing up and he was sitting down.
d) He always asked his landlady for milk.
   He was always asking his landlady for milk.
e) Someone has telephoned you.
   Someone has been telephoning you.
f) Patrick Peters painted some interesting pictures.
   Patrick Peters has painted some interesting pictures.
g) You have been yawning throughout the lesson.
   You were yawning throughout the lesson.
h) He thought himself intelligent because he was at University.
   He thought himself intelligent because he had been at University.

i) He had a lot to do so he wanted quietness.
He had had a lot to do so he wanted quietness.

j) He crossed the road when the lights changed.
He was crossing the road when the lights changed.

k) The elderly man had worked as a journalist on a local paper.
The elderly man had been working as a journalist on a local paper.

l) He went to Australia the following week.
He was going to Australia the following week.

m) She had gone to do some shopping when her friend called.
She had been going to do some shopping when her friend called.

n) His watch was being mended.
His watch had been mended.

B. ALL TENSES

*Reference material
pages 216-17*

Other forms

EXERCISES

1. (i) Answer the following questions, using in each case a complete sentence, and introducing the appropriate verb tenses.
   (ii) Explain the use of the tenses.

a) How long do you think it will be before man is travelling regularly to and from the moon?
b) Do you think that such problems as feeding the world's population adequately and curing diseases such as cancer will have been solved by then?
c) What kinds of useful things had you already learned before you started school?
d) How long ago did you buy the shoes you are wearing?
e) How long have you been wearing them since the first time you put them on?
f) How did you spend your school holidays?
g) What newspaper do you read?
h) What will you be doing at this time tomorrow?
i) What do you think the weather will be like tomorrow?
j) How many meals will you have eaten today by the time you go to bed?
k) Why do some young people get angry with society?
l) What qualities do you hope to find in your husband or wife?
m) Before you started work, had you been attending a boarding school?
n) What kinds of things were you always worrying your parents for when you were a small child?
o) What happening in childhood has remained most vividly in your mind?
p) Describe an occasion when you were expecting something unpleasant to happen and you had a delightful surprise.
q) What were you talking about while you were eating lunch yesterday?
r) How will most people be travelling to work in the year 2000?
s) By that time how long will people have been travelling by car?
t) What had you been dreaming about when you woke up this morning?

2. Explain the differences in meaning between the sentences in the following groups.

a) I'm sorry I can't come. I lecture to a group of students on Thursdays.
I'm sorry I can't come. I am lecturing to a group of students on Thursday.

b) Where have you been all this morning?
Where were you all this morning?

c) My foreign students wonder when they will see a sunny day in England.
My foreign students wonder when they see a sunny day in England.
My foreign students will wonder when they see a sunny day in England.

d) I had been walking through the park when it suddenly started to rain.
I was walking through the park when it suddenly started to rain.

e) He is always receiving extraordinary letters.
He always receives extraordinary letters.

f) He has had a free day. He has completed the report on his researches.
He has had a free day. He has been completing the report on his researches.

g) He was making a long speech when I asked the question.
He made a long speech when I asked the question.

h) They will take a test when they enter the class.
They will have taken a test when they enter the class.

i) He said he was working in Leeds.
He said he had worked in Leeds.
He said he had been working in Leeds.
He said he would be working in Leeds.
He said he would work in Leeds.

j) I'm always leaving my umbrella at my friend's house.
I always leave my umbrella at my friend's house.

k) Maria doesn't come to class today.
Maria isn't coming to class today.
Maria won't come to class today.

l) He assured me he always wrote to his mother.
He assured me he would always write to his mother.

m) He said he always paid for his friend's drinks.
He said he was always paying for his friend's drinks.

n) He will mend the roof in a week's time.
He will have mended the roof in a week's time.

o) He will be waiting for you in the hall.
He is waiting for you in the hall.

3. Insert the appropriate tense, active or passive, in place of the bracketed infinitives in the following exercise. Adverbs which may come between auxiliaries are bracketed with the verbal form. The exercise includes several future in the past forms.

I (arrive) at the small hotel at ten o'clock the previous evening. My room (reserve) a week before. After I (sign) the hotel register, I (pause) to speak to the receptionist on duty.

'(Arrive) any letters for me?'

'I (be) sorry, madam,' she said, 'I (forget). One (arrive) this afternoon.'

She (give) me a buff-coloured envelope with my name on it in sprawling capitals. It (obviously deliver) by hand. Momentarily I (wonder) who (write) to me in this way. Then I (stick) it in my pocket.

'(May) I have some sandwiches and a coffee?' I (ask).

'The kitchen staff (already go) off duty, madam,' (say) the receptionist.

'I (travel) all day and I (not eat) since lunch,' I (complain). 'I (be) much too tired to go out again.'

'The night porter (come) in a few minutes,' the receptionist (tell) me. 'I (make) a cup of tea for him. (Make) I one for you, madam?'

'I (be) very grateful.'

'I (see) whether there (be) any biscuits in the staff room, and if so, I (bring) some up to you. (Leave) you early tomorrow morning? (Ask) I the porter to call you?'

'No, thank goodness. I (think) I (sleep) till ten. I (get) up at five this morning as I (catch) the 6.30 train. I (always travel) so I (be) used to it, but a long sleep (do) me good.'

The receptionist (ring) a bell as soon as I (sign) the register and now a tall man with an almost unnaturally black beard (appear). Taking my luggage he (lead) me up to a room on the first floor. After he (put) down my suitcase, he (just leave) when he (pause).

'I (hope) you (have) a quiet night,' he (say) significantly.

I (think) of this rather odd statement as I (prepare) for bed. I (expect) him to wish that I (sleep) well.

I (wash) when the receptionist (bring) a pot of tea. I (know) that tea (not keep) me awake so I thankfully (drink) three cups. My train (not leave) until one o'clock the next day so I (have) time to see a little of the town after I (have) breakfast. It (be) best if I (have) lunch on the train.

I (fall) asleep almost immediately after I (get) into bed. I (dream) that I (run) up and down the train looking for a non-existent restaurant car when I (disturb) by a sound like the howling of a dog. I (be) suddenly wide awake. In the next room it (seem) a dog (howl) quietly, mournfully, restlessly.

But a notice on the receptionist's desk (state) that dogs (not allow) in the hotel.

I (not unpack) my dressing gown so I (pull) on my coat. As I (do) so, I (feel) in my pocket the note which I (forget). I (open) the envelope and (read) the enclosed paper.

'Tonight I (claim) what you (take) from me.'

Cameron.

But Cameron (be) no longer alive. Cameron (be) my unsatisfactory cousin who (gamble) away all his own money and much of his parents', who (imprison) for fraud and (drown) while escaping from prison three years before. The ownership of our grandfather's business concerns (leave) to me, the younger cousin.

In the next room, the dog (howl) again. And then I (remember) Macbeth, Cameron's dog, who (die) soon after his master.

I (throw) open my door, and (run) to the next room, the only other one along this corridor. The door (be) open, and as I (go) in, I (can) see by the light outside that the room (be) empty. Bare boards, uncurtained windows, no stick of furniture and a door which (close) quietly behind me. And then a faint sound, as of a dog panting softly just in front of me.

SECTION II PUNCTUATION

INVERTED COMMAS

Reference material
pages 231–32

EXERCISES

1. Copy the following sentences, adding inverted commas and related commas and changing small letters to capitals where necessary. Arrange in paragraphs where necessary.

a) He laughed unpleasantly and said yes, I was released from prison yesterday and then, after a pause, added or should I say I got out of prison yesterday?

b) Throwing down his coat he asked has anyone telephoned? Yes said his wife a man rang about an hour ago. He wouldn't leave a message but said he'd call again. I wonder who that could have been speculated Jonathan thoughtfully.

c) Shall we have a drink in The Red Lion Peter suggested. I want to discuss my new play Only Death is Endless.

d) The following statement appeared in yesterday's evening papers: the police would like to interview a tall dark man of about thirty-five, clean-shaven and with a cast in his right eye.

e) When I say three all push together.

f) Explain why the writer uses the word self-seeking rather than selfish.

g) Many hands make light work and too many cooks spoil the broth show contrasting attitudes towards the value of co-operation.

2. Make up a conversation of about 50 words between two people introducing the following expressions: 'I asked him', 'he explained', 'I agreed' and with direct speech within inverted commas.

SECTION IV   CHOICE OF EXPRESSION

CHOICE OF WORDS—A

Reference material
pages 240-41

EXERCISES

1. Replace 'nice' by a more effective word or phrase in the following word groups:

a nice boy; a nice day; a nice holiday; a nice book; a nice rest; a nice job; a nice teacher; nice food.

One may speak of 'a LOVELY girl' but not of 'a lovely time', 'a lovely car', 'a lovely surprise'. Suggest more suitable adjectives.

An invention can be WONDERFUL but not a cook, coffee, weather. Again suggest more suitable adjectives.

2. Rewrite the following sentences, correcting any of the faults dealt with in the reference material.

a) It is with infinite regret that I am constrained to impart such desolating information, but alas, the room which it is your custom to occupy is not at this present juncture available and I am in the position of being able to afford you only one of inferior amenities.

b) The conditions in which most servants lived and worked in the nineteenth century weren't very nice.

c) We are in receipt of your communication of the 12th inst. and wish to tender our thanks for same.

d) Our eyes were gladdened by the sight of woolly lambs frolicking gaily in the verdant meadows. We lifted our hearts in thankfulness to the benevolent heavens.

e) The gloomy outlook of the consumer public is manifest in the current downward trend in the retail trade. An easing of the burden of taxation would do much to encourage an upswing of confidence and hence increasedly favourable prospects for industrial production together with a welcome reprieve for those with redundancy threats hanging ominously over their heads.

SECTION VI   REPORTED SPEECH

STATEMENTS

Reference material
pages 247-48

EXERCISES

1. Convert the following examples of direct speech into reported speech. Suggest a suitable speaker where no one is mentioned.

a) 'I'm getting tired of waiting,' he complained. 'I've been sitting here for half an hour. The same thing happened when I came here yesterday. The next time it happens, I shall report it.'

b) 'It must be at least ten years since I last saw you.'

c) 'I had expected to see more people here tonight,' commented the secretary. 'We should have publicised the meeting in yesterday's paper.'

d) 'You ought to eat less, get up earlier in the morning and do plenty of exercise to get your weight down. I used to walk five miles a day when I was your age.' 'But you're not me,' I said.

e) 'We must arrange our holiday during the coming week. We should have done it a month ago.'

f) 'If you must keep three dogs, practise singing and cook such peculiar-smelling foods, you really ought to have a house of your own.'

2.   Rewrite the following sentences, giving the past form of the verbs underlined and making any other related changes.

    a) I know he telephoned an hour ago. He told me so himself.
    b) I shouldn't be surprised if you had to pay duty on that.
    c) It seems very likely that even if he gets a rise he will still give up his job.

Composition

IMPRESSIONISTIC DESCRIPTION

A PRACTICAL DESCRIPTION: A presentation of FACTS.
                                        ACCURACY, EXACTNESS, COMPLETENESS,
                                        LOGICAL ARRANGEMENT, EFFICIENCY OF
                                        EXPRESSION are the essentials.

AN IMPRESSIONISTIC DESCRIPTION: The creation of an IMPRESSION,
                                                ATMOSPHERE or MOOD.

The opening passage offers a comparison between the spring, symbolising youth and its qualities, and autumn, suggesting maturity.

APPROACH: Before beginning, decide what your main impressions are to be.
MATERIAL: SELECT those DETAILS which help to create these impressions.
EXPRESSION: Choose WORDS which by their MEANING, ASSOCIATIONS and
                        SOUND can deepen the impression.

Sentences

Even in one or two sentences, an impression, atmosphere or mood can be conveyed.

EXAMPLES:
1.   An impression of a persistent salesman.
    Suddenly he was at my elbow, sleekly smiling and overpoweringly servile, sallow of face, with pouched eyes and hair just that shade longer. He would make me a very special offer, exclusively for me, with instant delivery to my home and a discount that would rob him of the slenderest margin of gain.

2.   An impression of a descent in a chair-lift.
    Legs dangling in nothingness, one floated soundlessly and infinitely peacefully over forest green and meadow green, harsh rock and smooth grassy slope, towards a picture map of field and village. Here was a bird's delight in gliding lazily earthwards, borne aloft by space, a god in a mini-chariot, surveying indolently the engaging toybox world of Earth's children.

EXERCISES
Write one or two sentences which present a vivid impression of any of these topics.

    a) Describing a person who has just received some wonderful news.
    b) A dive into a deep pool.
    c) A smell of cooking that meets you as you enter a house.
    d) A space rocket ready for launching.
    e) An impression of the moon's surface.
    f) The moment when a football crowd acknowledges a goal.

A paragraph

The following paragraph conveys an impression of the Reading Room at the British Museum.

Immediately the neophyte enters the British Museum Reading Room he is aware that he has been admitted not to a mere library but to a major temple dedicated to the secluded goddess of erudition. The vast circular nave, crammed with a devoted congregation, is yet shrouded in meditative silence. At long radiating tables are stationed the worshippers, of all ages and races. Each sits in rapt contemplation of the holy and aged volumes surrounding him, a devout ascetic, islanded in the luminous circle shed by his reading-lamp. That his incantations are written not spoken is fitting in this hushed sanctuary. Attendants move discreetly, bearing more volumes from the underground repositories of secret lore. And among these living disciples wander the ghosts, revered authors and savants whose spiritual eternal home lies within these walls. Imperceptibly, living and dead draw more closely to the elucidation of the eternal mysteries of their chosen goddess, until, in the winter twilight, the living are ejected to the world of the evening paper, the Underground, and the self-service tea-shop, a little dazed by this sudden transition from the tranquil precincts of Academia to Chaos. The dead remain in their Elysium.

Vocabulary

neophyte	one recently converted to a religion or entering a monastery
secluded	enclosed apart
erudition	learning
nave	part of a church for the congregation
shrouded	covered, enveloped, wrapped round
rapt	completely absorbed in religious joy
incantations	words sung or recited as a magic spell
lore	learning
elucidation	explaining, making clear
Elysium	(Greek mythology) a heavenly home for the dead

This is clearly an example of an impressionistic description. The British Museum Reading Room is not described photographically; instead, a dominant impression, in this case of hushed, almost mystical devotion to study, is created.

Here are a few useful recommendations for writing a paragraph of this kind:

(i) Details, both visual and auditory, are selected for their relevance to the desired impression. In this case, vastness, silence, variety of readers, their isolation in a multitude, their absorbed concentration, the sense of tradition and of the past in the building, its associations, the contrast with the noisy world outside—all serve to deepen the impression of some temple of learning.

(ii) The choice of words and images. Here the impression of religious mystery is created partly by such words as 'neophyte', 'dedicated', 'goddess', 'nave', 'meditative', 'worshippers' and so on. As the whole passage is itself a form of image, no extra imagery is introduced, though the idea of a temple and devotion is maintained throughout the passage, extending to words like 'precincts' and 'devotion'.

(iii) In this paragraph the main theme is introduced in the first sentence and the rest of the paragraph consists of details which confirm the opening statement. The final short sentence acts as a firm conclusion.

EXERCISES

1. Write a paragraph about a slum street based on the following ideas. You can add one or two additional details if you wish.

District of the town near the river—low-lying—approached through district of neatly-painted carefully-kept houses—street deteriorates to unpainted dilapidated buildings with doors opening on to pavements—slatternly women of all shapes and sizes leaning against walls gossiping—small dirty children playing in gutters—boys in ragged clothes too big for them circling on rusty bicycles—stray lean mongrel dogs sniffing round piles of rubbish—dreary public houses on most corners with groups of men clustered outside—inhabitants all out of doors escaping from gloomy rooms within—yet sense of uncontrolled life and vitality absent from more conventional houses at respectable end of street.

2.   Here are some further subjects for descriptive paragraphs:

a) The general waiting-room at a provincial railway station.
b) A deserted sandy beach early in the morning.
c) A car ride by night.
d) A room used as a family nursery.
e) An almost deserted town square in the middle of a very cold Sunday.
f) A hospital ward on visiting day.
g) A small churchyard.
h) A town pavement café.
i) A school playground filled with children.
j) A classroom of students on a hot sleepy afternoon.
k) A theatre before the curtain goes up.

An essay

The comprehension passage is an example of the not very common essay that is entirely descriptive. Faced with a topic of this kind, it is advisable to decide first on the main impressions to be conveyed. Then the various aspects of the topic, each of which will be developed in a paragraph, are worked out and a plan devised. The essay is then embarked on.

Remember to choose WORDS carefully: for their relevance, associations and sound. Devices such as vivid metaphors, rhythm, sentence pattern can contribute to the overall impression.

But above all, THINK IN ENGLISH—with short controlled sentences and a SIMPLE STYLE OF WRITING ADAPTED TO YOUR CONTROL OVER THE LANGUAGE. DO NOT TRY TO TRANSLATE FROM YOUR OWN LANGUAGE.

Here are some suggestions of topics: A feasible length is six to seven paragraphs, between about 500 and 600 words.

1. A ruined cottage.
2. A kindergarten.
3. A painting that is well known to you.
4. A windy day.
5. A village shop.
6. Siesta in a sun-baked town.
7. The High Street at midday and midnight.
8. A short but unpleasant attack of influenza.

Descriptions of people

In this kind of description, it is equally necessary to decide on one dominant impression and to choose your details and arrange them so as to convey this impression vividly to the reader.

Consider this subject:

A description of an old sailor.

The obvious 'old sailor' would be found smoking his pipe on the quayside, with lively blue eyes and a suntanned face, fond of children, full of mythical accounts of his voyages, a companion to the older seamen and fishermen, an object of amused tolerance to the younger.

Less usual descriptions could be given:

a) The old sailor who works as a gardener—a morose taciturn man—warns young people against going to sea because of its discomforts and horrors.
b) The old sailor who keeps a dockside public house—now grown very fat—still enormously strong with loud voice—bars hung with objects from all over the world collected by self and customers—his stories.

c) The retired captain—lives with servant (member of former crew) in bungalow with distant view of sea—a quiet man much respected—member of parish council—keen golfer—interested in youth club work—churchman—strict disciplinarian, etc.

In each case, one impression is dominant. (a) an aversion to his former job, (b) joviality, (c) respectability. Your description will, of course, include details of the person's appearance, dress, personality, behaviour, interests and background.

Try one of the following descriptions:

   (i) Yourself at fifteen.
  (ii) The typical good sheriff of a Western film.
 (iii) A conceited and famous drama critic.
 (iv) An overworked mother of five children.
  (v) A middle-aged countryman who has spent all his life in the same village.
 (vi) A young man in rebellion against the world around him.
(vii) A thoroughly efficient person.
(viii) Sunworshippers.
 (ix) Visitors welcome and unwelcome.

PRACTICE PAPER 6

I READING COMPREHENSION

Section A

In this section you must choose the word or phrase which best completes each sentence. Write down each number and beside it the letters **A, B, C, D** and **E.** Then in each case cross through the letter before the word or phrase you choose. Give one answer only to each question.

1. Income tax rates are —— to one's annual income.

   A related   **B** dependent   **C** associated   **D** adapted
   E based

2. He went ahead with unpopular changes, —— to hostile criticism.

   A opposed   **B** indifferent   **C** sensible   **D** unaware
   E contrary

3. A sudden movement caught the antelope's attention and he instantly became —— and alert.

   A unsuspecting   **B** intensive   **C** superstitious
   D suspicious   **E** submissive

4. During their first teacher-training year, the students often visited local schools for the —— of lessons.

   A observation   **B** investigation   **C** inspection
   D examination   **E** observance

5. The teacher was —— both in his marking of homework and also in his treatment of offenders.

   A lenient   **B** merciful   **C** forgiving   **D** sympathetic
   E pitiful

6. Elegantly-dressed people were strolling along the many tree-lined —— through the park.

   A alloys   **B** allies   **C** avenues   **D** passages   **E** alleys

7. He is not one of those —— members of the staff who read 'The Times' and take an interest in art and philosophy.

   A clever   **B** erudite   **C** learned   **D** proficient
   E intellectual

8. The snake —— smoothly through the long grass.

   A crept   **B** skidded   **C** glided   **D** crouched   **E** strolled

9. The fire must have broken —— after the staff had gone home.

   A down   **B** in   **C** through   **D** out   **E** up

10. He came to inspect the house —— buying it.

   A in the event of   **B** with a view to   **C** with reference to
   D on account of   **E** in case of

II USE OF ENGLISH

Section B

Read the following passage and then answer the questions which follow it.

Many visitors to Great Britain who make a point of visiting the famous cultural shrines of Stratford, Oxford, Cambridge and Canterbury are less aware of the equally rewarding historical interest and the friendly individuality of the ancient capital, the city of Winchester.

This Hampshire centre of around 30,000 inhabitants has welcomed (and, on   5 various occasions, repulsed) a succession of visitors for nearly three thousand years. Early tribes occupied it from time to time, and much later the Roman colonisers established a commercial centre with solidly-constructed straight roads radiating from it. It was Alfred the Great who, in the ninth century, made the small town the national centre of learning, though his statue domi-   10 nating the main street recalls the warrior with raised cross-like sword. Norman succeeded Saxon and soon the cathedral, one of the loveliest and richest in architectural interest in England, was being erected. A College was founded in the fourteenth century and even though a decline in the wool trade led to a period of economic stagnation, the College maintained the town's tradition   15 of learning and is one of the most famous public schools of today.

Present-day traffic has destroyed much of the peace of the City centre. Private cars and buses which surge through the narrow streets at week-ends may be supplemented on weekdays by lorries roaring on their way to Southampton. And yet away from the busier roads, the prevailing atmosphere   20 remains one of calm meditation and contentment. From the smooth sun-flecked lawns of the Close, patterned with leaf-shadows from gently stirring foliage, rises the Cathedral, its comfortable, square, late-Norman tower, its Norman transepts and severe Gothic nave suggesting that the beauty created by man, though not imperishable, may survive wars and revolutions, and   25 represent the endurance of traditional values even in an age of undignified scurrying change. Certain houses round the Close may have provided homes for the loyal subjects of the first Queen Elizabeth when Shakespeare was learning to write. The Youth Hostel, a mill standing on the city's river, is more than two hundred years old. In well-mannered unobtrusiveness, the old   30 buildings of the main street blend with the new, and a walk through the town centre is one of enjoyable discovery.

The rounded hills of Southern England, among which the city is built, shelter a countryside of farms and picturesque villages, where, despite motor transport and television, many of the old rural traditions and mental attitudes   35 are preserved.

Winchester belongs to its surroundings: it is the appropriate centre of a region of prosperous, quiet, richly-green countryside. Lively, up-to-date and friendly, it maintains very many English traditions of fine domestic and ecclesiastical architecture, of graciousness and imperturbability, of richly inventive   40 variety and peaceful dignity which are among the highest achievements of all those English planners and designers who created the heritage we now enjoy.

1. What feature had the Winchester of Roman times in common with that of the Middle Ages?
2. What aspect of a previous period in the history of the town did the foundation of the College recall?
3. What obvious contrast is there between different parts of the modern town?
4. Suggest one of the traditional values referred to in line 26.
5. Why should a walk through the main street be one of enjoyable discovery?
6. In what ways does Winchester 'belong to its surroundings'? (see line 37)
7. The historical interest of Winchester is said to be 'equally rewarding' (line 3). What to?
8. Account for the use of brackets in lines 5-6.
9. Contrast the attitude of many of the visitors of the distant past with that of visitors of today.
10. Why is the word 'though' used in line 10?
11. What impression of Alfred the Great's statue does the word 'dominating' (line 10-11) give?
12. 'Yet' in line 20 could be replaced by a phrase of 5-7 words which would show what 'yet' is referring to. The sentence would then start with the word 'but'. Suggest a suitable phrase.
13. What aspect of modern times mentioned elsewhere in the passage is referred to by the word 'scurrying' in line 27?
14. Express in another way what is conveyed by 'mental attitudes' in line 35.
15. Quote a phrase of seven words that appears in the passage and suggests the spokes of a wheel.
16. Quote the single word from the first paragraph which indicates most convincingly the importance of Winchester in a past age.
17. In what way does the last paragraph relate Winchester to England as a whole?
18. In a paragraph of not more than 100 words suggest why a cultured tourist might enjoy a visit to Winchester. Your ideas should all come from the passage.

III   GENERAL PRACTICE

Section A

1. Copy the list of verbs preceded by THEY in *Column A*. After each verb write the word group from *Column B* which would normally follow it.

Examples: They persuaded   him to sing.
              They admired   his singing.

A	B
They made	
They knew	
They wanted	him sing
They advised	
They enjoyed	

They believed	him to sing
They saw	
They forced	
They let	that he would sing
They thought	
They realised	
They allowed	his singing
They appreciated	
They encouraged	
They dreaded	

2. Rewrite these sixteen sentences, giving the full written form for each bracketed numeral and adding any other words that in certain cases should precede the numeral. Notice whether the following noun is singular or plural as this may affect your decision. Underline the words you add.

Example: He bought (3) record he heard.
He bought the third record he heard.

a) Having flown (1), he refuses to fly again.
b) William (IV) reigned in (19) century.
c) The Mercury spaceship splashed down at (1.23) on (31) of February, (1999).
d) He was (2) agent, working simultaneously for Ruritania and Arcadia.
e) I haven't had a (1) minute to spare all day.
f) Newcastle United won the football match (3-0).
g) The score in the final game of tennis was (40-0).
h) He lives on (5) floor at (123) (4) Avenue and his telephone number is (0987).
i) He won (8) game.
j) The (3) countries, Northmark, Southland and Westalia, have established a (3) alliance.
k) According to the latest census, the population is (9,438,302).
l) Not many of them are employed. (¼) are housewives; (¼) are under (16) and (⅛) have retired or are incapacitated.
m) Only (.04) of the population have had this disease.
n) He made out a cheque for (£14.56).
o) Of his (4) brothers, (3) are married and (4) is engaged.
p) He has (10) sons and says he wants (11) boy to make up a football team.

3. The following is part of a possible dictionary definition. Read it through and then deal briefly with the exercises below.

IRON [áiən] 1. U. Common and useful metal from which steel is made: *wrought iron, cast iron, pig iron. As hard as iron. Strike while the iron is hot.*
2. C. A device made of iron, often of a type heated and used for smoothing clothes: *a curling-iron. To have too many irons in the fire.*
3. (pl.) Fetters restricting a prisoner's freedom of movement.

IRON [áiən] vt. Smooth a surface with an iron, usually heated, as to *iron a tablecloth, iron out difficulties,* i.e. remove difficulties.

a) Explain the words in square brackets.
b) Explain the mark over the 'a' in square brackets.
c) Give the full word or words for each of these abbreviations:
   (i) U. (ii) C. (iii) pl. (iv) vt.
d) What is the meaning of the letters i.e.?
e) What have all the expressions in italics got in common?
f) Explain the use of a curling-iron.
g) Explain the surface meaning and also the more generalised meaning of the two sayings:
   Strike while the iron is hot.
   To have too many irons in the fire.
h) Why should the expression 'iron out difficulties' have the meaning of 'remove difficulties'?

4. Each of the following commands can be expressed more politely and pleasantly. Rewrite the commands as polite requests but in such a way that while each is suitable for the occasion on which it is being said, no two are alike in form. The addition of the one word 'please' is not enough.

a) Help me. (you are trying to lift a heavy suitcase)
b) Write to me. (to a friend going on holiday)
c) Change a ten-pound note for me. (to a shopkeeper)
d) Have a cup of tea. (to a friend who has just dropped in)
e) Open this suitcase. (a customs officer is speaking)
f) Tell me the way to the station. (to a passing stranger)
g) Remember to post that letter. (a woman is speaking to her husband)
h) Read now. (a teacher is speaking to a student)

5. The exclamation 'Well' or 'Very well' can express a wide variety of meanings in spoken English. Ten of these are listed and numbered below. Write down these meanings, numbering them, and beside each, write the capital letter preceding the sentences illustrating that meaning.

   (i) hesitation
   (ii) surprise
   (iii) challenge
   (iv) a pause for thought
   (v) relief
   (vi) qualified approval
   (vii) agreement
   (viii) resignation
   (ix) decision
   (x) ironic surprise

A Well, thank goodness that's finished.
B Very well, you can have it.

C Well, I never thought it would rain.

D How long have you known her? Well, I should say about five years.

E How do you like this dress? Well, I like the colour.

F Oh, well, I suppose it won't take more than an hour.

G Well, well, look who's come to help!

H Do you enjoy chamber music? Well, no, not really.

I Well, what do you want?

J Well, I know what we can do. We can send him a greetings telegram.

IV   USE OF ENGLISH

Section A

1. Rewrite each of these sentences in such a way as to replace the existing participle by a clause. A slight change may be made in the other clause where this is necessary.

> *Example:* Examining the document carefully, he asked me where I had found it.
>
> *Answer:* As he examined the document carefully, he asked me where I had found it.

a) Feeling very tired, he sat down.

b) On hearing the news, he rushed to the hospital.

c) I waited in the passage, wondering what to do next.

d) He slept on a park bench, having nowhere else to go.

e) He went to live in Birmingham, opening a shop there.

f) I asked for help, doubting however whether anyone would volunteer.

g) The police left the house, having taken statements from everyone.

h) He worked very hard, making a fortune as a result.

2. Finish each of the following sentences in such a way that it means exactly the same as the sentence printed above it.

> *Example:* When the parents went out, the children were watching television.
> The parents left the. ....
>
> *Answer:* The parents left the children watching television when they went out.

1. He had already posted the letter when he remembered the extra stamp he should have stuck on.
   It was not ....

2. This letter was almost certainly posted weeks ago.
   This letter must ....

3. It wasn't necessary for you to hurry so much.
   You ....

4. He persuaded me to make further enquiries before paying the money.
   He convinced ....

5. Whenever I had been to the restaurant, it had always been full of people.
   I had never. ....

115

6. Even though I tried to understand the lesson, I learned almost nothing.
Despite ....

7. One of the features of his style is that the reader has to concentrate intensely to understand it.
His style demands ....,

8. He is unable to get about very much and this frequently makes him depressed.
His frequent. ....

9. You would not be so fat if you took more exercise.
Taking more exercise. ....

10. My parents always refrained from influencing me in any way.
In ....

V USE OF ENGLISH

Section C

The following are some notes about the structure of British education. Using them as your material, write an article on the subject for an educational periodical appearing in your own country. The beginning of the article has been written for you; write another 125 to 175 words.

THE STATE SYSTEM OF EDUCATION IN ENGLAND

Age Range

School attendance legally compulsory: 5 to 16.
1972: 29·3% stayed at school beyond 16—15% beyond 17.
Together with pupils in further education: 30% receiving full-time education till nearly 18.

Structure of School System

1. Nursery schools (3+)—voluntary attendance.
   Not sufficient provision for demand.
2. Primary schools:
   a) Infant: 5–7   b) Junior: 7–11.
3. Secondary schools: 11–19.
   These may vary in type, according to local education authority,
   Pattern 1
   a) Grammar schools: may prepare pupils for University entrance.
   b) Modern schools: for less academically gifted children.
   c) Technical schools: these provide some vocational training together with the normal school subjects.
   Pattern 2
   Comprehensive schools.
   These cater for pupils suited for all of above types of school.
   Often considerably larger and can offer wider subject range.
   Increasingly replacing other types of secondary school.

Recent Developments
Some local authorities experimenting with 'middle schools' (11–16) with various educational alternatives beyond.
Other have 'sixth-form colleges' for pupils over 16.

Here is the opening of the article:

The State System of Education in England

The legal age for school attendance is between five and sixteen years. In 1972, nearly 30% of pupils stayed on after sixteen, however, while 15% did not leave school before they were eighteen. If full-time attendance at Colleges of Further Education is included, this later percentage rises to thirty.
   Schooling is divided into two stages, Primary and Secondary, though

VI   INTERVIEW

Section D

   The fourth section of the Interview demands an ability on the part of the candidate to express his ideas suitably and fluently in one of a variety of situations in which he might find himself.
   The Syllabus stipulates the following:

(2–3 minutes) The candidate will be given a booklet containing a brief description of a number of situations and asked to turn to a particular passage, which the examiner will read aloud. The candidate should then make the appropriate response, paying due attention to tone and manner and the use of socially acceptable and appropriate forms; these are the basis of assessment in this part of the test. Each candidate will be given five of these exercises.

Notice the emphasis on TONE, MANNER and USE OF SOCIALLY ACCEPT-ABLE and APPROPRIATE FORMS.

Some useful expressions

REQUEST	I wonder if you'd mind helping me with this.
	Would you be so kind as to write it down.
	Would you mind wrapping this for me.
	Would you like to try this coat on?
	Would you be able to come back later?
	I hope you don't mind my glancing at your newspaper.
APOLOGIES	I'm so sorry I'm late. I just missed a bus.
	Please forgive my forgetting your birthday.
ADVICE	I should recommend going there quite early.
	(Don't you think) it might be a good idea to wait a little?

SUGGESTIONS	You know, I'd suggest going to see him yourself. It would/might be as well to see a doctor about it. How about putting it off till tomorrow? Shall we send them a telegram?
OFFER TO HELP	Would you like me to/May I/Couldn't I carry that for you? I'd be very willing to look after the children for you.
INVITATION	We're giving a party on Saturday evening. Would you be able to come?
ACCEPTANCE	Yes, I'd be pleased to. Yes, I'd love to.
REFUSAL	Oh, what a pity! I'll be away this week-end. I'd love to have come.

The best way to prepare for this test is to imagine as many situations as you can and to consider beforehand just how you would deal with them and what you would say. Here is one possible example:

You have bought a new light bulb but this has provided light for only half an hour. You have taken it back to the shop to claim a replacement.

Suitable answer:

Good morning. I bought this bulb here yesterday afternoon. It was the assistant over there with the glasses who served me; he may remember me as we discussed prices of colour TV sets. The bulb was all right when he tested it but in fact it lasted only half an hour and under these circumstances I think I have the right to a replacement.

Here are some other situations to deal with:

1. A friend who is spending a few days in a hotel in your town has written just before his arrival suggesting your meeting him for dinner. You have another engagement, so just before you leave, you telephone the hotel to suggest some other arrangement. Your friend however is not in. What do you say from the time you get through to the hotel?

2. You have a neighbour with a spoilt eight-year-old child whom you secretly dislike intensely. One day you see the child going out of your gate carrying a large bunch of the chrysanthemums you were especially proud of. You wish to keep on good terms with your neighbour but are quite furious about this. What do you say to the neighbour?

3. You are working as an au pair with an English family with duties arranged for certain hours. Several times the lady asks you to do a job that will extend well into your free time and finally you feel you must say something. What do you say?

4. Apologise to your boss or teacher who is annoyed with you for being late the third time in succession.

5. Explain to your teacher why you have given no homework in for the past three weeks.

6. You arrive alone at the only hotel in a town late at night to find that it is quite full. Plead with the manager or receptionist to accommodate you somehow.

7. An acquaintance invites you to her house by telephone at 8.30 p.m. You do not know whether this means you will be having dinner and also whether you are expected to dress suitably for the occasion. What do you say to find out tactfully?

8. You have to get in touch urgently with your teacher, but know only his or her surname. It is a small town you both live in so you decide to consult the telephone directory and telephone each of the people with that name, explaining what you want and (if the person rung is not the right one) if she/he knows your teacher. Suggest the conversation that takes place.

6
Reading, Vocabulary and Comprehension

A Factual Essay

Landscaping Yields a Harvest of Efficiency

When offices are planned the attention paid to the correct use of space, and individual and company needs, is often totally inadequate. Bad planning can frustrate the manager and employee and reduce their level of performance. This is why so much research has been undertaken since the war into effective
5 office planning.

There is a growing realisation that investment in people means that their needs should be thoroughly analysed and provided for. It has encouraged a number of office planning approaches. The best of these approaches take into account not just the physical aspects of a building but the complex individual
10 and group relationships which need to be understood before a plan is implemented.

A man's personal preference is always for his own separate office. Where this can be achieved it provides privacy and special advantages for him. However, it is quite uneconomic for most organisations to provide such
15 facilities on anything but a limited scale. Moreover the corporate needs for good communications, smooth exchange of ideas and paper work, and flexibility demand a different form of planning. Preoccupation with rental costs has led in the past to open-plan offices which in the worst circumstances are laid out in such a regimented fashion that the atmosphere is totally
20 impersonal.

Nevertheless, costs must be faced realistically. Perhaps the best balance between the needs of most of the employees and the needs of the company are to be found in landscaped offices.

Developed in Germany in the late 1950s, landscaping, or *Bürolandschaft*
25 as it is sometimes called, seeks to achieve good communications and information flow by the correct juxtaposition of departments. Its aim is to provide a pleasing working environment for all, coupled with economic use of space and the ability on management's part to alter office layout to cope with changes in working methods.
30 Ideally a floor area of not less than 6000 sq. ft. is required, generally in the form of a square or rectangle the sides of which have a ratio of less than two to one. Employees are grouped together in clusters, in accordance with a plan that takes into account work flow and desirable relationships across traditional organisational barriers. Such groups are identified and separated
35 by movable screens. An acceptable general noise level is achieved by careful acoustic control to provide aural privacy and mask intrusive noise.

* * *

The main disadvantage of landscaping, particularly to the manager who enjoys the privacy and freedom from disturbance of a private office, is that its implementation requires individuals to recognise the need to balance their 40 requirements with corporate needs. At first it might appear that all such people would react strongly to being wheedled out of their enclosed spaces. Recent research suggests this may not be so.

What may at first appear to be a second disadvantage of office landscaping is that it requires careful study of the company and individual requirements 45 before it is implemented. This calls for skills and experience which may not be possessed by a company's own office management or organisation and methods staff. The alternative is to call on the services of an outside consultant, but this service is often felt to be too comprehensive and too expensive. A less costly way of training and guiding the company is perhaps what is 50 needed, to avoid losing many times over the gains in short-term economies during the occupancy of a badly-planned environment.

Increasing information is becoming available about the effect of environment on the individual. In the past, ignorance about such effect has led to discontent and long-term detriment to people's performance. As the calibre 55 of employees increases, and as the computer absorbs routine tasks, there will be a parallel growth in the need to understand what men require in their surroundings to stimulate them to work effectively. Present office planning research can contribute benefits to both employee and employer.

Ultimately the refinements may lead to a situation in which an office 60 building will reflect even in its external appearance the activities of those who work within. The tall rectangular building may well give way to a more complex and exciting shape providing areas with which the individual can fully identify himself. (From supplement 'The Ideal Office', *The Times*: 6th September 1971—condensed as shown by asterisks)

Notes on the passage—General

This is an example of a straightforward presentation of facts. The vocabulary, though far from simple, is unadorned. The metaphorical title is an exception, though the 'harvest' metaphor is very conventional, in fact is more or less a cliché. Other single words which are in fact used metaphorically ('faced' in line 21; 'reflect' in line 61) pass unnoticed as such.

Special points

Line
6   There is a growing realisation
    'There' in such constructions is nearly always followed by some form of the verb 'to be': There seems to be (or exist) ——;
    There may be ——.
    Avoid such constructions as: 'There came a man' or 'There happened an accident'. The student is advised to use only 'be' forms after 'there'.
7   'It has encouraged'. What does 'it' refer back to?
8   'approaches'. One speaks of an approach to a problem or matter—a way of thinking about or dealing with it.

12 'his own personal office'. Remember the possessive adjective or form of a noun before 'own'—not an article.

14 Notice the following sentence openings:

However —— (l. 14)   Moreover —— (l. 15)
Nevertheless —— (l. 21)   Ideally —— (l. 30)
Ultimately —— (l. 60)

Explain the meaning in each case.

21-23 What grammatical error can be found in this sentence?

24 *Bürolandschaft*—with the use of italics to separate an unusual word. Inverted commas could also serve this purpose. This is an example of the introduction into a language of the foreign word first used for a new idea—sometimes with a snob-appeal, as an adequate native expression may exist side by side with it.

38-41 A rather long sentence, with a subject widely separated from the verb. It is best to avoid sentences of this kind as control can easily be lost and construction and meaning become confused.

'At first' (ll. 41 and 44)

Remember that 'at first' suggests that some kind of contradiction of the statement will follow soon. The contradiction is obvious in the first case. In the second it is implied: there is a suggestion that this may not actually prove to be a disadvantage.

Prepositions

pay attention TO   research INTO effective office planning
investment IN people   invest IN business
provide FOR a person's need   provide a person WITH what he wants
a preference FOR a separate office
prefer his own office TO working with someone else
it is uneconomic FOR most organisations to provide
it is difficult FOR me to understand
it is impossible FOR him to come
ON a limited scale

preoccupation WITH rental costs (interest IN rental costs)
IN the worst circumstances   IN such a regimented fashion
changes IN working methods   IN clusters
IN ACCORDANCE WITH a plan
freedom FROM disturbance   free FROM commitments
react strongly TO being wheedled
information ABOUT the effect of environment ON the individual
a growth IN the need to understand

Word distinctions

Totally   entirely   completely   quite   utterly   are all similar in meaning
'utterly' is the strongest and most dramatic—utterly exhausted
'quite' is the weakest
Effective control of the disease—reasonably successful
effectual eradication of the disease—completely successful

122

A *complex* matter of organisation   a complicated explanation of one's lateness

These are very similar in meaning—'complicated' could suggest more confusion

economic problems (financial)   an economical housewife (careful with money)
deal with situations and people in general   *cope with* difficult and demanding situations and people;

> *Group together* cluster join unite assemble gather link amalgamate meet

to —— a club;	The Great North Road ——
clouds ——;	Edinburgh with London.
different groups —— to achieve	firms ——;
something;	Parliament (the school) ——.
the children —— round the teacher	
groups —— to exchange	
information;	

Movable screens   a mobile library

Aural privacy   an oral examination

> *Wheedle* persuade convince coax urge
> The mother spent hours — the ailing child to eat.
> I — him I was right.
> His teacher — him to work harder but he was obstinate.
> We — him to come.
> With her sweetest and most appealing smile she tried to — him into buying her a fur coat

A *comprehensive* study of the problem (all-inclusive);   a comprehensible explanation (that can be understood)
There is no job *available* in an office accessible from my home.

Expressions to learn and use

All his attempts to secure a University place were *frustrated*;
a high *level of performance*;   *undertake* (carry out; do) *research*;
There is a growing realisation that scientific research must be controlled in the interests of humanity.
You should *take into account* the fact that he has had little training.
Implement a plan—put a plan into effect
The desperate shortage of homes *demands* immediate action
Complaints about overcharging have *led to* a thorough investigation.
Increased demand *coupled with* programmes for industrial expansion has lowered unemployment figures.
The company has at last *recognised the need for* overall modernisation.
This will *call for* considerable capital expenditure.
They have had to *call on* the services of an expert. (or: call in an expert)

123

An attractive shopping precinct can *contribute benefits* both to retailers and the public.

A child's behaviour may *reflect* his home environment.

Open fires are *giving way to* various forms of central heating.

Explaining the meaning of words and phrases

Explain the following words and phrases in such a way as to bring out their meaning clearly.

a) investment in people (l. 6)   b) the complex individual and group relationships (ll. 9–10)   c) flexibility (l. 17)   d) preoccupation with rental costs (ll. 17–18)   e) uneconomic (l. 14)   f) in such a regimented fashion (l. 19) g) intrusive (l. 36)   h) to balance their requirements with corporate needs (ll. 40–41).

Short answers to questions

The following exercises, based on the reading passage, should be dealt with in complete sentences. Only a little information is needed in each case. As far as possible your answers should be expressed in your own words.

1. What psychological and practical effect can bad office planning have?
2. What two factors must be considered when a plan for a new office layout is being prepared?
3. Summarise in one sentence the principles of the open-plan house or office.
4. What has been in the past a consideration that has led to possible inflexibility in open-plan schemes?
5. In what other spheres of modern life is landscaping made use of besides in offices? (Give your own ideas here)
6. What may be one of the main difficulties of working in a large open-plan office?
7. Why may individuals resist the conversion to an open-plan working arrangement?
8. For what economic reason may a company hesitate to consider this conversion?
9. What may be a further development of this trend?

Longer answers

These answers should be expressed within the number of words stated. Use only information found in the passage but express your answers in your own words as far as possible.

1. What is it suggested will be achieved by the introduction of effective office planning? (not more than 80 words)
2. How may some of the problems of office organisation be eliminated by office landscaping? (not more than 90 words)
3. What difficulties may confront a company which decides to introduce office landscaping? (not more than 100 words)

Practice

A. CONDITIONS

Reference material
page 218

EXERCISES

1. Complete the following sentences, with due regard to the tense you use.

a) If we were always to tell the exact truth, . . .
b) A considerable improvement can be seen in a student's work if . . .
c) If refrigeration had not been developed, . . .
d) People would be better-tempered if . . .
e) Had primitive man been able to leave written records, . . .
f) Julius Caesar would not have been assassinated if . . .
g) If all husbands helped their wives in the home, . . .
h) Smallpox can be practically eliminated if . . .
i) If the people of the world are to be better fed, . . .
j) The ordinary person in my country would be happier if . . .

2. Answer the following sentences, each answer in one or more complete sentences. Give careful consideration to the tense used.

a) What would you do if you met a being from outer space?
b) If you had been born a hundred years earlier, what job do you think you would have been doing?
c) If children are spoilt, what are they like?
d) If you just miss the bus or train home tonight, what will you do?
e) In what ways would the world have been a better place if motor cycles had never been invented?
f) What would you say if a stranger were to ask you whether you would invest in a business he was starting?
g) If you had to give a talk to the class on any subject you liked, what would you choose to talk about?
h) What circumstances in your home or school life during childhood would you have liked to have been different?
i) What problems will the community have to face if people in future live much longer?
j) Describe one important development or achievement in your life which would not have taken place if you had not been in the right place at the right time.
k) What will happen if during the coming year there is a prolonged period of heavy rain, drought, high wind, or other form of exceptional bad weather in your country?
l) If you were asked whether you would train as an astronaut why would you agree to or turn down the suggestion?
m) If you were dictator, what would be the first great reform you would introduce into your country?
n) If you were asked to define your philosophy of life in one sentence, what would you say?
o) If we had all been born perfect, what kind of place would the world have been?

B. THE IMPERATIVE AND SUBJUNCTIVE MOODS

Reference material
pages 218-19

EXERCISE

In each of the following sentences only the infinitive of some of the verbs is given. Suggest the form of the verb suitable to the context. An extra modal verb might be needed.

1. I'm feeling tired, aren't you. (Sit) down. (IMPERATIVE)
2. Supposing he (be) to die suddenly.
3. I wish I (be) young again.
4. If I (be) you, I should turn down the offer.
5. He looks as guilty as if he (murder) his rich uncle.
6. You're always grumbling about the cold. Suppose you (live) in Siberia.
7. Even if the nation's wealth (be) shared equally, it wouldn't make much difference to most people.
8. I wish the weather (be) not so cold.
9. It's time we (have) something to eat.
10. He put down his suitcase so that he (help) me with mine. (not 'could')

C. VERBS USED AS AUXILIARIES

Reference material
pages 219-20

EXERCISE
Explain the difference in meaning between the sentences in each of the following pairs with special reference to the significance of the verb form.

a) He stated that the men were to do overtime.
   He stated that the men were doing overtime.
b) What could have happened? She was to have telephoned the manager this morning.
   What could have happened? She telephoned the manager this morning.
c) I am going to finish this homework in half an hour.
   I shall finish this homework in half an hour.
d) Captain Rodney used to command a ship.
   Captain Rodney is used to commanding a ship.
e) When he gets home he will light the fire.
   When he gets home he is to light the fire.
f) When he was angry, he would go white and clench his fists.
   If he were angry, he would go white and clench his fists.
g) He was going to act the part of Falstaff when he fell ill.
   He was acting the part of Falstaff when he fell ill.
h) I said I was going to come back when I had further instructions.
   I said I was going to come back but I had further instructions.

D. NOTES ON SOME   MODAL VERBS AND ON 'NEED'

Reference material
pages 220-21

EXERCISES
1. Write the following sentences supplying the tense suggested in brackets at the end for the verb given.

a) He was irritable because he (can—negative) sleep the previous night. (Past Perfect)
b) All his life he (must) obey orders. (Past Perfect)
c) He said he (must) travel to Cardiff during the following week. (Future in the Past)
d) The children slept late as they (may) to stay up till midnight. (Past Perfect)
e) I'm sorry I'm late. I (must) make an urgent telephone call. (Present Perfect)

2. Suggest whether the action expressed by the main verb in each of the following sentences actually (or possibly) happened.

a) You could have been much earlier if you had hurried.
b) You might have been killed.
c) He didn't need to use his dictionary.

d) He must have run all the way.
e) You ought to have been more careful.
f) That letter should have been posted yesterday.
g) You needn't have shouted.
h) You shouldn't have thrown it away.
i) He may have left a message. He usually does.
j) You should have stayed at home.

SECTION II PUNCTUATION

A. BRACKETS AND DASHES

Reference material
page 232

EXERCISE
Insert brackets or dashes where these are needed in the following sentences.

1. 'No, I don't think there's a vet. living in the village, not since Wait a bit though. How about Mr. Marchant?'
2. A few charred sheets with illegible writing, a heap of black flakes all that remained of three years' patient research and creation.
3. He was born in Afghanistan eighty years ago at least that's what he says.
4. 'Could you please speak a little more loudly David, do turn that radio down it seems to be a very bad line.'
5. The country had recently achieved independence previously it had formed part of the Ottoman Empire and there was as yet no written Constitution.

B. THE PUNCTUATION OF LETTER HEADINGS AND ENDINGS

Reference material
page 233

EXERCISE
As Mrs R. Feather you are writing to Mr H. Lead of the Pressed Steel and Alloy Company, 19-31 Greatburn Street, Crusham, Lancashire, 6OV 4T9. Your address is Honeysuckle Cottage, Fairview Gardens, Sunnyvale, Hampshire, HE2 34L. Address an envelope suitably and head and send a possible letter, using the current date.

SECTION IV CHOICE OF EXPRESSION

CHOICE OF WORDS B

Reference material
pages 242-3

EXERCISE
Rewrite the following sentences, correcting any of the faults mentioned in the reference material.

a) Every year greater armies of tourist cars throng the overburdened arteries of the kingdom and saturation point in the near future must surely be on the cards.
b) Wet rain streamed in torrents from the grey vaporous clouds above him.
c) I have a high opinion of that fine Finnish bass Kim Borg who I think is an outstandingly good and competent singer.
d) He had an arresting face. A snow-white thatch of hair surmounted a deeply-furrowed brow; ice-blue eyes burned fanatically in an ashen face and an aggressive beak of a nose overshadowed a receding rabbit-like mouth and chin.
e) We shall fight the decision tooth and nail and shall leave no stone unturned in upholding the sacred cause of Justice.
f) On a sea as calm as a millpond the boat was as steady as a rock, but he stood there with a face as white as a sheet wishing vainly he were back on dry land.

g) The countryside of England is disappearing far too rapidly. Main roads bring noisy traffic to the countryside. New housing development, the concentration of industry, caravan sites, all are disfiguring the quiet beauty of the countryside.

SECTION VI REPORTED SPEECH

B. QUESTIONS; COMMANDS; EXCLAMATIONS; SPECIAL EXPRESSIONS; OTHER POINTS

Reference material
pages 248–50

EXERCISES

1. Express each of the following exclamations in the form of reported speech, supplying a suitable introduction.

a) 'What a day!'
b) 'How annoying!'
c) 'What nonsense!'
d) 'What a stupid thing to say!'
e) 'What big teeth you have!'
f) 'How ill you look!'

2. Express the following sentences in the form of reported speech, dealing with the various expressions they contain as effectively as possible.

a) 'Good dog! Here's a biscuit for you.'
b) 'You do look beautiful, Eileen!'
c) 'Bother! I've left my address-book at home.'
d) 'Attention! Eyes right!'
e) 'You idiot! You're sitting on the eggs.'

3. Convert the following sentences into reported speech.

a) 'These liqueur chocolates are delicious. Would you like some?'
b) 'What a cold day! I need warmer gloves.'
c) 'When did you get back? Did you have a good journey?'
d) 'Speak more slowly! You will not make so many mistakes then.'
e) 'Would you mind posting this air letter for me, Don't forget it.'
f) 'If you need help, you can telephone me. Here is my number.'
g) 'How about a cup of tea? Or would you prefer coffee?'
h) 'Have you a copy of today's paper? Lend it to me when you have finished with it.'

4. Convert the following passages into reported speech.

a) 'Who lives in that dilapidated house on the corner?' Robert asked his landlady.
'At the moment, nobody,' she replied, 'An elderly bachelor, rather eccentric, who had four boxer dogs, lived there till a few months ago, but he died mysteriously. His nephew, who should inherit, lives in Bechuanaland.'
'What happened to the dogs?' Robert asked.

b) 'A pot of tea for two,' said the stout lady to the waitress, after settling herself comfortably on her chair.
'Not for me, dear,' interposed her companion. 'I no longer partake of such stimulants. So bad for the heart, you know. Have you any lemon juice? And a glass of hot water?'
'Really, Eliza,' exclaimed her friend, 'Whatever absurd fad will you adopt next? How about some of that delicious chocolate cake?'
'Chocolate cake! Shocking for the digestion. May I have a couple of dry biscuits, please. Mark my words, Clara. Within a year you will be a martyr to gout. Quite apart from high blood pressure and excessive overweight.'
'Better a little pain and discomfort in a year's time,' said Clara, popping two sugar lumps into her mouth, 'than death from starvation in a couple of months.'

c) 'Furthermore, gentlemen,' said the Member for South Northend, 'my party intends to bring to your notice a grave scandal. All of you must know by now that the number of new houses erected last year was the lowest in the past ten years. Yet two years ago, the present Prime Minister promised that if his party were returned to power, more houses than ever before would be completed. I challenge him to deny this statement. I ask him to explain why in this age of prosperity thousands of people should still exist in miserable conditions. Has his family ever been forced to live in one room? Must the less privileged of our society continue to exist in misery? Yet I was informed just two days ago that plans exist for building new headquarters for the party now controlling the Government. If these plans are accepted, the new building will cost around half a million pounds. Gentlemen, I shall say no more.'

d) 'What will be your next production?' asked the television interviewer.

The famous producer saw a good opportunity for publicity. 'We have been rehearsing "Candida" since Christmas,' he said. ' "She Stoops to Conquer" is coming off at the end of this month and the Shaw should open a week later.'

'Who will be taking the part of Candida?'

'We had originally hoped to have Miss Angela Siddons, but, you will remember, she was involved in a car crash a few weeks ago. She is now convalescing in Switzerland. However, we have discovered a charming Irish actress, a Miss Deidre O'Donovan. She has a warm attractive Irish voice and has so delightful a personality that I believe she will prove one of the loveliest Candidas we have ever seen.'

'Are you yourself taking any part in the play?'

'Not this time. I'm doing some filming just now as well as producing, and if I tried acting too, I should wear myself out completely.'

'I think you're right. You must often feel quite exhausted. How about your book of memoirs? Is it completed?'

'That was finished last month, but I shall be revising it in my spare moments. I'd like to include some reference to this new production.'

'Well, Mr Barrington-Barnes, may I, on behalf of all our listeners, wish you every success with your many new ventures. Thank you so much for coming along tonight. Goodbye for now.'

'Goodbye. It's been nice having a chat.'

e) The young man with neatly-waved hair and an ingratiating smile beamed patronisingly at us from the television screen.

'Examine this photograph,' he suggested. 'This is a picture of Miss Madeline Maxim as she was a month ago. Do you see those disfiguring wrinkles round her eyes? Look at the slightly sagging chin-line. And I can assure you that her naturally lovely skin had been roughened by the bitter cold of last winter.

'Last week Miss Maxim started applying Peachmelba Cream each night before she slept. She gently massaged her face with this vitamin-charged skin food. Now you must meet Miss Maxim herself. How beautiful she is! Observe in close-up this satin-soft radiance of skin texture. Every line has been quietly smoothed away by Peachmelba's magic caress. Do you want to share Miss Maxim's entrancing loveliness? Buy a jar of Peachmelba today. If you apply a little each night, within a few days you will have a skin softer than a June rose-petal. Fifty pence invested in beauty, in endowing your weather-tired skin with a glowing freshness and allure you would never have believed it could possess.'

Composition

FACTS EXPRESSED IN SENTENCES: DEFINITIONS

Summing up the essentials of an idea and expressing them in the minimum number of words but in good English is useful practice and training for dealing with facts at greater length. The writing of definitions provides this practice.

Study the following definitions:

Pasteurisation is a process for sterilising milk by heating it to destroy germs.
A solicitor is a person qualified to give advice on legal matters.
Oxygen is a gas which sustains both life and combustion.
A bookcase is a piece of furniture with shelves for holding books.

Notice

    (i) Each consists of one sentence only.
   (ii) In each case the class of things to which the object belongs is mentioned first.
  (iii) The individual characteristic which distinguishes the object defined from all others of its class completes the definition.
  (iv) A definition is not the same as a description.
       Compare these examples:
          Coal is a black mineral fuel formed by the prolonged compression of decayed vegetable matter.
          Coal is a hard, black, often shiny substance, which is extracted from the earth.
       The first of these is a definition; the second is a short description.
   (v) A definition should apply to all examples of the object being defined but should not apply to anything else.

We might say:

A lift is a device for taking people from one level to another.

Such a definition could equally apply to an escalator so this interpretation is too wide.
On the other hand, not all lifts are designed to carry people, so the definition is too narrow.

Here is a more satisfactory definition:

A lift is a device whereby people or objects are raised or lowered vertically from one level to another.

  (vi) A definition should be no longer than is needed for an exact classification.
 (vii) Occasionally the individual quality may be expressed in the form of an adjective defining the classifying noun.
       Hydrogen is the lightest gas known.
(viii) Try not to repeat any form of the word being defined in the definition itself. Occasionally such repetition is inevitable.

Some common classifications

a person; a worker; a craftsman; a clergyman; a liquid; a gas; a chemical compound; a fuel; a food; a drink; a cereal; a garment; a piece of furniture; a musical instrument; a form of lighting; a form of heating, a profession; an occupation; a tool; an instrument; a device; a container; a piece of kitchen equipment; a mineral; a metal; a substance; a material; a piece of jewellery; a game; a toy; a building; a construction; a vehicle; a means of communication; a geographical feature; a geometrical figure; a process; a system; a quality; a form of literature; a document; a subject; a means; a place.

EXERCISE
Write definitions of the following:

a thermometer; water; a passport; a handkerchief; a triangle; a loom; a canal lock; a mule; a prima donna; a policeman; a driving licence; a convector heater; wine; porridge; a wardrobe; obstinacy; a waiter; baking; a cinema; irrigation; a precipice; an electric torch; a spanner.

LONGER EXERCISES DEALING WITH FACTS

Writing a factual essay needs little imagination or invention and vocabulary and style are plain and straightforward. Yet many students find an imaginative or impressionistic description or a story far easier to produce.

Discipline and control are essential in dealing with facts. Thinking must be accurate, exact and logical—and this needs very much practice and training. These are the characteristics of any work in which facts are being dealt with:

1. A clear knowledge and understanding of the material to be presented.
2. The ability to assess what must be included and what is irrelevant.
3. The power to arrange this material logically, step by step, so as to convey it intelligibly.
   In the case of an essay, this involves overall planning of paragraph sequence together with the logical development of ideas within each paragraph.
4. The expression of the material in words chosen for their exactness and in simple but well-constructed sentences.

The arrangement of ideas in a single paragraph

Study the following paragraph in which advice about motorway driving is given.

> Certain features of the motorway undoubtedly ease the strain of driving. Gradients and bends are so controlled as to obviate the necessity of sharp braking and the absence of traffic approaching from the other direction removes one of the commonest sources of accidents. Many dangers remain, however, made more terrible by the high speeds of vehicles. A collision at seventy miles an hour is almost inevitably appalling in its results. A mechanical defect in the car or a puncture can lead to loss of control and catastrophe. The car should be completely roadworthy and tyre pressures and treads have been checked. Clear and early signalling of lane changing is essential, though this cannot be taken for granted in other drivers: watch the driver who is approaching a car ahead who may suddenly pull out without even signalling. Use your own mirrors continually and above all well before changing lanes, calculating the speed and distance of traffic coming up behind you. If you must use the motorway in fog keep far enough behind the preceding vehicle to minimise the possibility of a pile-up. Be especially careful when joining the motorway and adapt yourself to other road conditions immediately on leaving it. Concentrate the whole time; remain calm and unemotional whatever the provocation; be ready for immediate action in an emergency and use your commonsense.

This is an unusually long paragraph which is intended to show how many ideas can be assembled, clearly and simply.

Study the paragraph. You will see that it is constructed as follows:

1. Introductory statement on value of motorways.
2. Contrast—the dangers that remain and their extreme seriousness.
3. The importance of a roadworthy vehicle.
4. Signalling and use of mirrors.
5. Driving in fog.
6. Joining and leaving the motorway.
7. Concluding general advice.

EXERCISE

Write a paragraph on one or more of these topics.

List the points you intend to introduce. Bear in mind the characteristics of a good paragraph: the clear logical development of ideas, a beginning and conclusion, sentences of varying length and construction.

a) The winter climate of the district you live in.
b) Instructions for the correct feeding of an animal or bird.
c) Advice on how to lose weight.
d) The danger to health of smoking.
e) The qualities of a first-class wine.
f) Driving a car on an icy morning.

131

g) A radio news bulletin on an important item of world news.
h) Advice to a person who is unhappily shy in company.
i) On the care of a gramophone record.
j) How to fry an egg.
k) Keeping a pair of shoes smart.
l) The duties of an air hostess.
m) The function and working of a canal lock.
n) Advice on choosing stationery for personal correspondence.
o) The main purpose of a Trade Union.

An essay which presents facts

The features of the single paragraph will apply equally to the essay, consisting as it does of a sequence of paragraphs, each on its own related topic, and each carrying forward logically the thought that is being developed. Study the following plan, which refers to the comprehension passage at the beginning of the chapter.

1. Introduction to the idea of office planning.
2. Planning applies to staff grouping as well as the use of the building.
3. Reasons for good office planning.
4. Best way of reconciling costs and staff needs is by landscaping.
5. The purpose of office landscaping.
6. The nature of landscaping.
7. A possible drawback: resistance of occupants of private offices.
8. A second drawback: need for special skills in such planning with expense of employing consultant or difficulty of training the company.
9. Importance of understanding effect of environment on work achievement.
10. Future extensions of principle of office landscaping.

EXERCISE
Prepare and discuss a suitable plan for several of the following essay topics. Then extend this into an essay of about 500–600 words (six to seven paragraphs) on any one of them.

1. The training of future business men and secretaries.
2. The future of the giant aircraft.
3. The theatre in my country.
4. The value of refrigeration.
5. Dealing with ONE of these natural disasters: a flood, a famine, an earthquake. (Notice that this concerns only measures for dealing with the disaster.)
6. Earning one's living on or in water.
7. Opportunities for exploration today.
8. Factors to be considered in planning schools for the future.
9. International sport.
10. Private charity in a Welfare State.
11. Careers for women.
12. The exploration of the moon and planets.
13. Services that a bank can render the individual as distinct from the business concern.
14. The press in your country.
15. Problems that an insurance company has to cope with.
16. The qualities of a good teacher.
17. Archaeology as a hobby.
18. A career in the hotel industry.
19. The control of pests.
20. Aids to the housewife that may be developed during the next ten years.

Presenting a case

This type of composition shares the characteristics of the presentation of fact and that of opinion. The writer is not only expressing what he thinks but is trying to induce the reader to share his opinion and quite possibly do something about it.

He should therefore concentrate on these things:
a) A good background knowledge of the subject he is dealing with.
b) Selecting those facts that support his argument, and being prepared to deal with any likely criticisms.
c) Persuasiveness in presenting his case.

His method of presentation must depend on the type of person he is addressing. A businessman or professional person will need clear well-substantiated facts to support the argument. A more emotional appeal may be made to the readers of the more popular newspapers or listeners to commercial television. Humour, with the so-called 'human touch', appeals to self-interest or duty, are among the many other devices which may help to push home an idea and produce the desired results.

It is therefore necessary to decide first the possible audience and then to consider the best method of convincing that particular group. Here is a paragraph in which a case is made for increased advisory services and clubs for young foreigners.

Many visitors to Britain are astonished at the extraordinary variety of help available to citizens in difficulties: charitable organisations catering for all kinds of physical and mental afflictions and official and semi-official bureaux with advice about citizens' rights, hospitals and other provisions for common needs, marriage difficulties—most of the problems of everyday life. It may seem understandable that the foreign student or young temporary resident is less well provided for. His problems are different, or, as in the case of accommodation, are shared by too many British nationals. But the problems are no less worrying. The foreign student is young, sometimes not more than eighteen or nineteen, in many cases poor, possibly with little or no knowledge of the language, often lonely, with almost no British acquaintances and, especially in that overpoweringly impersonal colossus London, very likely to be bewildered and miserable. Most European girls are doing domestic work, either in hospitals or in families which vary from the benevolent to the slave-driving. Here and there advisory services and clubs exist and many colleges have their student advisers. But far more should be done. Every borough in which there are a fair number of foreign students should have advisory bureaux, advertised as widely as possible, where not only information about education and daily needs could be given but also where young people could talk over the problems which they normally discuss with their own families. And could there not also be some kind of local clubroom available with its own refreshment canteen, where British and foreign students could meet, discuss, enjoy themselves and learn from each other? Why not extend the ideals of the European Community and the United Nations Organisation to the individuals whom these giant complexes are intended to represent?

Characteristics of this type of paragraph

The above paragraph is clearly considerably longer than one which would normally form part of an essay but it shows in a condensed way a possible development of thought in this kind of writing. It is written presumably by a student or someone interested in student welfare and intended for those of the general public who might feel responsible for helping to promote some such service.

The development can be summarised:
a) Introduction—the variety of welfare and advisory services available for British people.
b) Why less is done for foreign students and young workers.
c) The need for such services—the youth, poverty, helplessness, bewilderment and possible exploitation of these people.
d) Some services exist but more should be done.
e) Suggestions: local advisory services and clubrooms.
f) Conclusion: an appeal to ideals of international co-operation.

EXERCISE
Discuss several of these subjects. Then develop one or more into a paragraph.
a) That many more houses specially suited to old people living alone should be built.

b) The importance of a cheerful congenial atmosphere and environment in hospital wards.

c) That boys and girls should (should not) be expected to help equally in the home.

d) That a person is as young as he feels.

e) Private cars should be excluded from the centre of all very large towns.

f) Defend your own extravagance.

g) In defence of beards.

h) You are writing a letter to a local Polytechnic asking whether a course in English for Foreign Students can be organised there. One paragraph states that there are many foreigners working in the town, including au pair girls, who are anxious not only to learn the language but also to study English life and culture. Many foreigners have been forced to leave the town in order to attend classes elsewhere. Write this paragraph.

i) You are writing an article for a local newspaper criticising the conditions under which many Au Pair girls are having to work. One paragraph states that most of the girls come from well-educated families and are willing to work for a small wage in order to continue their education. Yet in some cases they are forced to work so many hours a day that they are too tired to study. Write this paragraph.

Each of the stages in the development of the foregoing paragraph could form the subject of a whole paragraph. A similar kind of plan could form the basis of an essay.

Exercises in essay writing

Choose several of the following topics and discuss a suitable approach and plan. Then write an essay on one of the topics, not necessarily one with which yourself agree.

The essay should be addressed to a reasonably intelligent and objective reader and obvious emotional appeals avoided.

1. English spelling should be simplified.
2. All areas of beauty should be protected by the government from industrial, housing, or non-essential road development.
3. Far more time should be given in all schools to practical subjects such as housekeeping, repair jobs, child rearing, car driving and maintenance and careers guidance.
4. In countries where there is no conscription, all young men should spend one year between the ages of 18 and 25 in some form of community service.
5. Politics should be kept out of sport.
6. Medical treatment should be free to all.
7. Marriage and a family should cause the minimum interruption to a woman's career if she wants to go on working.
8. Suggestions about the kind of taxation that will stimulate not inhibit industrial growth.
9. Workers' control in industry.
10. Some methods of promoting growth in a stagnant economy.
11. The importance of a branch of science in which you are interested.

Business letters

Though a long and interesting letter sent to a friend may be classified as essay rather than composition, letters which have some practical purpose share most of the characteristics of a composition.

Accordingly such letters are expressed clearly and briefly, with the additional quality of courtesy. This latter quality is observed (possibly with considerable coldness) however exasperated one may feel at incompetence and rudeness. If your correspondent is known to you personally, the essential request or information may be expressed in a style adapted to the reader and irrelevant news and greetings will probably be added.

PARAGRAPHING is important. Each subject needs a separate paragraph. A short business letter often shows the following arrangement:

1. a) Reference to previous letter if there has been one.
   or b) Circumstances leading to the main subject.
   or c) The main subject.
2. a) The main subject (following from 1a or 1b).
   or b) Circumstances applying to main subject, modifications, additions, comments (as suitable) (from 1c).
3. Conclusion
   a) Asking for an early reply.
   or b) Requesting immediate action.
   or c) Sending greetings, etc.

A longer letter introducing more than one main topic will require additional paragraphs according to the number of subjects dealt with.

Letter paragraphs tend to be *shorter* than those in other forms of writing.

It is still customary to *leave a space* at the beginning of each paragraph in English correspondence.

VOCABULARY AND SENTENCE CONSTRUCTION should be as simple as is consistent with exactness. Write what you have to express plainly, avoiding such out-of-date jargon as 'I beg to acknowledge . . .', 'In re your communication . . .', '. . . tender our thanks . . .', 'we are of the opinion that . . .'. The expressions 'inst.', 'ult.' and 'prox.' (for 'this month', 'last month' and 'next month') have almost disappeared nowadays. It is far better to state the name of the month.

But remember COURTESY. 'Would you please send' is better than 'Please send' and 'I regret' (or: I am sorry) that we cannot supply' preferable to 'We cannot supply'.

There is a convention determining the arrangement of the address on an envelope, letter headings and endings. Certain full stops and commas are optional, but otherwise it is necessary to be familiar with the accepted forms.

Read the following notes for a letter which you, as an au pair girl wanting to obtain full-time employment, are writing to a hospital.

Present employment (au pair looking after two children under five and helping in the house)—age 22 years—nationality German—engaged to Englishman and anxious to earn more to save for a house—studying for Proficiency Certificate—one year already in this country—would like to undertake full-time domestic work—live in—enquiry about jobs available (wages and hours)—(free time for study?)—working permit.

The letter itself could be paragraphed as follows:

1. Description of self and present post.
2. Reasons for wishing to change to full-time employment.
3. Enquiry about conditions of work in a hospital.
4. Working permit.

Here is the letter:

4, Ash Grove Crescent,
Silverlake,
Southshire.
16th October, 19-.

The Matron,
Everley General Hospital,
Rannoch Avenue,
Southshire.

Dear Madam,

I am a German girl aged twenty-two who for the past year has been employed by an English family at the above address to help with two young children and with domestic duties.

As I have recently become engaged to an Englishman and we are saving for a home. I should like to undertake a full-time job which will provide a higher

135

salary than my present one. I understand that full-time domestic work in hospitals is often available for foreign girls and that there may be hostel accommodation.

If there is an opportunity to undertake work of this kind in the Everley General Hospital, would you please inform me of the conditions of employment, including the wages, weekly hours and living accommodation. Is it possible to attend an English language course at the Everley Polytechnic, where I have enrolled in an afternoon class preparing for the Proficiency examination?

I am registered here as an au pair girl. I believe that a different kind of permit is required for full-time work. If you can offer me a job in the hospital, could you please let me know how I should apply for my new permit.

Yours faithfully,
Heidemarie Holz.

Heidemarie received a reply from the hospital three days later. The following notes give the substance of the reply:

A job available at a salary of £16.32* for a 40 hour week with 3 weeks' holiday after a year's service.

Hostel accommodation provided £2.50* deducted from weekly wage.

Rises are given at certain intervals—hostel fee then increased slightly.

Most evenings and two full days are free.

If applicant accepted, she is given note to Aliens Office which will normally issue full-time working permit.

The letter is signed by Mary Gamp, Domestic Superintendent.

Write the above letter in full. The letter heading will be as follows:

THE EVERLEY GENERAL HOSPITAL
RANNOCH AVENUE, EVERLEY, SOUTHSHIRE

EXERCISES

Write one or more of the following letters:

1. a) You have been living as a student in London for six months and attending daily classes in English in a local College. Now you are offered a very pleasant au pair job in a provincial town but are unwilling to take it without knowing whether you can continue your studies there. Write a letter to the Registrar, The Polytechnic, Midton, Northshire, asking whether the College has any courses in preparation for the next Proficiency Examination. Make up your present London address.
   b) A reply from the Registrar stating that classes may be started at the beginning of the next session but at present the most advanced course is a twice-weekly class in preparation for the Lower Certificate examination.
   c) A letter to the family in Midton regretting that as no suitable course exists, you cannot take the job.

2. a) You have recently returned by coach from Farhaven to your home in Mapsley. You find you have left an umbrella in the coach which was travelling to the Panther Line Coach Station at Nearport, fifty miles farther on. Write to this coach station reporting your loss, giving details of time, place of alighting and the coach service. Give a description of the umbrella and ask how you may reclaim it.
   b) A letter from the coach company stating that the umbrella has been found and will be sent by the coach which reaches Mapsley cross-roads at 1.30 p.m. on the 10th April. It asks that you will confirm that you can collect it there.
   c) A letter from you thanking the coach company and stating that you will collect the umbrella.

3. Before you returned home from England you bought a coffee service which the shop assistant promised to have packed securely and sent to your address. When it arrives you find that one of the cups is chipped. Write to the shop giving details of your purchase and of what has happened, stating that you are returning the cup separately and asking for it to be replaced.

* As at January 1972

136

4. Write a letter to the Youth Hostels Association, St. Albans, Hertfordshire, England asking for information about the association to be sent to you together with a list of prices of such things as maps, rucksacks and sleeping-bags. Ask also for an enrolment form.

5. You wish to prepare for the Cambridge Proficiency examination in your own country. Write to the nearest British Council office enquiring about classes and also how to enter for the examination.

6. a) An English person is writing to a travel agency in your country asking about an interesting area in which she (he) could spend ten days and how to get there from London. Write this letter, stating the type of holiday you prefer (cultural, enjoyment of scenery, beaches, etc.)
   b) The reply sent by the agency.

7. a) You have heard a B.B.C. broadcast about your country and consider that part of the programme gives a false impression. Write to the B.B.C. stating in what way you thought the programme was unsatisfactory.
   b) The reply from the B.B.C.

8. This advertisement has appeared in the *Grasmere Gazette*.

> HOLIDAY CARAVAN TO LET. SLEEPS FOUR PERSONS.
> IDEAL LAKE DISTRICT SURROUNDINGS.
> FOURTEEN POUNDS WEEKLY. BOX 111.

Three of your friends and you had planned to visit the Lakes and think you would enjoy renting a caravan. Write to the box number given to ask whether the caravan will be available at the time you wish and to find out other essential details.

9. An English firm is sending a consulting engineer to your factory to advise on new techniques. You have had the responsibility for arranging his journey and accommodation. Write to him (Mr A. Wright, The National Steelworks, Stockborough, Bradshire) giving him details of his journey (air ticket to be collected at London Airport), where he will be met, and his local accommodation.

Testimonials

A testimonial is that written account of your present position and the writer's estimate of your ability and character which is given to you by your employer shortly before or at the time when you leave your job. When another job is being applied for a copy of the testimonial is usually submitted with the application.

A reference (or referee) is a person who is willing to supply additional information and answer questions about you if this is required by your possible new employer.

A testimonial is in fact a summarised report. It usually consists of three or four paragraphs, the first stating your position, the second your experience and/or qualifications (sometimes these two paragraphs are combined), the third summarising your character and/or ability as revealed in your job and the fourth a short sentence relating to your suitability for another job.

A writer of a testimonial rarely says anything really damaging though there may be allusions to unpunctuality, lack of enthusiasm or real incompetence. On the whole statements are favourable though not necessarily enthusiastic It is often said that a testimonial is a poor guide to a person's qualities as many writers hesitate to commit themselves too strongly and usually the tone of the statement is determined by the temperament of the writer. In any case few people will be completely hostile in a document to be handed to its subject.

The following might be an example of a reasonably favourable testimonial. It might have been given by a Swiss travel agency to one of their Italian employees who is applying for a post as an information clerk at a big British airport.

EDELWEISS REISEBÜRO

31st January, 19-.

Mr. A. Fiore joined the staff of this organisation in 19-. He was appointed as an Assistant Clerk in the Seat Reservations Department and after eighteen months was transferred at his own request to the position of Counter Clerk where he dealt specifically with seat and sleeper reservations.

Mr. Fiore is a fluent linguist with an excellent practical knowledge of French and German. I understand that he has been attending English classes and has made good progress in that language. He has a thorough knowledge of all aspects of travel by rail and sea and has successfully given assistance in our air section when this has been necessary.

I can say that he is polite, pleasantly helpful and patient in his dealings with clients. He is of good appearance, intelligent and always ready to learn.

I can fully recommend him for any post for which his ability and experience qualify him.

K. Alpenblume.

Write the kind of testimonial which might apply in one or more of the following cases:

a) The testimonial that you would like to receive from your employer or class teacher. (Do not be too ambitious.)

b) The testimonial which might be given to a girl leaving a Commercial School to become a junior secretary.

c) The testimonial that might have been given to a teacher in the secondary school you attended.

d) A postgraduate wishes to undertake advanced research in England and is applying for an appropriate scholarship. Prepare the testimonial that might be submitted by the firm or professional organisation with which he is working.

The same technique could be applied to a review of a textbook:

1) Aim of the book 2) Contents of the book 3) Your opinion 4) Recommendation.

Write a review of any textbook or journal on these lines.

PRACTICE PAPER 7

I READING COMPREHENSION

Section A

In this section you must choose the word or phrase which best completes each sentence. Write down each number and beside it the letters **A, B, C, D** and **E**. Then in each case cross through the letter before the word or phrase you choose. Give one answer only to each question.

1. On Labour Day the workers will march in —— through the town.

    A process   **B** procedure   **C** procession   **D** progress
    E progression

2. The ink had faded with time and so parts of the letter were ——.

    A illiterate   **B** illegible   **C** illegitimate   **D** inscrutable
    E indelible

3. He has read widely but seldom thought deeply so his apparent learning is really quite ——.

    A superior   **B** superficial   **C** supercilious   **D** superfluous
    E supernatural

4. Driving with —— brakes endangers not only yourself but also all other road users you encounter.

    A deficient   **B** insufficient   **C** inadequate   **D** defective
    E degraded

5. Poisons should be kept in a place that is —— to children.

    A unavailable   **B** insurmountable   **C** inaccessible
    D impracticable   **E** inapplicable

6. One of the problems local authorities have to deal with is the —— of plastic containers.

    A dispersal   **B** disposition   **C** disposal   **D** disappearance
    E dissolution

7. The law proved so unpopular that it was —— by the Government a year later.

    A repelled   **B** repulsed   **C** taken back   **D** repealed
    E reinforced

8. The floods did not start to —— until two days after the rain had stopped.

    A retire   **B** recede   **C** retreat   **D** depart   **E** sink

9. I doubt whether he can keep —— his efforts much longer as he looks very tired.

    A in   **B** up   **C** on   **D** on with   **E** at

10. The tenant must be prepared to decorate the property —— the terms of the agreement.

    A with regard to   **B** in relation to   **C** in accordance with
    D provided by   **E** by way of

II READING COMPREHENSION

Section B

In this section you will find after each of the passages a number of questions or unfinished statements about the passage, each with four suggested ways of answering or finishing it. You must choose the one which you think fits best. Write the numbers 1–10 and beside each the letters **A, B, C** and **D**. Then in each case, cross through the letter you choose. Give one answer only in each case. Read the passage right through before choosing your answers.

    With its common interest in lawbreaking but its immense range of subject-matter and widely-varying methods of treatment, the crime novel could make a legitimate claim to be regarded as a separate branch of literature, or, at least, as a distinct, even though a slightly disreputable, offshoot of the tra-
5 ditional novel.
    The detective story is probably the most respectable (at any rate in the narrow sense of the word) of the crime species. Its creation is often the relaxation of University dons, literary economists, scientists or even poets. Fatalities may occur more frequently and mysteriously than might be expected in
10 polite society, but the world in which they happen, the villlage, seaside resort, college or studio, is familiar to us, if not from our own experience, at least in the newspaper or the lives of friends. The characters, though normally realised superficially, are as recognisably human and consistent as our less intimate associates. A story set in a more remote environment, African jungle
15 or Australian bush, ancient China or gaslit London, appeals to our interest in geography or history, and most detective story writers are conscientious in providing a reasonably authentic background. The elaborate, carefully-assembled plot, despised by the modern intellectual critics and creators of 'significant' novels, has found refuge in the murder mystery, with its sprinkling
20 of clues, its spicing with apparent impossibilities, all with appropriate solutions and explanations at the end. With the guilt of escapism from Real Life nagging gently, we secretly revel in the unmasking of evil by a vaguely super-human sleuth, who sees through and dispels the cloud of suspicion which has hovered so unjustly over the innocent.
25   Though its villain also receives his rightful deserts, the thriller presents a less comfortable and credible world. The sequence of fist fights, revolver duels, car crashes and escapes from gas-filled cellars exhausts the reader far more than the hero, who, suffering from at least two broken ribs, one black eye, un-countable bruises and a hangover, can still chase and overpower an armed
30 villain with the physique of a wrestler. He moves dangerously through a world of ruthless gangs, brutality, a vicious lust for power and money and, in contrast to the detective tale, with a near-omniscient arch-criminal whose

140

defeat seems almost accidental. Perhaps we miss in the thriller the security of being safely led by our imperturbable investigator past a score of red herrings and blind avenues to a final gathering of suspects when an unchallengeable 35 elucidation of all that has bewildered us is given and justice and goodness prevail. All that we vainly hope for from life is granted vicariously.

1. The crime novel may be regarded as
   A a not quite respectable form of the conventional novel
   B not a true novel at all
   C related in some ways to the historical novel
   D an independent development of the novel
2. The detective novel may be considered respectable in the sense that
   A people need not feel ashamed of reading one
   B there are often some well-drawn characters in it
   C it deals with conventional people and scenes
   D it is written by people of culture and intelligence
3. The passage suggests that intellectuals write detective stories because
   A the stories are often in fact very instructive
   B they enjoy writing these stories
   C the creation of these stories demands considerable intelligence
   D detective stories are an accepted branch of literature
4. Which of the following are the only unlikely aspects of the average detective novel?
   A its characters   B its setting   C its incidents
   D its authorship
5. What feature of the detective story is said to disqualify it from respectful consideration by intellectual critics?
   A the many seemingly impossible events
   B the fact that the guilty are always found out and the innocent cleared
   C the existence of a neat closely-knit story
   D the lack of interest in genuine character revelations
6. According to a suggestion in the passage, detective story readers feel guilty because
   A they should be devoting all their attention to the problems of the world around them
   B they should have a more educated literary taste
   C they become aware that they too share some of the guilt of the criminal
   D they would hesitate to admit the considerable enjoyment they get from these stories
7. Which of the following is mentioned in the passage as one of the similarities between the detective story and the thriller?
   A both have involved plots
   B both are condemned by modern critics
   C both are forms of escapist fiction
   D both demonstrate the triumph of right over wrong

8. One of the most incredible characteristics of the hero of a thriller is
    A   his exciting life   **B**   his amazing toughness
    C   his ability to escape from dangerous situations
    D   the way he deals with his enemies
9. One of the most incredible characteristics of the thriller plot is
    A   the eventual defeat of the villain
    B   the type of society described
    C   the effect of the story on the reader
    D   the fact that the villain is clever
10. In what way are the detective story and the thriller unlike?
    A   in introducing violence
    B   in providing excitement and suspense
    C   in appealing to the intellectual curiosity of the reader
    D   in ensuring that everything comes right in the end

III   COMPOSITION

Section B

Read the following passage and then answer the questions on it.

We descended into a deep narrow valley, to the road-junction and the canteen house, then up again, up and up sharp to Tonara, our village we had seen in the sun yesterday. But we were approaching it from the back. As we swerved into the sunlight, the road took a long curve on to the open ridge
5 between two valleys. And there in front we saw a glitter of scarlet and white. It was in slow motion. It was a far-off procession, scarlet figures of women, and a tall image moving away from us, slowly, in the Sunday morning. It was passing along the level sunlit ridge above a deep, hollow valley. A close procession of women glittering in scarlet, white and black, moving slowly in
10 the distance beneath the grey-yellow buildings of the village on the crest, towards an isolated old church: and all along this narrow upland saddle as on a bridge of sunshine itself.
    Were we not going to see any more? The bus turned and rushed along the now level road and then veered. And there beyond, a little below, we saw the
15 procession *coming*. The bus faded to a standstill, and we climbed out. Above us, old and mellowed among the smooth rocks and the bits of flat grass, was the church, tanging its bell. Just in front, above, were old half-broken houses of stone. The road came gently winding up to us, from what was evidently two villages ledged one above the other upon the steep summit of the south
20 slope. Far below was the south valley, with a white puff of engine steam.
    And slowly chanting in the near distance, curving slowly up to us on the white road between the grass, came the procession. The high morning was still. We stood all on this ridge above the world, with the deeps of silence below on the right. And in a strange, brief staccato monody chanted the men, and in
25 quick, light rustle of women's voices came the responses. Again the men's voices! The white was mostly men, not women. The priest in his robes, his boys near him, was leading the chanting. Immediately behind him came a small cluster of bare-headed, tall, sunburnt men all in golden-velveteen corduroy,
142

mountain peasants, bowing beneath a great life-size seated image of Saint Anthony of Padua. After these a number of men in the costume, but with white linen breeches hanging wide and loose almost to the ankles, instead of being tucked into the black gaiters. So they seemed very white beneath the black kilt frill. The black frieze body-vest was cut low, like an evening suit, and the stocking-caps were variously perched. The men chanted in low, hollow, melodic tones. Then came the rustling chime of the women. And the procession crept slowly, aimlessly forward in time with the chant. The great image rode rigid, and rather foolish.

D. H. Lawrence, *Sea and Sardinia*

a) The writer was a visitor to this area. Suggest why he should call Tonara 'our' village?
b) What effect is given by the expression 'a glitter of scarlet and white' (line 5)?
c) 'It was in slow motion'. What word does the pronoun 'it' represent and what is the effect of the idea thus expressed (lines 5–6)?
d) Suggest two contrasting pairs of abstract nouns which would apply to the ridge as compared with the valley.
e) In what way was the procession moving 'on a bridge of sunshine' (line 12)?
f) (i) Explain why the word 'coming' in line 15 is italicised.
   (ii) What does this idea suggest about the route being followed by the bus?
g) What effect have the words 'faded to a standstill' in line 15?
h) What does the word 'tanging' (line 17) suggest about the sound of the bell?
i) Why does the writer prefer the expression 'the deeps of silence' (line 23) to 'the silent valley'?
j) In what ways are the men's and the women's voices in contrast?
k) What details give an impression of vividness amid isolation?
l) 'The writer has a painter's vision'. Justify this statement, using between 40 and 50 words.

IV   USE OF ENGLISH

Section A

1 Write the numbers of the following sentences and beside each the phrase from those grouped above the sentences that in each case most suitably replaces the dotted line.

in contrast——besides——beside——except——on the other hand——on the contrary——also——without——excluding——apart from——but.

1. Even .... the poverty of its ideas and originality, the dreary style makes this book almost unreadable.
2. He does nothing .... grumble.

3. Applications are invited from all citizens between the ages of 18 and 20, ... members of the armed forces, for scholarships in the U.S.A.
4. The people of his village had been friendly to the point of interference; .... his neighbours in town seemed unaware of his very existence.
5. He is an unusually tolerant ànd easy-going person .... for his fanatical anti-feminism.
6. He never goes anywhere .... taking his camera with him.
7. He is a strict and domineering teacher but .... he takes a keen interest in his pupils' progress and welfare.
8. The inhabitants of this region suffer not only the immediate havoc caused by violent storms but............ the effects of the soil erosion which they bring about.
9. .... working as a garage mechanic during the day, he undertakes many repair jobs in his spare time.
10. You claim that by travelling by boat I am wasting part of my holiday: .... I regard the sea journey as the most enjoyable part of it.
11. The painter had set up his easel .... a sparkling swiftly-flowing stream.

2 For each of the numbered blanks suggest one suitable word.

—— (1) accumulation of —— (2) knowledge is —— (3) part of —— (4) education but this kind of learning can be and often —— (5) carried —— (6) excess in many countries so that —— (7) time for other interests is available to young people. Not only —— (8) they —— (9) school —— (10) five-hour periods —— (11) six days of the week, studying possibly as many as thirteen different subjects, but —— (12) addition they may even go to afternoon institutes for further instruction. They have almost no —— (13) of taking —— (14) any of —— (15) own hobbies or becoming familiar —— (16) the plants and wild life of the —— (17) except during their summer holidays. —— (18) youth should be a time of exploration and adventure, of reading books for —— (19) as well as study, of freedom to enjoy —— (20) before the responsibilities of working for a living and raising a family put an end to study, to freedom and only too often to carefree enjoyment.

3 Each of the following clauses should be expanded into a complete sentence by preceding it with a group of not more than 6 words. Write the full sentence in each case.

1. ————————————— that was badly in need of repair.
2. ————————————— when it will be ready.
3. ————————————— who rarely reveal their thoughts.
4. ————————————— that I could barely hear him.
5. ————————————— as I could.
6. ————————————— which are quite common in this part of the country.
7. ————————————— if the weather would be fine.

8. ———————————— that I could do.
9. ———————————— what most people wanted.
10. ———————————— in whose change I had left Mary.

V VARIOUS TOPICS

1 Express each of the following telegrams in one or more sentences. Only articles, verbs and other words essential for a complete grammatical sentence should be added.

1. Father in accident. Emergency operation on spine. Asking for you.
2. Regret match postponed. Pitch waterlogged. Suggest fixture Saturday week or when convenient later.
3. Accept post offered. Thank you. Can start 1st March. Writing to confirm.
4. Consignment due yesterday not received. Urgent. Cancel order if not already despatched.
5. No money left. Angry landlady. Examinations next month. Please send £100.
6. Please undertake assignment Ruritanian earthquake. Accompany star photographer Porlock. Charter plane London Airport 6 pm. today. Cover especially human interest features and relief schemes.
7. No key to filing cabinet. Harper in hospital. Emergency operation appendicitis. Nobody in his flat. Second key missing. Please send yours immediately. Enjoy your holiday.
8. Please extinguish gas left burning kitchen. Key at 32. Check sitting-room window. Horrible crossing.

2 Write advertisements on the following topics for inclusion in a newspaper. As many useful details as possible should be given but the advertisement should be limited to 15 words. Your own address, box number or telephone number need not be included.
   a) You have just arrived in London and want to find a furnished flat.
   b) You are living in a country other than your own and would like to give private lessons in your own language.
   c) You want to find a job for your long summer holiday.
   d) You have lost a dog.
   e) You are travelling a long distance by car and wish to find a companion to share the cost of the petrol.
   f) As secretary to a Dramatic Society you are advertising for new members.

Suggest some reasons for assuming that this photograph was taken in Great Britain.

Explain what is happening to the traffic in the two sections of the street.

Describe the buses shown here and suggest why they are constructed in this way.

What are some of the difficulties of shopping in this street?

What advantages has a traffic-free shopping area? Are there any disadvantages?

Do you like or dislike shopping in a large town centre? Explain your preference.

Say something about two of the main traffic problems of your country.

What are some of the reasons for which people come to London from other countries.

Tell me some interesting things about the capital of your own country.

7
Reading, Vocabulary and Comprehension

An Essay on a Generalised Topic

Family Reunions

Before the Industrial Revolution scattered populations and steam and later
petrol engines ensured easy mobility, there could have been few family
reunions as we know this ceremony at the present time, with its assembling of
infrequently-encountered but still familiar figures and the consequent getting
5 up to date with the events in other people's lives. There must have been indeed
a good deal of 'dropping-in', for if members of a family did not actually live
in the same house, they were within easy walking distance of one another. A
man rarely went very far to look for a wife and the girl who married someone
from elsewhere almost certainly said a final goodbye to her parents when she
10 was taken off to her husband's home.

It was the Victorians who firmly established the family reunion. Present-day
impressions of this important occasion are of a strange blending of formality,
plain speaking with hovering dissension and a general lack of natural warmth.
The rarer such meetings, it would seem, the more important it was to reflect
15 prosperity and propriety. Firm attention was paid to suitable clothes and
decorum while hostesses must demonstrate their ability to provide abundant
meals in dignified surroundings. Children eyed little-known cousins with
distrust and they, together with grown-up daughters, had to entertain the
company with piano-playing or recitations while their own parents beamed
20 complacently. There was the barbed exchange of news, gossip, gloomy
prognostications about absent relatives, reminiscences of Uncle Albert and
shared memories of childhood. The mask of formality gradually slipped and
the natural individual, self-satisfied or envious, charitable or spiteful, assumed
control. Half-forgotten feuds glowed again, the quarrels and rivalries of
25 childhood clamoured only just below the ruffled surface. Goodbyes might be
colder than greetings and unflattering assessments of the hosts occupy the
return journey. But these less than perfect connections were, after all, part of
oneself: unattractive and unsympathetic perhaps, rarely seen but in some
indefinable way necessary.

30 The ritual of the family reunion is less rigid nowadays but, despite the
availability of the private car, meetings are probably more infrequent.
Summer week-ends offer the pleasures of the sea and countryside and in
winter television adds to the attractions of a home which may be warmer
and more comfortable than Cousin Linda's. In any case there are fewer
35 opportunities for visiting. Small families have been the fashion for more than
fifty years and even uncles and aunts are in short supply. There is a good
chance moreover that the nearest family member lives two hundred miles
away or even in another continent.

148

Special occasions however still seem to gather a sizeable contingent of relatives near or further removed. Few young couples even today marry without a united family blessing and a wedding affords an ideal family reunion. Everyone preens in lounge suit, new gown and eye-alluring hat: food and drink mellow and enliven. That compact privileged group, the family, surrounded by mere friends, probably gets the greatest pleasure out of the celebrations. Note is taken of how Uncle Richard has aged and Aunt Margaret is putting on weight—wherever did she get that absurd little-girl dress? In-laws on the outer fringes regard one another vaguely and those more closely allied with some suspicion, but the mood is relaxed, genial and harmonious.

Funerals have their own atmosphere and come nearest to Victorian tradition. The family is on its very best behaviour. Clothes are conventionally sombre and faces decently composed. A feeling of guilt waits to pounce: a sudden burst of conversation or unfortunate laugh draws shocked attention. The near relatives of the deceased are handled cautiously with hushed voices and patronising solicitude. A careful muted conviviality accompanies the following baked meats: voices are louder now and somewhat more cheerful: a cheerfulness that perhaps tries to dispel the chill of the empty place, the moving-up one degree towards the position of dear-departed.

Christenings, Christmas, comings-of-age cast no shadows and probably see the family at its happiest and friendliest. The pride of being an incontestable member of this biologically-linked group, for all its irritations, demands, eccentricities, is blended with a feeling of safety that goes back to early childhood. And while much has been written of family frictions, bullying and all uncharitableness, most people have at least some relations they enjoy meeting because they can feel more at ease with them than with all but the most enduring friends. There is a deep feeling of sharing many things—physical and often mental and emotional inheritances, absent from the closest friendship.

So it seems likely that perhaps to a more limited extent than earlier family reunions will continue to flourish, superficially different from those of our ancestors but in fact with many things in common. But can we be sure of this? Marriage, we read, is an outmoded institution. Children with anonymous fathers, uncles and aunts will be brought up collectively and, supposedly, relatives will just become other people. We shall miss, I think, Uncle Jim with his oft-repeated anecdotes, Aunt Jill with her knitting and home-made wines and Cousin Philippa with that awful little Derek. Most of all we shall miss the presence with us of that little-loved, internationally-derided and very unfairly underrated mother-in-law.

Notes on the passage

Line
6   A GOOD DEAL OF 'dropping-in'—remember that MUCH while normal in negative statements and all question forms is rare in affirmative statements, though 'very much', 'too much' and 'so much' are certainly used. Replacements are 'a good (great) deal of', 'a lot of', 'plenty of'. But notice that 'much' is used in line 63 'Much has been written'—partly for emphasis. The student is advised to avoid this however.

11– PRESENT-DAY impressions—impressions of the present time. 'Today's
12 news' means the news of this same day. 'Today's' is not normally used
adjectively in this way especially when the present time is being referred
to.

16 ABILITY to provide—'capability' is far more rare.
'able to' is a general expression of possibility:
     'He is able to come today' . . . (he is free to do so)
'capable of'—having the necessary power, strength, intelligence, etc.
. . . 'but he is not capable of making the long journey'. (he is ill)

32 COUNTRYSIDE 'Country' is commonly used: 'He lives in the country.'
'The country may be as noisy as the town.'
'Countryside' may emphasise its special characteristics: agriculture or
the world of nature, but may be used for rhythmic purposes.

44 MERE friends—slight contempt: inferior beings outside the important
family circle.

52 DECENTLY 'Decent' is a common colloquialism: 'That's decent of you'
= 'kind' Here the original meaning of 'proper and suitable' is expressed.

52 COMPOSED—The features are arranged to express gravity.

56 BAKED MEATS refers to a quotation from 'Hamlet'. The prince is criticising his mother's hasty remarriage:
    Thrift, thrift, Horatio! the funeral baked meats
    Did coldly furnish forth the marriage feast.

58 DEAR-DEPARTED refers to a common inscription on a tombstone:
'dear-departed husband of ——'

64 ALL UNCHARITABLENESS—a quotation from the Book of Common
Prayer of the Church of England, where deliverance is asked from:
    envy, hatred, and malice, and all uncharitableness.

Metaphors

Explain the significance of the capitalised words which are used metaphorically in the following expressions:

 plain speaking with HOVERING dissension (l. 13)
 the BARBED exchange of news (l. 20)
 the MASK of formality gradually SLIPPED (l. 22)
 half-forgotten feuds GLOWED again (l. 24)
 The quarrels of childhood CLAMOURED only just below the RUFFLED
  surface (ll. 24–25)
 a feeling of guilt waits to POUNCE (l. 52)
 the CHILL of the empty place (l. 57)
 Christenings — — — CAST NO SHADOWS (l. 59)
 family FRICTIONS (l. 63)

Prepositions

Notice the following:

 They, TOGETHER WITH grown-up daughters, had to entertain the family
 WITH piano-playing

there are fewer opportunities FOR visiting
to have few opportunities OF visiting
get pleasure OUT OF (or FROM) something
see the family AT its happiest
all BUT the most enduring friends
different FROM those of our ancestors

Word distinctions

SCATTERED (l. 1)—breadcrumbs scattered for the birds.
Pepper is sprinkled. Fruit-trees are sprayed.

ENSURE (l. 2) Soundproof walls ensure quietness.
He insured his house against fire. He assured me that there was no danger.

TAKE (l. 10) from here to there. BRING from there to here.

FETCH BRING TAKE LEAD CONDUCT
The dog was —— the blind man.
—— your dictionaries to class tomorrow.
The footman —— the statesmen to the President's room.
I hope he —— me to the cinema.
The photographs should be ready tomorrow. I must —— them from the shop.

BEAMED (l. 19) His face beamed with satisfaction and triumph. The schoolboy grinned cheerfully. I sneered at his feeble attempt. The poor imbecile leered at us hopefully.

REMINISCENCES (l. 21) exchange reminiscences of one's schooldays. To have pleasant memories of the past. To buy holiday souvenirs.

JOURNEY (l. 27) trip outing expedition excursion voyage
an old people's ——;   an —— to the South Pole;
a —— in the South Seas;   cheap —— tickets;
an evening —— to the seaside;   the —— home.

NECESSARY (l. 29) indispensable vital essential.
Arrange these words in order of emphasis, beginning with the weakest. Two have almost the same meaning but different aspects, connected with the origin of the words, are referred to. Which two words are these and what are their exact meanings?
OPPORTUNITIES (l. 35)—possibilities that one can take advantage of.
Bear in mind the possibility that it may rain.
There is a possibility that you will be awarded the prize.
You will have an opportunity of taking the examination.
Opportunity knocks only once. (Proverb.)

AGED (l. 45) Past form of the verb 'to age'—one syllable.
This applies also to the verbal forms of 'blessed' and 'learned'
Adjectival 'aged', 'blessed' and 'learned' are pronounced with two syllables.

MOOD (l. 48)—in a cheerful, depressed, thoughtful, good and bad mood. But only—in a good temper (cheerful and not angry)—in a bad temper (angry)

Additional word distinctions

MEND   REPAIR   OVERHAUL   RECONSTRUCT   DARN   PATCH   RENOVATE

to —— a sock;   to —— the sleeve of a worn jacket;
to —— a broken cup;   to —— a faulty machine;
to —— a damaged building;   to —— old furniture.
to —— shoes (two possibilities);

KILL   MURDER   ASSASSINATE   COMMIT SUICIDE   MASSACRE   SLAUGHTER   EXECUTE   SACRIFICE

to —— a statesman;   to —— an army;
to —— a murderer;   to —— a hated enemy;
to —— a lamb;   to —— a fly;
to —— cattle;   the desperate man ——.

INSOLVENT   INSOLUBLE
The business is now hopelessly ——. The problem of making any real profit seems ——.

ALTERNATE   ALTERNATIVE
As the boat leaves only on —— days, you have no —— but to stay here overnight.

INDUSTRIAL   INDUSTRIOUS
The inhabitants of the —— North are independent, enterprising and ——.

RECOMPENSE   REWARD
He has given two hundred pounds as —— for the damage done to his boat. The men whose lives he had saved gave him a —— of a gold watch.

It is altogether impossible.
All together the money amounted to ten shillings.
It is already midnight.
They were all ready to go.
That is an everyday occurrence. (Adjectival.)
That happens every day. (Adverbial.)
He works in a factory where a certain fabric is made.
He came in to see me.
He came into the room.
The cat jumped on to the table.

Expressions to learn and use

The house is WITHIN EASY WALKING DISTANCE OF the town centre.
THE RARER such meetings . . . THE MORE IMPORTANT it was . . .
(The sooner the better. The more difficult the work the less trouble you take.)

| ATTENTION WAS PAID TO . . . | IN SOME INDEFINABLE WAY |

A coal fire ADDS TO THE ATTRACTIONS OF a winter evening indoors.
Small families HAVE BEEN THE FASHION
Owing to the strike, petrol is IN SHORT SUPPLY.
He is ON HIS VERY BEST BEHAVIOUR.
A SUDDEN BURST OF CONVERSATION.
He wears odd clothes so as to DRAW ATTENTION TO himself.
We FEEL AT EASE WITH our friends.
TO A MORE LIMITED EXTENT.
American English is only SUPERFICIALLY DIFFERENT FROM British
English.
The Alsatian dog and the wolf HAVE MANY THINGS IN COMMON.

Explaining the meaning of words and phrases

Explain the following words and phrases in such a way as to bring out their
meaning clearly.

  a) plain speaking with hovering dissension (l. 13)
  b) to reflect prosperity and propriety (ll. 14–15)
  c) reminiscences (l. 21)
  d) ritual (l. 30)
  e) internationally-derided and very unfairly-underrated (ll. 77–78).

Short answers to questions

The following exercises, based on the reading passage, should be dealt with
in complete sentences. Only a little information is needed in each case.
Express your answers in your own words as far as possible.

  1. Why did the girl who in earlier times married a husband from a long way
     off have to say a final goodbye to her parents?
  2. What were the main impressions that Victorian families who rarely met
     tried to give?
  3. What were the commonest topics of conversation at such gatherings?
  4. What half-forgotten memories of childhood came alive again at such
     gatherings?
  5. What was the general feeling about such reunions that was experienced
     after they had ended?
  6. What pleasures do families derive from wedding receptions?
  7. How do people at funerals behave to the relatives most closely affected?
  8. What is one possible reason for the cheerfulness of the meal that follows
     the funeral?
  9. What picture is suggested of the future family?

Longer answers

These answers should be expressed within the number of words stated. Use
only information found in the passage but express your answers in your own
words as far as possible.

1. In what ways does the Victorian family reunion seem to have been unpleasant? (not more than 60 words)
2. Why are family reunions possibly less common nowadays? (not more than 65 words)
3. What links keep families in touch with one another and what are the special characteristics of each of these? (not more than 90 words)

Practice

SECTION I GRAMMAR

VERBAL CONSTRUCTIONS   *Reference material*
                                                   pages 221–7

EXERCISES

I. For each of the dashes in the following sentences substitute as many words as you wish to continue and complete the meaning of those given. Each word group supplied should contain a verbal form (gerund, infinitive, or finite verb in a clause) dependent on the verb or adjective already provided. In some cases a preposition will precede the appropriate verbal form.

1. Many old people are interested —— and they enjoy ——.
2. The guide suggested —— but we thought ——.
3. If that book is worth —— I should like ——. The last one that author produced —— too obscure ——.
4. The matron does not allow visitors —— but some people insist ——.
5. Marie Curie succeeded ——, Her husband helped her ——.
6. The bad weather prevented us ——. We had been looking forward ——.
7. After Mrs White had finished ——, she felt like ——.
8. Fishermen don't mind —— but most other people would loathe ——.
9. The young motor cyclist was boasting ——. If what he said was true, he should be punished ——.
10. The bus conductor accused ——. He made her ——.
11. The education committee spent an hour ——. It was then agreed to postpone ——.
12. The people in the bus queue were watching ——. They were tired ——.
13. If you arrive late you had better ——. Mr Smith does not like ——.
14. The sales manager doubts ——. He insists ——.
15. Our cat is sitting ——. She objects to ——.
16. When the house decorator had finished ——, he intended ——.
17. Most small boys prefer ——. They never complain ——.
18. You had better not ——. If you do, you risk ——.
19. The old lady said she remembered —— but she refused ——.
20. Persevere —— and you will not fail ——.
21. In spring birds are busy ——. By instinct they know ——.
22. The accused man denied —— but the police took him to headquarters ——.
23. It is so warm I should like ——. But I expect ——.
24. I could not help —— but I soon regretted ——.
25. Would you rather —— or have you definitely decided ——?
26. He apologised profusely —— but I told him ——.
27. The heckler kept ——. When he challenged ——, he was asked ——. He then apologised ——.
28. His parents did not forbid —— but they discouraged ——. He finally promised ——.

154

29. When I visited London I missed ——.
30. My sister wanted —— but I forgot ——.
31. You will be very ill if you stop ——. It is most important ——.

II. a) From the four words or phrases listed in each of the following sentences, indicate the one which belongs there grammatically.

b) Modify each sentence in as many ways as are necessary to incorporate each of the other three words in a grammatical construction.

1. He $\begin{matrix} \text{is} \\ \text{makes me} \\ \text{lets me} \\ \text{had better} \end{matrix}$ to study Mathematics.

2. I $\begin{matrix} \text{avoided} \\ \text{postponed} \\ \text{happened} \\ \text{insisted} \end{matrix}$ to meet him.

3. Do you $\begin{matrix} \text{mind} \\ \text{persist} \\ \text{object} \\ \text{dare} \end{matrix}$ to go home alone?

4. He $\begin{matrix} \text{suggested} \\ \text{is used} \\ \text{promised} \\ \text{succeeded} \end{matrix}$ to calculate how much it might cost.

5. I $\begin{matrix} \text{should like} \\ \text{remember} \\ \text{deny} \\ \text{missed} \end{matrix}$ to have played with trains as a child.

6. He $\begin{matrix} \text{knows} \\ \text{spends time} \\ \text{would rather} \\ \text{is learning} \end{matrix}$ to play chess.

7. The retired boxer $\begin{matrix} \text{suggests} \\ \text{means} \\ \text{thinks} \\ \text{had better} \end{matrix}$ to buy a public house.

8. The harbour master $\begin{matrix} \text{wants} \\ \text{thinks} \\ \text{will allow} \\ \text{prefers} \end{matrix}$ that the boat will arrive early.

9. He $\begin{matrix} \text{feels like} \\ \text{has finished} \\ \text{enjoys} \\ \text{has decided} \end{matrix}$ to eat a ham sandwich.

10. He seldom $\begin{matrix} \text{fails} \\ \text{forgets} \\ \text{troubles} \\ \text{suggests} \end{matrix}$ sending news to his brother abroad.

11. I $\begin{matrix} \text{apologise} \\ \text{cannot help} \\ \text{regret} \\ \text{prefer} \end{matrix}$ that I am late.

12. I $\begin{matrix} \text{am looking forward} \\ \text{long} \\ \text{enjoy} \\ \text{imagine myself} \end{matrix}$ to ski through the forest.

155

SECTION II PUNCTUATION

HYPHENS

Reference material
page 232–3

EXERCISE

All or some of the words in each of the following groups should be:

    a) written as one word OR
    b) hyphenated OR
    c) remain separate.

Write each word group in the way in which you think it would normally appear.

a coming of age party; an old age pension; he dreads old age; a bus stop; heat resistant glass; under ground; present day tendencies; anti vivisectionist; a one year old child; he is one year old; the room was rarely occupied; four hundred and thirty two; a mouth organ; mid night; ex president; a three sided figure; a looking glass; a light house; a non stop train; anti social; a general hospital; medium sized; all right; a playwright; washing up; roast beef; a cat burglar; a many coloured vase; a department store; a road junction; every day life; he comes every day; a hire purchase agreement; an estate agent; a football match; a look out; dairy farming; he is very highly strung; a public library; panic stricken flight; the starting point; a seaside resort; a hard boiled egg; a grape fruit; hard wearing cloth; a multi storey car park; mean while; a water proof raincoat.

SECTION IV   CHOICE OF EXPRESSION

SENTENCE PATTERN

Reference material
pages 243–4

EXERCISE

Rewrite the following sentences and sentence groups so that the ideas are expressed more effectively and pleasantly.

    a) The daily newspaper has become an essential part of our lives. What would we do without it? How much we owe to those who first established it!

    b) Scientists and agronomists are devising methods of producing additional food but the world's population is increasing far more quickly than the supply of food available. What is to be done about providing adequate living standards for future generations? No one can say. And time is running out!

    c) She was determined that her suitcase should be light enough to carry easily, so, having decided that it would be best to fit all the heavier objects into a hold-all, she packed her lightest clothes in the case, only to discover that by the time the hold-all had been crammed with two novels, a guide book, a medium-sized dictionary, fruit, biscuits, a thermos flask, a dressing-gown, a mackintosh, shoes, two cameras and a miscellany of small heavy objects, while she would be able to carry the suitcase for miles without noticing it, she could hardly lift the hold-all from the ground.

SECTION VI   REPORTED SPEECH

C. CHANGING FROM REPORTED TO DIRECT SPEECH

Reference material
pages 250–1

EXERCISES

I. Convert the following sentences into direct speech.

    a) She implored them to be careful and not to leave the mountain hut the next day if the weather got worse.

b) He asked me if I would telephone him as soon as I got home.

c) I promised that I would lend him the duplicator when I had finished with it.

d) She exclaimed in wonder at the beauty of the miniature and said how much she would love to wear it.

e) He grumbled about the noisy aeroplanes and said that something ought to be done about them.

f) He said that if I had asked his advice about the type of car I was buying he would have recommended an estate car.

g) He asked in what century I should like to have been born and whether I thought I would have been happier then.

2. Convert the following sentence groups into direct speech where necessary, remembering to start a new paragraph for each fresh speaker.

a) Mrs Minton asked her guests what they had been doing for the past hour. They said they had just bought a map and then had found a quiet café. They had been planning the tour they would be making the following week.

b) He advised me not to speak so loudly because the chauffeur might be listening. What I had just said was confidential. I reminded him that I had been speaking in a whisper and that anyhow the chauffeur had arrived in England only a fortnight before and could speak no English. He said I must never take anything for granted.

c) He shouted to attract our attention and asked us whether we had won the previous day's match. When we said we had not, he expressed his sympathy and wished us better luck the next time.

d) The dealer patted the car bonnet affectionately and murmured that she would sail like a bird. Ninety miles an hour she would do, like a dream.

The poker-faced man said that birds did not sail and that ninety miles an hour was a nightmare.

The dealer drew his attention to the various gadgets: the retractable ash tray, the fitted radio, the highly efficient heating system.

The poker-faced man said that he did not smoke, was stone deaf and was taking a job on the Equator.

The dealer then asked him just what sort of car he was looking for.

The poker-faced man said he wanted one that the dealer could guarantee would get him from place to place without breaking down, that would carry his luggage, his dog and his wife over desert tracks and jungle trails, that would not deteriorate in heat, disintegrate in dust or dissolve in tropical storms and that would not cost more than £700.

The dealer regarded thoughtfully the sleek bonnet, the gleaming radiator, the luxurious upholstery, the whole symposium of varnish and chrome and told the man he could not help him. He recommended his trying the garage round the corner as they had a few pre-war models in stock.

e) I rang him up this morning at the number he had given and a girl asked if she could help me. I asked if I might speak to George. She wanted to know which George I wanted as there were five Georges in the office. I told her that I did not know his second name but he had red hair. She said that that was George Murphy, the junior clerk. She asked my name and when I told her, she requested me to wait and she would put me through. I heard George answer abruptly and the girl reply that Mr Marvin Newman would like to speak to him. George's tone changed immediately. He thanked the girl courteously and greeted me respectfully, giving his full name. I replied by stating my surname and said I hoped I was not disturbing him. He assured me that this was not the case as he had everything under complete control.

I went on to explain that I had telephoned about a certain financial matter that concerned us both. George had some difficulty in finding words and then stammered out a question as to whether this meant that his application for promotion had been approved. I said that I knew nothing about promotion. I was referring to the ten pounds he had borrowed from me a year previously. He repeated my words incredulously and sought confirmation of the fact that I was Mr Marvin Newman, Personnel Manager at Headquarters. I said that I was Mr Martin Newnham of Norbury and that he would remember he had borrowed money from me on the way to the Derby of the previous year.

His tone changed again. With a non-committal exclamation he said that he was an extremely busy man and implied that I was wasting his time. He suggested my ringing at some more convenient time and closed the conversation forthwith.

Composition

Writing on a general topic

Some essay topics escape the classification of factual account, expression of opinion, an attempt to convince, description, imaginative reflection. The following titles are examples of an essay of this kind:

Week-ends
The art of bargaining
The clever shopper goes early to market.

The subject may be a proverb:

All that glisters is not gold.

lines of verse or a quotation:

'He that fights and runs away
May live to fight another day.'
Musarum Deliciae, 1656

'For fools rush in where angels fear to tread.'
Alexander Pope

The immediate reaction to a topic of this kind may well be blankness of mind. How best can the subject be approached: what should be included and what ignored?

Some advice on dealing with this kind of subject

Decide on ONE single line of approach.

In the case of the comprehension passage, different kinds of family reunion are dealt with, with the shared characteristics of lack of warmth and formal behaviour barely concealing ill-feeling, but at the same time a sense of belonging based on childhood memories and a common inheritance.

WEEK-ENDS—possible approaches:

1. The changing attitudes to week-ends through history.
2. Changing attitudes to week-ends through a person's own life.
3. The frequent disillusionment produced by the longed-for week-end.
4. Contrasting week-ends.

The essay itself may be a blend of description, fact, opinion and even imagination. Here is a SUGGESTED SCHEME for an essay on 'The Art of Cooking':

1. There are many good cooks: i.e. those ready to take time and trouble achieving flavour, lightness, etc. Examples. But these are technicians, not artists.
2. True artist must be creative—have a vision of a hitherto untried dish and ready to take infinite trouble to achieve it. Shares enjoyment, frustration, frequent disappointment of all artists.
3. An illustration of a cook artist at work (description).
4. The serving of a newly-created dish (description).
5. Many types of painters and writers and also of artist cooks—meticulous, slapdash, eccentric, specialist etc. Possible anecdote.

6. But cooking a limited form of art. True art should appeal to intelligence and emotions, awakening deeper understanding of problems and feelings of mankind. Beyond powers of cook. And true art has some degree of permanence.

Other approaches to the same topic could be

a) A largely factual presentation of advice on how to cook really well.
b) A description of the preparation of an extremely good meal.
c) An expression of contempt for the fashionable view of this art in newspapers or on television, as this is only a form of social snobbery. What you yourself would accept as the art of cooking.

EXERCISE
Prepare and discuss plans for several of the following topics. Write an essay of around 600 to 700 words on one or more of them.

The art of bargaining.

The clever shopper goes early to the market.

He that fights and runs away
May live to fight another day

For fools rush in where angels fear to tread.

The pleasures of writing and receiving letters

Getting to know people

Home

Fashion

Holiday resorts

Caravans

DIALOGUE

A *conversation*, when recorded in writing, is set down as direct speech accompanied by such tags as 'he said', 'the guide explained'.

A *dialogue* normally resembles the script of a play, with the name of each speaker at the left-hand side and movements and possibly facial expressions indicated in brackets as part of the text.

When creating a dialogue remember the following characteristics of conversation:

a) Sentences are nearly always short and simple and often incomplete. Direct questions and exclamations are quite common.
b) Question tags and short answers, often inverted, e.g. 'So do I'.
c) Short simple words including common colloquialisms, possibly some slang.
d) Language adapted to the person speaking (the way he speaks is often influenced by the person he is speaking to). A university professor will not speak in the same way as a stevedore and a middle-aged housewife will have a different kind of vocabulary from a teenager. Even the professor, however, would use a simpler form of language when speaking than when writing, especially when addressing someone considerably less educated than himself.

The following example illustrates these suggestions.

A dialogue between a teacher and an eleven-year-old boy who has secretly brought a white mouse to school and is playing with it under the desk.

Teacher: You're not attending, Potter. What are you up to?
Potter: Nothing, sir.
Teacher: Then what was my last remark?
Potter: Er ... well, sir—yes, sir, you were talking about the Amazon Indians. Yes, that was it, sir.
Teacher: That was ten minutes ago. What have I said since then?

Potter: Well, sir, you were speaking a bit softly. I didn't like to interrupt, but I couldn't quite hear.

Teacher: Very thoughtful of you, Potter. And just what have you got under your desk?

Potter: Under my desk, sir? Well, sir, my feet I suppose. Oh yes, sir, it's my handkerchief here. I thought I might sneeze, sir, you know, unexpectedly. It's always as well to be ready for emergencies, sir.

(He lifts a grubby handkerchief into view, and, at this point, the mouse which he has transferred to his other hand, escapes. After an exciting five minutes the mouse is recaptured and handed back to Potter, who holds it up and strokes it soothingly. The class are back in their places under the teacher's hostile eye.)

Teacher: Now Potter, we've had just about enough. Kindly restore that rodent to its box, or whatever conveyance it travelled here in, and we'll go on with the lesson.

Potter: It's awfully upset, sir. Don't you think——?

Teacher (*fiercely*): Potter, if I ever see, hear or smell that mouse again, it will disappear for good. I've a small son who would appreciate having a white mouse—in his own home.

Potter (*slipping the mouse into a cardboard box*): Oh, sir, would he? I could sell him this one. Only twenty-five pence to you, sir.

Teacher: Tomorrow morning I shall receive a five hundred word composition from you, Potter, entitled 'The Proper Care of White Mice'. And any other animal, bird or insect of yours that I ever set eyes on again will be confiscated at once. And now, boys, besides coffee, what are the main products of Brazil?

Rewrite the above dialogue as it would appear in a short story.

Suggestions for other dialogues.

1. An English lady is instructing an au pair girl how to make a cup of English tea. (Or the girl is telling the lady about the making of coffee in the girl's country.)
2. An English person visiting your town stops you and asks the way to the Post Office. You volunteer to accompany him or her. Your conversation on the way.
3. You are inspecting a room that is to let. Your conversation with the English-woman who is showing it to you.
4. A barber and his customer are talking (the weather, football, boxing, the newspaper, etc.).
5. A door-to-door salesman wants to sell a vacuum cleaner and a lady wants to get rid of him.
6. A wife is trying to persuade her husband to buy a new suit.
7. A TV interview between a lady and an au pair girl introducing some of the complaints of each. A Chairman is present.
8. You are in a train with a fellow-passenger who has visited the town you live in.
9. Two waiters are discussing difficult customers.
10. Two young people are disagreeing about abstract art.
11. An opera enthusiast tries to convert an admirer of pop music.

DEBATES

In a general discussion, various aspects of a subject are dealt with and though there is a tendency to take sides, there need be no division of opinion. A discussion, for example, on the merits and defects of a certain scheme under consideration need not be narrowed down to the proposed adoption or rejection of the scheme.

A debate, however, presupposes a division into those in favour of and those against a certain proposition, often termed a motion. Some debates deal with essential issues, as in the case of Parliamentary debates when bills are under discussion or in the local Council chamber. Less formal debates, while serving no

160

practical purposes, have a value in encouraging clear and logical thinking, in presenting other viewpoints and in providing training in fluency and persuasiveness.

The Chairman controls the debate. The motion has probably been announced previously and one speaker is ready to propose and another to oppose the motion, in other words, to make a speech in favour of or against the proposition to be discussed. Each speaker usually has a seconder, who speaks more briefly, supplementing what the main speaker has said and possibly dealing with some of the points already made by the opposing speaker. The normal programme for a debate is as follows:

1. The Chairman opens the debate, announces the motion and introduces the speakers.
2. He calls upon the proposer of the motion, and, after this speech, upon the opposer.
3. He calls upon the seconders in the same order.
4. He throws open the motion to general debate.
5. At about ten minutes before the end of the allotted time he calls first on the opposer and then upon the proposer to sum up for their sides.
6. He takes a vote. The motion is carried or rejected by (for example) 33 votes to 20.

Throughout the debate, everyone who speaks starts by addressing the Chair: 'Mr Chairman, . . .' Anyone failing to do this can be called to order by the Chairman. If two people try to speak at the same time, the Chairman decides the issue. In all, the Chairman has the responsibility of seeing that the debate is conducted in a correct and orderly manner.

Suggestions for making speeches

The ability to make a good speech depends fundamentally on personality. Anyone who has plenty of self-confidence and perhaps some acting ability is likely to hold his audience more surely than the shy nervous person who hardly dares to make himself heard. Yet practice can help. Even the shy person can become the confident lecturer or teacher. The unhappy novice should remember that most beginners feel as he does and that even some very experienced actors are said to dread every entrance they make on the stage. Once they are there, the part and the atmosphere absorbs them and they find acting enjoyable. Facing a hostile crowd of hecklers at a political meeting may well be an ordeal even for the most seasoned party candidate but the average group participating in a debate is docile and not too critical. One of the secrets, if it can be mastered, is to look at one's audience all the time and speak directly to them, feigning an ease and confidence one is far from feeling.

Certain features distinguish the speech from the essay or composition. Much depends, of course, on the voice, personality and ideas of the speaker but the following suggestions may be usefully borne in mind.

1. A speech being obviously spoken English, the usual colloquial abbreviations are normal. Some speakers seek to enhance the dignity of their words by always using the extended form: 'We do not think that . . .', 'It is not necessary . . .' This style may seem strained and artificial unless it blends ideally with the general tone of the speech.
2. Sentences are usually short and direct. Listeners would find it far more difficult to follow the involved thought of a long sentence. Moreover short sentences often have a more dramatic appeal.
3. Other dramatic devices may be introduced. The rhetorical question and personal challenge tend to draw the feelings of the listener into the argument.

   'How can we condemn a young person who gets into trouble in this way? I expect most of you remember a contented childhood with affectionate parents. Inhabitants of a secure world, you felt little need to rebel. I ask you to consider. If you had come from a miserable home wouldn't you have turned against an indifferent society? Mightn't you also have been in trouble with the law?'

Another device is climax:

'Man can irrigate the desert; he can control the flood; he can fertilise the unproductive soil. Couldn't he, if he really wished, satisfy also the hungry millions of the world?'

And balanced antithesis:

'We, the fortunates of Europe and America, enjoy a standard of living never achieved before: they, the deprived of the greater part of the earth's surface, still live in near-starvation and squalor.'

A pause effectively inserted at appropriate points can achieve emphasis, dignity and emotional appeal.

4. Repetition is common, each important idea being repeated at least once, in other words or by means of an illustration or anecdote. A listener needs this repetition, especially in an obscure argument; he cannot, like the reader, re-read the passage.

'Man's life is gradually being dominated by the machine: these efficient devices he created to achieve greater freedom are increasingly determining how he shall spend his time.'

5. Vivid illustrations, striking phrases, clever anecdotes can all help to hold the listeners' attention.

6. Above all, audiences enjoy humour, particularly quick clever repartee, humorous absurdity and exaggeration, parody and any original ironical turn of speech.
   A quick, witty, relevant retort in general debate can establish a speaker's reputation for cleverness.

7. Remember, however, that a clear, logical exposition, delivered in a firm, friendly, pleasant voice at a moderate to slow speed, and (this is very important) directed towards the audience and not towards the paper in the speaker's hand, should be quite effective, even though some of the other suggestions may seem beyond the speaker's power. Nervousness does usually disappear once one has started speaking and sincerity, individuality, common sense (and audibility) will certainly win respect.

The preparation of a speech

Given notice, one has the opportunity of assembling one's ideas so as to be able to secure the maximum effect. An impromptu speech by anyone but an expert is likely to be diffuse, rambling and at the same time sparse in ideas. But it is as well to avoid the over-prepared speech and, unless the speech is unusually important, it should never be read from the paper. Few things are more boring than being read to by the top of a person's head. Ideally one speaks without notes but this requires considerable confidence and a good memory: notes, set out so that each point can be seized at a glance, and available merely for consultation at intervals without distracting attention, are a valuable support. In the example below, merely headings of the points to be made are given. Other useful references might be included: examples to be mentioned, anecdotes, and, naturally, figures and details difficult to memorise.

The introduction and conclusion are very important. The first captures or loses the audience's interest; the second may finally engage their support for the author's point of view.

Here are some ideas for preparing speeches for and against a topic. The motion is:

'That the use of transistor radios should be made illegal in public places.'

The *proposer* listed these subject headings.

1. Selfishness—other people's enjoyment and peace spoilt.
2. Merely for show—rarely listened to.
3. Usually only less-educated people use them.

4. If everyone had one!—all tuned to different stations!
5. Far too much noise in the world already.

He devised an introduction on these lines:

'Mr Chairman, Ladies and Gentlemen. The poet Keats wrote an ode to the nightingale while Shelley praised the skylark. Music (in its right place) has inspired poetry and song. But surely no poet who has sensitive ears attuned to the gentle sounds of Nature could ever find inspiration in a horrible, perambulating, wailing box. We linger by the quiet lake: we listen to the soft lapping of the waves: we luxuriate in peace. It is just then that a noise approaches: an abominable, discordant, tinned sound of jerky ugliness. A transistor-armed picnic group is just arriving, about to settle down. We turn and flee.'

Here is his conclusion:

'The transistor age is upon us. Within a few short years we shall exist in a blaring jungle of transistors. Every single person in the crowd around us will have a transistor radio tuned to a different station. Faces will glare at us from transistor televisions. Walkie-talkie transistors will transmit loud-voiced messages between friends. For all I know, transistors may be producing unending quantities of ice-cream, weak tea and cans of beer. Save us good people from this nightmare! Let us start here a monster petition which will be signed by all normal citizens to restore some measure of peace and sanity and rid all places where people meet of the menace of the transistor.'

The *opposer* based his speech on these points:

1. People complain only because envious of gaiety of younger generation.
2. Grumblers often talk loudly themselves.
3. Usually set owners obliging—will turn down volume if asked.
4. Objectors can always go elsewhere.
5. No such ban could be enforced.
6. Usefulness of transistor—sports scores and commentaries, news, talks, plays, etc., always available.
7. Music adds to the enjoyment of our leisure. Happiness always enhanced by music.

(The speaker would also deal with points raised by the proposer.)

This introduction was as follows:

'Mr Chairman, Ladies and Gentlemen. Tonight we have all had a most interesting experience. We have heard the last lingering survivor of a long-past generation, he who regards laughter and gaiety as wicked, who forbids us to sing and dance and show our enjoyment of life when we are free to do so. His secret aim is to destroy all gaiety. Not only for his narrow, miserable self but for all who enjoy rhythm, melody and singing, who like to walk to the beat of music and relax to the soothing sweetness of a song.'

His conclusion:

'All of you in front of me are young at heart. You are happy and want to share your happiness with others. Those who wish to destroy your simple pleasures, common to all, are the old, the lined, the embittered. Show that you are among those who are gay and young and vote to have the right to carry and enjoy your transistor night and day, wherever you are and however many your company.'

(There is a possibility that both proposer and opposer are speaking with their tongues in their cheeks.)

Suggested motions for debate

1. That old people should receive much higher pensions.
2. That any person found driving a car under the influence of alcohol should be disqualified from driving for three years.

3. That husbands and wives who are both wage-earners should share equally domestic chores.
4. That prize fights (boxing) are dangerous and should be banned.
5. That public transport is a national service to the community and should be State subsidised.
6. That all Parliamentary candidates should have to pass an examination in History and Economics.
7. That all workers should have at least four weeks' annual holiday.
8. That English people give far too much attention to animals.
9. That members of a less highly developed nation may well be happier than those in a very prosperous community.
10. That 'Live for the Day' is the best motto for life.
11. That a person achieves greatness only if he is born at a suitable time.
12. That we condemn most in others our own besetting faults.
13. That 'Early to bed and early to rise' is not a good motto for life.
14. That reading detective stories is a waste of time.
15. That the money spent on space research should be devoted to human need.
16. That a feeling of superiority or hatred towards another race or class of people is primitive and absurd.
17. That the tramp is the happiest member of the community.
18. That the popularity of many modern art forms depends entirely on fashion.
20. That the human race is no more intelligent now than in the days of ancient Egypt.
21. That material success rarely brings happiness.
22. That the desire for fame can rarely produce great art.
23. That the fundamental purpose of education is the adaptation of the child to his social environment.
24. That most people nowadays are largely able to shape their own destinies.
25. That a young person of sixteen years and over should be left free to make all his own decisions.
26. That all children should attend school until they are at least sixteen.
27. That happiness lies in the person and not in his surroundings.
28. That man will eventually be exterminated by the robots he has created.
29. That civilisation has passed its peak.
30. That a highly intelligent and sensitive person is rarely happy.
31. That telepathic communication is possible.
32. That ghosts do exist.
33. That political affiliations are motivated by psychological rather than environmental conditions.
34. That all human actions are motivated ultimately by self-interest.
35. That there is little relation between popularity and character.
36. That it is society that produces the criminal.
37. That environment is more important than heredity in forming character.
38. That the most underprivileged group all over the world is that of women.

PRACTICE PAPER 8

I READING COMPREHENSION

Section A

In this section you must choose the word or phrase which best completes each sentence. Write down each number and beside it the letters **A, B, C, D** and **E**. Then in each case cross through the letter before the word or phrase you choose. Give one answer only to each question.

1. Medieval travellers' tales of fantastic creatures were often fascinating but not always ——.

   A credible   **B** creditable   **C** conceivable   **D** credulous
   E imaginable

2. He had always had a good opinion of himself, but after the publication of his best-selling novel he became unbearably ——.

   A bigoted   **B** proud   **C** conceited   **D** exaggerated
   E cocksure

3. He made some —— sketches which would serve as guides when he painted the actual portrait.

   A primary   **B** elementary   **C** fundamental
   D introductory   **E** preliminary

4. No human being is —— but Alistair Allington made very few mistakes

   A fallacious   **B** false   **C** plausible   **D** infallible
   E correct

5. After his long illness, the old man appeared so thin and —— that a gust of wind might have blown him away.

   A flimsy   **B** powerless   **C** frail   **D** withered   **E** faint

6. The Romans —— a large part of Europe and the Middle East.

   A submitted   **B** subdued   **C** surpassed   **D** oppressed
   E predominated

7. He is considered to be an outstanding artist but I consider his work to be quite ——.

   A mediocre   **B** medium   **C** moderate   **D** intermediate
   E common

8. —— lighting has made an important contribution to the cultural development of humanity.

   A synthetic   **B** false   **C** imitation   **D** counterfeit
   E artificial

9. He lives entirely alone —— the rats, bats, moths and mice.

   A in spite of   **B** besides   **C** allowing for   **D** apart from
   E let alone

10. Many countries have now succeeded in —— the malarial mosquito.

    A erasing   **B** eradicating   **C** abolishing   **D** obliterating
    E demolishing

II COMPOSITION

Section B

Read the following passage and then answer the questions on it.

She stood before us looking very composed as she gave us good morning. Sabri cleared his throat, and picking up the great key very delicately between finger and thumb—as if it were of the utmost fragility—put it down again on the edge of the desk nearest her with the air of a conjurer making his opening
5 dispositions. "We are speaking about your house," he said softly, in a voice ever so faintly curdled with menace. "Do you know that all the wood is . . ." he suddenly shouted the last word with such force that I nearly fell off my chair, "rotten!" And picking up the key he banged it down to emphasise the point.
10 The woman threw up her head with contempt and taking up the key also banged it down in her turn exclaiming: "It is not."

"It *is*," Sabri banged the key.

"It is *not*." She banged it back.

"It *is*." A bang.
15 "It is *not*." A counter-bang.

All this was certainly not on a very intellectual level, and made me rather ill at ease. I also feared that the key itself would be banged out of shape so that finally none of us would be able to get into the house. But these were the opening chords, so to speak, the preliminary statement of theme.
20 The woman now took the key and held it up as if she were swearing by it. "The house is a good house," she cried. Then she put it back on the desk. Sabri took it up thoughtfully, blew into the end of it as if it were a six-shooter, aimed it and peered along it as if along a barrel. Then he put it down and fell into an abstraction. "And suppose we wanted the house," he said, "which we
25 don't what would you ask for it?"

"Eight hundred pounds."

Sabri gave a long and stagy laugh, wiping away imaginary tears and repeating, "Eight hundred pounds" as if it were the best joke in the world. He laughed at me and I laughed at him, a dreadful false laugh. He slapped his
30 knee. I rolled about in my chair as if on the verge of acute gastritis. We laughed until we were exhausted. Then we grew serious again. Sabri was still as fresh as a daisy, I could see that. He had put himself into the patient contemplative state of mind of a chess player.

"Take the key and go," he snapped suddenly, and handing it to her,
35 swirled round in his swivel chair to present her with his back; then as suddenly he completed the circuit and swivelled round again. "What!" he said with surprise. "You haven't gone." In truth there had hardly been time for the woman to go. But she was somewhat slow-witted, though obstinate as a mule:
166

that was clear. "Right," she now said in a ringing tone, and picking up the key put it into her bosom and turned about. She walked off stage in a some- 40 what lingering fashion. "Take no notice," whispered Sabri and busied himself with his papers.

The woman stopped irresolutely outside the shop, and was here joined by her husband who began to talk to her in a low cringing voice, pleading with her. He took her by the sleeve and led her unwillingly back into the shop 45 where we sat pointedly reading letters. "Ah! It's you," said Sabri with well-simulated surprise. "She wishes to discuss some more," explained the cobbler in a weak conciliatory voice. Sabri sighed.

"What is there to speak of? She takes me for a fool." Then he suddenly turned to her and bellowed, "Two hundred pounds and not a piastre more." 50

It was her turn to have a paroxysm of false laughter, but this was rather spoiled by her husband who started plucking at her sleeve as if he were persuading her to be sensible. Sabri was not slow to notice this. "You tell her," he said to the man. "You are a man and these things are clear to you. She is only a woman and does not see the truth. Tell her what it is worth." 55

Lawrence Durrell, *Bitter Lemons*

1. Sabri used various dramatic devices in trying to secure an advantage. Suggest four of these and the effect each was intended to produce.
2. Explain the suitability of the metaphor "curdled" as it is used in line 6.
3. In what various ways is it made clear that Sabri intended to give tremendous emphasis to the word 'rotten'?
4. Justify the writer's remark: 'All this was not a very intellectual level.' (line 16)
5. 'The preliminary statement of theme': what musical reference has this expression and how can it be applied in the situation being described?
6. Explain the symbolical uses of the key throughout the first stage of the proceedings.
7. With what purpose did both sides make use of simulated laughter and why was the laughter more effective in one case than in the other?
8. The writer clearly viewed the interview partly as some kind of theatrical entertainment. Quote from the passage three words or expressions which highlight this connection with the world of the theatre and entertainment.
9. Define three succeeding stages of emotion which the woman experienced during the events of the passage.
10. Explain the writer's purpose in choosing to employ each of the following words:
    ringing (line 39); irresolutely (line 43); pointedly (line 46); conciliatory (line 48); plucking (line 52).
11. What details give the impression that the woman will finally be defeated in the bargaining?

III USE OF ENGLISH

Section B

Read the following passage and then answer the questions which follow it.

Caracas has been called the Los Angeles of South America. At first sight this seems reasonable enough, for this brash modern city on the fringe of the Orinoco wilderness is dominated by a profusion of motor traffic winding its way along numerous urban motorways, sprawling interchanges and curving
5 distributors. Railways have completely disappeared from this part of the world, and Venezualan oil, which fuels the multitude of cars, has been the source of wealth on which the city has developed and spread.

But in complete contrast to Los Angeles and many other Western cities, the motor car in Caracas has in no way stimulated residential sprawl at very
10 low densities. Indeed, the city shows every sign of a tightening in densities of development as population growth sends the numbers of inhabitants rocketing. By 1950 about 700,000 people lived there; today the figure is nearer 2,000,000—or about one-fifth of all Venezuala's inhabitants. A marked land shortage has arisen and, partly as a response, much of the rapid urban expan-
15 sion of the past twenty years or so has seen the townscape transformed by a rash of tall apartment and office blocks to moderate the increasing demands for more building space. This veritable concrete jungle is, in fact, the epitome of the so-called 'primate' city—a city completely overshadowing the country's economy.
20 For the urban geographer, nowadays less convinced by the supposed importance of physical constraints, these conditions once again give some life to the long-discarded concept of environmental determinism. The city has a quite remarkable natural setting. Cradled in a valley nearly 1000 metres in height between the sheering coastal range of the Andes and the more
25 broken mountains to the south, its climate is superb and air pollution almost non-existent, in spite of the swarms of motor vehicles. But what this excellent location gives with one hand it takes away with the other. To the north, the built-up area comes to a complete and abrupt end against the steeply rising slopes of the coastal range. A motorway carved out of the mountainside marks
30 the building boundary as clearly as a line ruled on paper. To the south, the hills are less precipitous, and apartment blocks and individual houses have gained a sometimes precarious foothold as development has pressed ever outwards.

The rate of building comes as something of a surprise to anyone who has been inured to the idea that England has a problem of urban expansion un-
35 paralleled anywhere else in the world. On every side there is the constant turmoil of new high-rise blocks being erected and new shopping centres and roads being constructed. Yet, in all this fever of activity to extend the area, one predicament so relevant to so many Western cities just does not exist at all. This is the competition and conflict with agricultural land. Around Caracas,
40 the fertile farmland of the valley floor, originally cropped with sugar cane and coffee, was soon absorbed by the early extension of the city, and now the urban spread takes in largely unutilised hill lands. There is no real agriculture within a radius of many kilometres.

168

The immense growth of the city is certainly not just in sophisticated housing or other developments. Like all expanding cities in developing countries, Caracus also has its share of squatter settlements, or ranchos as they are called there. Over one-quarter of the population lives in these small dwellings built with the occupiers' own hands. They now take up as much as one-fifth of the built-up area and are often poised hazardously on steep, eroded slopes, particularly at both ends of the Caracas valley. The ranchos of Catia at the western extremity of the city are perhaps the most noticeable, for they are the first sight one has of Caracas from the breath-taking twenty kilometres of access motorway through the mountains which connects the airport and the coast with the city.

1. What is one feature that Caracas and Los Angeles have in common?
2. What are the reasons for the land shortage in Caracas?
3. In what ways are the northern and the southern limits of the city in sharp contrast?
4. The word 'this' in line 2 ('this seems') refers to ....
5. The expression 'residential sprawl at very low densities' (lines 9–10 can be expressed more simply as ....
6. The word 'rocketing' in line 11 gives the impression that ....
7. What conspicuous recent development has recently occurred 'partly in response to the land shortage' (lines 13–14)?
8. Why does the writer use the word 'rash' (line 16) to refer to the apartment and office blocks appearing in Caracas?
9. A simple explanation of the expression 'the long-discarded concept of environmental determinism' (line 22) is ....
10. 'Cradled' (line 23) is a misused participle as in this sentence it is wrongly related to ....
11. What are the two reasons for a land shortage in this area?
12. Give an illustration to each part of these contrasting statements: 'But what this excellent location gives with one hand it takes away with the other' (lines 26–27)
13. The apartment blocks and houses are described as having 'a precarious foothold' (line 32) because ....
14. What adverb in the fifth paragraph has a similar meaning to 'precarious' (line 32)?
15. There is no 'competition and conflict with agricultural land' (line 39) because ....
16. The expression 'sophisticated housing and other developments' refers to ....
17. What is a 'squatter settlement' (line 46)?
18. In a paragraph of not more than 100 words explain the effects of the geographical location of Caracas on the appearance of the city and the well-being of the inhabitants.

IV INTERVIEW

Section C

(The student should prepare to read the part of Lady Bracknell. The teacher will read the parts of Cecily and Jack.)

LADY BRACKNELL I beg your pardon?

CECILY Mr Moncrieff and I are engaged to be married, Lady Bracknell.

LADY BRACKNELL (*with a shiver, crossing to the sofa and sitting down*). I do not know whether there is anything peculiarly exciting in the air of this particular part of Hertfordshire, but the number of engagements that go on seems to me considerably above the proper average that statistics have laid down for our guidance. I think that some preliminary enquiry on my part would not be out of place. Mr Worthing, is Miss Cardew at all connected with any of the larger railway stations in London? I merely desire information. Until yesterday I had no idea that there were any families or persons whose origin was a Terminus. (*Jack looks perfectly furious, but restrains himself.*)

JACK (*in a clear cold voice*). Miss Cardew is the granddaughter of the late Mr Thomas Cardew of 149 Belgrave Square, S.W.1; Gervase Park, Dorking, Surrey; and the Sporran, Fifeshire, N.B.

LADY BRACKNELL That sounds not unsatisfactory. Three addresses always inspire confidence, even in tradesmen. But what proof have I of their authenticity?

JACK I have carefully preserved the Court Guides of the period. They are open to your inspection, Lady Bracknell.

LADY BRACKNELL (*grimly*). I have known strange errors in that publication.

JACK Miss Cardew's family solicitors are Messrs. Markby, Markby, and Markby.

LADY BRACKNELL Markby, Markby, and Markby? A firm of the very highest position in their profession. Indeed I am told that one of the Mr Markby's is occasionally to be seen at dinner parties. So far I am satisfied.

JACK (*very irritably*). How extremely kind of you, Lady Bracknell! I have also in my possession, you will be pleased to hear, copies of Miss Cardew's birth, baptism, whooping cough, registration, vaccination, confirmation, the measles; both the German and the English variety.

LADY BRACKNELL Ah! A life crowded with incident, I see; though perhaps somewhat too exciting for a young girl. I am not myself in favour of premature experiences. (*Rises, looks at her*

	watch.) Gwendolen! the time approaches for our departure. We have not a moment to lose. As a matter of form, Mr Worthing, I had better ask you if Miss Cardew has any little fortune?
JACK	Oh! about a hundred and thirty thousand pounds in the Funds. That is all. Goodbye, Lady Bracknell. So pleased to have seen you.
LADY BRACKNELL	(*sitting down again*). A moment, Mr Worthing. A hundred and thirty thousand pounds! And in the Funds! Miss Cardew seems to me a most attractive young lady, now that I look at her. Few girls of the present day have any really solid qualities, any of the qualities that last, and improve with time. We live, I regret to say, in an age of surfaces. (*To Cecily*) Come over here, dear. (*Cecily goes across.*) Pretty child! your dress is sadly simple, and your hair seems almost as Nature might have left it. But we can soon alter all that. A thoroughly experienced French maid produces a really marvellous result in a very brief space of time. I remember recommending one to young Lady Lancing, and after three months her own husband did not know her.

Oscar Wilde, *The Importance of Being Earnest*

V USE OF ENGLISH

Section A

1 In some of the following sentences HIMSELF, HERSELF or EACH OTHER are not essential in conveying the meaning. Copy all the sentences, omitting any of the above three expressions where these are not essential to the exact meaning.

1. They wrote to each other regularly.
2. He tired himself out.
3. She dressed herself in a hurry.
4. She made herself a dress.
5. He behaved himself fairly well.
6. They greeted each other when they met.
7. She prepared herself for the party.
8. He resigned himself to a long wait.
9. They helped each other at all times.
10. They are not speaking to each other now.
11. He looked at himself in the wing mirror of his car.
12. They fought each other with bare fists.
13. He cleared himself of the accusation.

2 In each of the phrases below the adjective can be expressed by a clause beginning with 'that' which has the same meaning. Rewrite each of the

phrases in such a way as to explain the meaning of the adjective by using 'that' clause. In a few cases a verb different from the adjective may be preferable.

Example: drinking water
Answer: water that can be drunk
Example: an interminable journey
Answer: a journey that never seems to end.
Notice that it is not sufficient to write: a journey that is interminable.

a) a misused word
b) a disused factory
c) incomprehensible instructions
d) an incredible story
e) a worrying situation
f) an unthinking action
g) an anti-war demonstration
h) a cloudless sky
i) a non-inflammable substance
j) irrevocable decisions

3 a) Some of the following sentences can be changed by the addition of the name of the person doing the action described. Change and write ONLY those sentences where this is possible. No other words should be added or omitted.

Example: The envelope burnt quickly.
Answer: Fred burnt the envelope quickly
Example: The envelope fell into the fire.
    This sentence cannot be changed in the same way.

1. The museum opens on Sundays.
2. The light shone in my eyes.
3. The train moved into a siding.
4. The bus stopped at "The Swan".
5. The newspaper described the riots.
6. The castle stood on the side of the mountain.
7. The kettle boiled quickly.
8. This cake tastes good.

b) These sentences should where possible be changed in the opposite way to those above. The person doing the action is no longer mentioned. No other words may be omitted, added or changed.

Example: Father dropped his wallet into the river.
Answer: His wallet dropped into the river.

Example: The ferry crossed the river.
This cannot be changed in the same way.

1. They raised the water level by several inches.
2. Mother washed this blouse perfectly.
3. She is cooking the dinner slowly.
4. They spread the news throughout the town.
5. Francis saved his money for a holiday.
6. They run the trains all night.
7. People will understand the problem.
8. They changed the timetable last month.
9. The men will lay a new carpet in the hotel lounge.

172

4 Finish each of the following sentences in such a way that it means exactly the same as the sentence above it.

The car driver asked the way from there to Rochester.
1. "How ....

2. He forced the chest open but was disappointed when he found it empty.
2. He forced the chest open only ....

He fell asleep during the discussion on overwork.
3. He fell asleep while ....

He would rather work with his hands than with his brain.
4. He prefers ....

She was extremely tired after the party but she still washed the glasses and tidied the room.
5. Tired ....

I should like to be beautiful.
6. If ....

The journey home will last about three hours.
7. It will ....

People say that Peter, who is quite deaf, can lip-read perfectly.
8. Peter, who ....

Only after they had examined every room did the police leave the house.
9. It was ....

5 Fill each of the numbered gaps with one suitable word or phrase.

1. If you had taken that job in Munich, you .... to learn some German.
2. Only after Simon's visitors had left, ... the opportunity of reading his letter.
3. "Did you lock the door when you came out?" "Well, I ...., but I'm not quite sure."
4. Turn off that television. It's time you .... your homework.
5. He took a lot of food with him in .... feel hungry.
6. The research chemists did not foresee the effects of the drug, and .... the doctors who prescribed it.
7. There's no harm .... one cup of coffee a day.
8. Everybody turned up for the meeting with .... the Mayor, who was too ill to come.

6 For each of the sentences below, write a new sentence as similar as possible to the original sentence, but using the word or words given in capital letters.

1. He started talking to the man sitting next to him.
   GOT INTO
2. Overcrowding in schools demands immediate attention.
   DONE

3. He first introduced himself and then explained the purpose of his visit.
   WENT
4. The Leader of the Opposition said that the Government was doing nothing to help the homeless.
   ACCUSED
5. His scheme finally gained the Committee's approval.
   AGREED
6. It is now your job to decide how the money should be spent.
   LEAVE
7. You cannot do less than visit him once a week.
   LEAST
8. He grumbled the whole time.
   NOTHING

VI USE OF ENGLISH

Section C

1 These are some of the inducements offered by a certain post. Suppose you are writing to a friend overseas who might be interested in the job and are trying to explain them more simply as part of the letter. Write the part of the letter in which you do this. Begin with the words: 'If you get the job . . .'

   a) An initial salary of £2000 per annum payable in arrears in twelve equal parts on the last day of each calendar month.
   b) An additional allowance of £200 for the possession of a University degree or its equivalent.
   c) An annual increment of £75 extending over a period of 20 years.
   d) Consideration for promotion at the end of five years' satisfactory service.
   e) A pension payable at the age of sixty or thereafter on retirement based on graded contributions supplemented by an equal amount paid by the firm.
   f) Provision of furnished family accommodation at a subsidised rental.
   g) Twenty-one days' annual vacation.

8
Reading, Vocabulary and Comprehension

An Imaginative Essay

Mirrors

On one wall of most of the rooms in a modern house hangs a picture whose subject and composition can be changed instantaneously whenever we wish. Yet it is a meticulously exact rendering of the domestic interior it portrays. Walk a few steps and the softly-gleaming bowl of fruit on the sideboard is re-placed by a garden landscape, framed by an open french window with roses   5 and lupins radiant in sunlight. But it is a strange picture, for we ourselves are moving about in it: we can eat that fruit and can walk in a copy of the garden.

The mirror world is essentially an irrational one. What lies behind us is assembled before our eyes; we gaze critically at a face we shall never be able to see. This awkward world of objects which we fall over and knock into,   10 which have to be lifted and dragged about for cleaning, becomes a serene, polished mirror-world of the ideal home, or at worst, a scene of casually elegant disorder. In this untroubled other world, live, one feels, creatures of a dream world, who can appear and disappear silently; our other ideal selves, untouched by emotion or human weakness.   15

But all this is foolish whimsical speculation. A mirror is merely a piece of clear glass coated with mercury. Dentists stick it into the mouth to examine tooth decay and men scrape the beard from their chin with its assistance. A car mirror warns of the following lorry and a dressing-table looking-glass reveals the texture and curve of a lipstick. The shop-lifter is detected, the sea   20 surface scanned from within a submarine, the line of a skirt hem adjusted: all with the aid of this utilitarian device. But even in its most practical applications, the mirror can suggest the fundamental or the infinite. The misting of its glass is evidence that life still exists; when mounted in a telescope such glass can gather the faintest light from outer space so that the scientist   25 can analyse factually what lies beyond his remotest imagination. The modern magician is well aware of the uncanny power of reflecting glass in causing people and objects to materialise and vanish merely by a shift of light. In the night-coated train window we survey our fellow-passengers unobserved and make disagreeable unexpected encounters with a repellent creature which   30 with a shock we suddenly recognise as ourselves.

Curve your mirror by a fraction and it acquires a sinister malice. The normally-proportioned human being becomes a grotesque, leering from the gently moulded surface, an obese rolling monstrosity or a hideous stalk nine feet high. Bodies enlarge and legs compress: a balloon-like head surmounts a   35 squashed body ending in massive pillar-shaped legs. A spoon of mirror-brightness reflects an inverted turnip face while chromium-plated taps specialise in perversions, all of them hideous.

And yet the water-mirror adds a strange beauty. Snow-peaked mountains
40 clothed with forests and framed by a cloud-flecked sky rest on the dark
waters of a lake. Even reflections of factories and warehouses have a tranquil
graciousness, the drabness of industry washed away. Swans move through a
coloured kaleidoscope of quivering square, triangle and ellipse. They pass
and the restless fragments reassemble into a landscape so apparently real that
45 we half-accept the myths of valleys and villages submerged as the result of a
curse and lying forever unchanged below the surface. This water world we
feel has its own silent inhabitants with their secret life, infinitely less troubled
than our own.

To the superstitious the mirror has evil powers, punishing anyone who
50 breaks it with years of ill luck. For the story-teller too the mirror has a
strange magic. It is the wicked queen in Snow White who seeks the reassurance of her cruelly truthful looking-glass. The Lady of Shalott may
view the world only in her mirror; when she turns to see without its aid, the
mirror cracks and her death is decreed. Alice steps into the looking-glass and
55 finds herself in a surrealist universe full of frustrated intentions, shattering
conflicts and a fantastic assortment of figures that later psycho-analysts might
well have detected deep in the human psyche.

It is surely the mystic who is most attracted by the mirror, that product
of the interaction of silicate and quicksilver, of liquid sand and dancing
60 metal. With its power of displaying a reality that has no tangible existence
and of showing us our other self, silent and apparently with its own separate
individuality, the mirror could symbolise the mystery of the universe. As we
scan this unattainable world, we feel that if only in some way we could
escape from material fact, could disengage ourselves from ourselves, we
65 could step through yielding glass to the other unknown side of reality. But
the conscious material mind is already speculating on angles of light con-
verging and other half-forgotten details of the physics we learned at school.
Science has intervened again, explained away magic, fantasy, illusion and
left us with angles of incidence, calculations of focal points and captured
mercury.

Notes on the passage

Line
5   french window—one of the few cases when an adjective of nationality
has a small letter. Glass doors, usually opening into a garden, are
referred to.
9-10 shall never be able to see—'can' may often express the future: especially
when it has the meaning 'may': 'You can qualify for promotion in three
years' time' (ability). 'He can come and see me after the summer holidays' (permission). Here however the true future is essential for the
meaning.
32   by a fraction—very slightly indeed.
54   her death is decreed—this refers to the Lady of Shalott, in Arthurian
legend, who had to view the world only through reflections in her
mirror. When she turned away to look at Sir Lancelot riding by, the
mirror cracked, announcing her death.

54 Alice—of 'Alice through the Looking-Glass', sequel to 'Alice in Wonder-
land.'
60 tangible should mean touchable. Here it suggests 'real'.

Prepositions

fall OVER / knock INTO   something IN the way
coated / covered WITH mercury   clothed WITH forests (dressed IN black)
(used only in literary style)
WITH its assistance   WITH the aid OF
warns OF the following lorry
unexpected encounters WITH
WITH a shock
recognise AS ourselves
ending IN
specialise IN
full OF / filled WITH frustrated intentions
IN some way
escape FROM material fact
speculating ON angles of light

Word distinctions

INSTANTANEOUSLY (l. 2) at the same instant—stronger than 'immediately'
or 'at once'
GLEAMING (l. 4) water in moonlight   GLOWING red-hot coals
SPARKLING dewdrops in sunlight   GLITTERING diamonds
TWINKLING stars
POLISHED (l. 12)—literally, 'having been rubbed with polish' and so shining
mirror-like: a person may have polished manners.
The basic meaning of these is SHINE.
I REPLACED the small cup WITH a large one.
I SUBSTITUTED a large cup FOR a small one.

LANDSCAPE (l. 5)   SCENE (l. 12)   scenery   outlook   view   sight
spectacle
the —— from the top of a church tower.
Constable and Turner were —— painters.
the wonderful —— of the Scottish Highlands.
to visit the —— of the accident.
The —— from my window is of a brick wall.
The meal awaiting us was a welcome ——.
The pageant was a gorgeous ——.

Notice also: a scene in a play
a scene shifter in a theatre
a beautiful scene
short-sighted   in sight
a gloomy outlook (for business; for the weather)
a view = an opinion

177

What is the difference between a viewpoint and a point of view?

STRANGE (l. 6) UNCANNY (l. 27) odd peculiar weird inexplicable eerie queer quaint

Notice: strange; odd, peculiar and queer are often used interchangeably. In each of the four cases below in which they could be used, one is more likely than the other three.

the —— cry of a lonely owl;
a —— three-headed monster;
an —— fire in the factory;
This fish has a —— taste. Is it good?
an —— ability to foresee the future;

a —— old-fashioned cottage;
a —— pointed hat on his head;
a —— tropical fruit with a fresh unusual taste;
an —— taste in pets.

Notice also: a strange house (unknown to someone); an odd number; odd man out; odds and ends; the odds are five to one; at odd moments; characteristics peculiar to a horse; to feel queer (ill).

IRRATIONAL—not in conformity with logic and reason
UNREASONABLE—not sensible or justified

GAZE (l. 9) for some time steadily   SCAN (l. 21) a large map
SURVEY (l. 29)—look at carefully and often over a wide area—survey the surrounding countryside
OBSERVE (l. 28)—carefully and usually for some time
STARE—boldly or in surprise   PEER—look with difficulty
DISCERN—see with difficulty   PEEP through a half-open door
CATCH SIGHT OF a distant eagle
CATCH A GLIMPSE OF (GLIMPSE) someone in a fast car
EYE with suspicion   GLARE angrily

DRAG (l. 11) a heavy table   DRAW a wheeled vehicle.

REVEAL (l. 20) show disclose uncover unveil publish expose
    to —— scandalous corruption;   to —— the true story in print;
    to —— facts hitherto known only to the authorities;
    to —— a far-reaching plot;   to —— a sacred mystery;
    to —— an unsuspected sense of humour;   to —— holiday photographs.
Notice that these words are often interchangeable.

HIDE conceal cover up camouflage hush up disguise cloak
    to —— a scandal in high places;   to —— a military objective;
    to —— behind a tree;   to —— a friend's mistake;
    to —— handwriting;   to —— one's identity;
    to —— one's evil intentions with apparent friendliness.
Notice: hide-and-seek.

UTILITARIAN (l. 22)—useful and practical—sometimes opposed to 'romantic'
REPELLENT (l. 30) and REPULSIVE both suggest a drawing back in dislike or disgust. 'Repulsive' is stronger. A cold repellent manner. A repulsive crime.

MALICE (l. 32). He is well-known for his malicious scandalmongering.
WITTY. She is clever, witty and always entertaining.
Do not mix a WAREHOUSE (l. 41) and a DEPARTMENT STORE.
The GRACIOUSNESS (l. 42) of a charming older actress
The GRACEFULNESS of a dancer.
QUIVERING (l. 43). An arrow QUIVERS as it enters its target.
People SHIVER with cold or fear and SHUDDER with disgust.
SUPERSTITIOUS (l. 49) of omens and believing in good and bad luck.
SUSPICIOUS of strange behaviour.
UNATTAINABLE (l. 63)—too high for one to reach (ideals, ambitions).
INACCESSIBLE—in any place that cannot be reached.

Words and expressions to learn and use

untouched by emotion, age, life   with its assistance   this utilitarian device
in its most practical applications   well aware of   by a fraction

Explaining the meaning of words and phrases

Explain the following words and phrases in such a way as to bring out their meaning clearly.

  a) whose subject and composition can be changed instantaneously (ll. 1–2);
  b) it acquires a sinister malice (l. 32);
  c) surmounts (l. 35);
  d) who seeks the reassurance of her mirror (ll. 51–2);
  e) science has intervened again (l. 68).

Short answers to questions

The following exercises based on the reading passage should be dealt with in complete sentences. Only a little information is needed in each case. As far as possible your answers should be expressed in your own words.

  1. 'A picture whose subject and composition can be changed instantaneously.' Explain the relevance of this statement to a mirror.
  2. How do the reality of a room and its mirror-picture differ?
  3. In what way do people and their mirror counterparts differ?
  4. 'The misting of its glass is evidence that life still exists.' Explain this statement.
  5. In what way does the curved mirror reveal its sinister malice?
  6. Explain what causes the 'coloured kaleidoscope' which later reassembles into a landscape.
  7. Why is Alice's looking-glass world described as surrealist?
  8. How far is it true to describe a mirror as a product of liquid sand and dancing metal?
  9. Why has the mirror reality 'no tangible existence'?

Longer answers

These answers should be expressed within the number of words stated. Use only information found in the passage but express your answers in your own words as far as possible.

1. In what ways is the mirror world irrational? (not more than 90 words)
2. What other surfaces that reflect but are not normally accepted as mirrors are mentioned and what is the special characteristic of each? (not more than 85 words)
3. In what ways can mirrors suggest the remote and the mystical? (not more than 110 words)
(This is an especially difficult question.)

Practice

SECTION I GRAMMAR

A. SHORT ANSWERS IN SPOKEN ENGLISH *Reference material page* 227

EXERCISES
Answer the following questions, using only the shortened verbal form.

a) Do you get much snow in your country in winter?
b) Could prehistoric cavemen read and write?
c) Are dogs more intelligent than cats?
d) Will man ever grow wings?
e) Did you enjoy your schooldays?
f) Should people save money?
g) Would you like to marry a film star?
h) Have guinea pigs got tails?
i) Do you have to get up early?
j) Had railways been built in your country a hundred years ago?
k) Must your fellow-countrymen train as soldiers?
   (Remember: You must not = You are forbidden to.
              You need not = It is not necessary to.)
l) Have I given you enough sentences here?

B. QUESTION TAGS *Reference material page* 227

EXERCISES
Add a suitable question tag to each of the following statements. Read each aloud when it is completed, indicating by the rise or fall of your voice whether the question tag implies confirmation or doubt. The question mark indicates cases where doubt is to be expressed.

a) That is your brother,
b) We can't go somewhere else,   ?
c) We may go home now,
d) I ought to work harder,
e) Those tropical plants should be in a greenhouse,   ?
f) They've not put up the bus fares again,   ?
g) You will remember to lock the door,
h) He was spring-cleaning all day yesterday,   ?
i) You never told me you got kept in,
j) I must hurry up,

k) He didn't back a winner,　?
l) He lives in a houseboat,　?
m) You don't serve coffee here,　?
n) The dinosaur existed in prehistoric times,
o) That jockey rides superbly,
p) The experiment didn't succeed,　?
q) You did knit that cardigan yourself,　?
r) Close that door,
s) So I'm expected to clear up after you,　?

C.　ADVERBS

Reference material
pages 227-8

EXERCISES

1. Use each of the following adverbs (a) to modify the verb in a phrase, clause or sentence and (b) to qualify an adjective or other adverb.
   unduly; practically; fundamentally; slightly; substantially; widely; thoroughly; seriously; strictly; absolutely.
2. Use each of the following adverbs to modify any adjective or another adverb: inordinately; comparatively; merely; wholly; largely; virtually; inherently; partly; incredibly; essentially.
3. Use each of these adverbial phrases in a sentence:
   on the whole; by and large; now and again; broadly speaking.
4. Use each of the following adverbs as a sentence opening:
   incidentally; certainly; surely; really; actually; eventually; finally; seriously; obviously; evidently; apparently; primarily; moreover; nevertheless.
5. Notice the use of 'else' in the following phrases: Who else? What else? everything else; someone else. And also: I must complete it by tomorrow or else it will not be accepted.
6. Copy the following table into your exercise book and complete it with words related to those given. Do not suggest participles. Then write sentences incorporating each word in the table.

	NOUN	VERB	ADJECTIVE	ADVERB
a)			substantial	
b)				simply
c)		provoke		
d)			solemn	
e)	table			no adverb
f)				sufficiently
g)			practical	
h)	enthusiasm			
i)			necessary	
j)		repel	(2 possibilities)	(2 possibilities)
k)				finally
l)		memorise		
m)			strong	
n)	school			
o)	system			

D.　PREPOSITIONS

EXERCISES

1. Each of the following words can be used either as an adverb or as a preposition. Write sentences illustrating the different uses.
   near; along; before; down; round; through.
2. Write sentences which show the differences in meaning between the words grouped together when they are used as prepositions.
   a) for, during, since, in.
   b) between, among.
   c) in, into.
   d) on, on to.

e) out of, outside.
f) beside, besides.
g) through, throughout.
h) to, towards, up to, until.

3. Supply a preposition in place of each of the dashes in the following sentences:
a) The mirror is hanging —— the wall.
b) People are standing —— the street.
c) The stick is leaning —— the wall.
d) We are reading 'Candida' —— Bernard Shaw.
e) The train arrived —— Victoria Station —— Southend.
f) He travelled to England —— Paris and Dieppe.
g) He was a man —— dark eyes who spoke —— a low voice —— a foreign accent.
h) The shortsighted student is sitting —— the front of the class.

4. Distinguish carefully between 'due to' 'owing to' 'thanks to'.
'Due is an adjective so there must be a noun or pronoun in the sentence which it is clearly qualifying. Otherwise the prepositions 'owing to' or 'thanks to' must be used. 'Thanks to' suggests that there is some cause for gratitude towards the noun or pronoun governed by the preposition, though sarcasm may also be suggested.
Use the correct expression in each of the following sentences:
a) His ill-health may well be —— malnutrition.
b) —— a prior engagement, the Chairman cannot come tonight.
c) —— rigorous training, the football team has secured promotion.
d) Outbreaks of violence, —— racial antagonisms, have caused several tragic deaths.
e) Many animals can blend with their surroundings, —— their protective colouring.
f) All air services have been suspended —— fog.
g) —— your idiotic blundering, the whole scheme will come to nothing.

5. Pronouns such as 'all', 'anything', 'nothing', 'everybody', 'anybody', 'nobody' may be followed by the preposition 'but' instead of 'except'.
'He'll say anything but the truth'.
'Nobody but the cleaners was in the buildings.'
Notice the colloquial 'all but' meaning 'nearly'.
'I've all but finished.'

6. Use each of these prepositional phrases in a sentence.
apart from; in addition to; on account of; with a view to; with reference to; in spite of (despite); in accordance with; by means of; in touch with; with the exception of; in the event of; by way of; in search of; free of; in return for; as a result of; provided that; for the purpose of; in favour of; in case of.

SECTION II PUNCTUATION

REVISION

EXERCISES
1. Explain clearly the differences in meaning caused by changes in punctuation in the sentences grouped together.

a) 'He said that someone had stolen his watch,' explained my cousin, 'and he looked very accusingly at me.'
'He said that someone had stolen his watch,' explained my cousin, and he looked very accusingly at me.

b) His car, which he uses only for travelling between his home and his office, is a two-seater convertible.
His car which he uses only for travelling between his home and his office is a two-seater convertible.

c) The largest piece of furniture was a walnut panelled cupboard.
The largest piece of furniture was a walnut-panelled cupboard.
d) We get most of our fish from River's.
We get most of our fish from rivers.
e) I saw 'Silas Marner' in the library.
I saw Silas Marner in the library.
f) He was speaking, naturally, to an admiring audience.
He was speaking naturally to an admiring audience.
g) He often drank to excess (this was a habit he had contracted during his early days in the theatre) when he was worried about his future career.
He often drank to excess: this was a habit he had contracted during his early days in the theatre when he was worried about his future career.
h) Did he say, 'Who was there?'?
Did he say who was there?
i) He is lecturing on Twelfth Night.
He is lecturing on 'Twelfth Night'.

2. Punctuate and paragraph the following passages:

a) mr matthews what would you say were the main causes of traffic accidents asked the b b c announcer the causes fall for the most part into two groups road and traffic conditions and careless driving was the experts reply would you give some examples of the latter please the announcer requested yes indeed careless overtaking faulty brakes failure to signal early enough lack of consideration these i should say are among the most common is there any class of pedestrian especially accident prone undoubtedly childrens and old peoples reactions can be unpredictable im not saying though that other people also cant be careless the highway code and in addition all motorists organisations stress the need for constant observation and concentration

b) sitting in the city of london club he scanned the advertisements listed under situations wanted in the evening standard he paused at one what do you think of this he demanded oxford graduate ex public school french and german honours highly intelligent and adaptable widely travelled considerable journalistic and office experience interested in politics economics psychology and law keen yachtsman and big game hunter seeks post in which he can make use of his abilities whatever post do you think that might be interesting commented his companion let me see with so much brilliance he will easily qualify as home secretary foreign secretary chancellor of the exchequer minister of education and of course prime minister in fact his intelligence and adaptability will fit him for all other cabinet posts too create a one man cabinet and let him run the country think of the time and money the country could save

c) Rewrite the advertisement referred to in the above example in three complete sentences, retaining all the information given and adding only such words as are necessary to the sentence construction. The word order may be changed.

d) 15 roman avenue oldchester yorks 2nd september 19—the manager scholastic books ltd college street reading dear sir would you please send me a copy of archaeology as a hobby by r digger ph d publisher mowbray trench ltd i should be pleased to receive details of any other of mr diggers books including the price of his peoples guide to roman mosaic i enclose a postal order for £1.50 in payment for the copy ordered yours faithfully a learner.

e) he crossed the river dee by ferry although it was well after nine oclock in june darkness fell slowly in this northern country the sun was still sinking through a crimson barred sky its lower rim had not yet touched the darkening horizon the small boat the golden glen was the name on its side chugged quietly through the rippled water the boatman he was a grizzled but sturdy fellow gazed thoughtfully ahead at first donald moved restlessly about the small deck then he sank down on a square locker the past months experiences which had at first exhilarated and then exhausted him seemed now almost incredible the day when through wind and sleet he had reached the mountain summit the wet night when he had slept under a hedge the english boy who had stolen his watch and the scotswoman who had given him a meal all these were already dream pictures which he had imagined at some time in his childhood in a few hours time he would be on the london bound express mechanical noises the rhythmic clatter of wheels the train whistle the slamming doors would surround him as the boat approached the shore where immense shapeless tree shadows now darkened the white road and nearby fields he knew that already the world of bustling routine of planned boredom was again closing round him

SECTION IV CHOICE OF EXPRESSION

REVISION EXERCISE

Read the following two passages. The second is a paraphrase of the first and contains very many faults of expression. Give examples of all the faults you can find, stating why you think the expression an unfortunate one.

a) It was not only during the Crimean War that Florence Nightingale showed extraordinary qualities of determination and organising ability, although it was at this time that the most exacting demands were made on her physical stamina and strength of character. At Scutari she found appalling conditions of dirt and disease among the wounded soldiers in the insanitary and dilapidated military hospital. Equipped with medical and cleansing supplies and aided by a highly-disciplined nursing staff she succeeded in reducing the death rate from forty-two to two per cent and, by establishing tolerable conditions, alleviated the sufferings of the men. She then exhausted herself by her travels and unremitting exertions in the Crimea where she set up further adequately-equipped hospitals.

Even as a young woman, however, she had had to struggle against very strong opposition from her wealthy family in achieving her ambition of becoming a nurse, and it was only by ruthless perseverance that she managed to undertake this career. After her return to England she devoted herself to improving army hospitals and barracks. Perhaps her most celebrated achievement, apart from her work in the Crimea, was the organisation of a nurses' training school, whose ideals were to transform the nursing profession everywhere. Even when her health deteriorated, Florence Nightingale continued to plan and advise. There can have been few people who achieved so much for humanity.

b) Florence Nightingale manifested unprecedented attributes of dogged determination and drive during the hideous holocaust of the Crimean War and at lots of other times too. It was then that she had to put her shoulder to the wheel and come to grips with an awful lot of really tough jobs, which, it goes without saying, took a lot out of her. At Scutari, the stricken warriors were languishing in a foul den which was really falling to bits and wasn't at all suitable for a hospital. A ministering angel, she descended upon them, armed with medicines and detergents and supported by a devoted band of dedicated heroines. Not only did she drag helpless thousands from out of the gaping jaws of death but she did a real good job in spreading comfort and healing in every direction. And was she content with this? Did she remain satisfied? No. For next she roamed through the length and breadth of the battle-torn Crimea, until she was quite worn out, and everywhere she went, decent hospitals sprang up in her path.

Even in her girlhood she had pitted her stubborn determination against the conventional conservatism of her well-off family and it was only by digging in her heels that she got what she wanted. After her return she didn't lay down her self-imposed mission but threw herself wholeheartedly into the job of cleaning up the substandard army barracks and hospitals. What was her finest achievement apart from her hour of glory in the Crimea? It was the setting up of a nurses' training school which blazed the trail for all later institutions of its kind. Her health began to go downhill but she never let up but bravely struggled on to conquer fresh fields against tremendous odds. An exalted place is hers among the noble and selfless benefactors of their suffering fellow-men.

SECTION V SPELLING AIDS

Reference material
pages 245-6

EXERCISES
1. Each of the following words is followed by a letter or letters in brackets, which should be added to the word. Letters may have to be changed or omitted to achieve satisfactory spelling. Some of the letter groups have no meaning but will become words only when the ending is added.

country(s)	country(fied)	repay(ed)	alley(s)
alley(s)	rely(able)	spy(d)	unpronounce(able)
cure(able)	charity(s)	deny(al)	die(d)
dye(d)	die(ing)	dye(ing)	chimney(s)
fortify(cation)	use(able)	sponge(able)	curtsey(ed)
destroy(er)	arrange(ment)	immediate(ly)	advertise(ment)
notice(able)	ski(ing)	supply(er)	polite(ness)
awe(ful)	measure(able)	delay(ed)	irreplace(able)
remove(able)	bath(ing)	bathe(ing)	

2. Two letters, an 'e' and an 'i', are omitted from each of the following words. In some words the 'e' precedes the 'i'; in others it comes after. Write each word as it should be spelt.

br—f	r—ndeer	sl—gh	sl—ght
dec—t	p—ce	bes—ge	ach—ve
b—r (a stand for a coffin)	v—n	fr—ght	
rec—t	y—ld	t—r (row)	h—ress
n—ghbour	p—rce	v—l	conc—ted

Composition

IMAGINATIVE EXPRESSION

Most writers feel more at ease with one type of essay than any other. The practically-minded look for the factual topic, while those with ideas on many subjects probably prefer to express an opinion. Those with visual imagination may create an impressionistic description, or, if they are also dreamers, will enjoy exploring the philosophies and fantasies suggested by a less precise topic. Anyone who does not belong to this last category of writers is well-advised to leave alone imaginative exploration.

The imaginative paragraph—the reverie

This is a form of writing which fulfils no definite function. It is often no more than a vehicle for the expression of the writer's thoughts and fantasies, the association of ideas, the undirected exploration of a topic which may appear quite commonplace and probably has no utilitarian importance. It is the treatment of the topic that matters. The simplest theme may be developed in any of a score of ways: humorous, inconsequential, original, nostalgic, astringent, fantastic, provocative, absurd. It may incorporate description, personal anecdote, opinion, fact or often superficial philosophising, and may blend several of these into a highly individual vignette. It is a paragraph of this type which may reflect most faithfully the personality and skill of its author.

The following paragraph deals with a mundane topic.

(Fried fish and chips, wrapped in a newspaper and ready to eat, are bought at a fried fish shop. Long a favourite meal of working-class people, they have also proved acceptable to hungry students who are just forgetting their evening meal two or three hours earlier and fortify themselves from the newspaper on their way back to a hostel or lodgings. The following paragraph records nostalgically the memories of a one-time student.)

FISH AND CHIPS

The heavy, oily but comfortable smell seeps round windy corners so that the hungry tired stroller is caught up in an aromatic current which draws him to its source. Pale anxious faces under cold strip lighting watch the gradual disappearance of the golden fish wedges, estimating whether there will be a wait for the next frying. A two-shilling batter-coated haddock, unrecognisable to any of its erstwhile free-swimming companions, a scoopful of oil-mellow chips, topped with salt and vinegar, are engulfed in 'News of the World' pages. The warm slow-greasing sheets are comforting to cold hands and one strolls contentedly through the drizzling dark, past the shuttered wet-fish shop, the steamed windows of the snack bar, the Methodist chapel, humble brick outcroppings against a cloud-swept sky. Snugly back in the early days of man, one tears with fingers the succulent freshly-cooked food, and eyes in the lamplight smeared photographs of bored public idols and tales of murder and war. The empty paper is screwed up and deposited but the cold and dark no longer depress. It is a genial satisfied giant who treads the street for home.

EXERCISES

Write a paragraph on one or more of the following topics:

a) The thrill of water-skiing.
b) Looking for a missing door key when one is in a hurry to go out.
c) Thoughts while waiting for a bus.
d) Saying goodbye to friends at the station.
e) Thoughts on one's way home after a day's fishing.
f) Visiting the village shop.
g) Doing homework.
h) Thoughts on dressing for a formal evening party.
i) The unexpected examination result.
j) Youth and the motor-cycle.
k) Café conversation.
l) Alone in a crowd.

The imaginative essay

The comprehension passage at the beginning of the chapter is an example of the imaginative essay. It wanders, apparently aimlessly but in fact under careful control, through descriptive, practical, speculative, romantic, mystical, scientific and vaguely philosophical aspects of the subject. At the end the reader has learned nothing new, gathered no new ideas or opinions although perhaps he discovered fresh ways of considering the subject.

As in the case of the more general essay, the greatest difficulty is deciding on a method of approach. Here is a possible scheme for the treatment of the subject of 'Darkness':

1. Introduction—Darkness always associated with danger and evil (preying animals, crime, fear of attack, etc.)
2. The quiet darkness of a summer night
3. The perpetual darkness of a Polar winter
4. The darkness of caves, tunnels, primeval forests, etc.
5. The legendary darkness of the underworld
6. The death of the sun
7. Conclusion—light is associated with growth: in this respect darkness is rightly associated with decay and death.

Write an essay of between 500 and 700 words on one or more of the following subjects:

1. The fascination of maps.	2. Sunlight.
3. Castles in the Air.	4. Islands.
5. Loneliness.	6. In Praise of Escapism.
7. Cats.	8. Ruins.
9. Bells.	10. Black magic.
11. Dreams.	12. Clouds.

Narratives

Narrative covers several different types of writing. It may take the form of a report which has to be delivered to someone in authority, of a newspaper article for public interest, or part of an exciting story. Each form will differ considerably in style from the others.

A report, for example, is concerned to give exact facts with relevant details, all assembled in chronological order. The reports from two people who have observed carefully the same incident should be fairly similar both in style and content.

The story written for enjoyment, however, requires far more creative skill. The style, choice of words, sentence length and atmosphere generally vary according to the nature of what is being related. Tense, fast-moving or mysterious situations usually demand simple words and short sentences with possibly some sudden questions or exclamations, abrupt incomplete statements, repetitions—devices which would be out of place in most other forms of writing.

Consider the following passage. Notice how the narrative—of an au pair girl whose twin charges mysteriously disappear from a train—centres on the girl herself —what she sees, feels, experiences. The short, agitated sentences record her thoughts. This presentation of events through the eyes and feelings of a participant adds vividness to any account.

In a longer passage, naturalistic conversation would also play an important part.

'With a lemon drink carton in each hand, she returned to the compartment where she had left them, the nearest to the driver's cab. It was empty. But they had promised not to move. She looked along the almost deserted platform. No sign of a pair of blue-coated children. They could not be hiding: there was no corridor and not enough room under the seats. She rushed to the barrier. No children had passed through. A porter accompanied her down the train, examining each compartment. A few men; a few women with children. No nine-year old boy and girl alone. Where had they gone? Where could they have gone? The driver had only just arrived, had seen nothing. Ahead, the bare grey platform sloped to meet the rain-washed tracks. On the far side of the train and the far side of the platform, nothing but empty lines racing out into the ordered tangle of metal beyond the station roof. At eleven in the morning, the station seemed asleep. But no children anywhere, anywhere.'

Another characteristic of a paragraph or essay of this type is the choice of descriptive detail which may emphasise the dominant impression (here: the empty lines, the deserted platform) or may contrast strongly with it (the homely lemon drinks she had bought: the everyday things of the station).

The newspaper account should combine certain characteristics of the two, the preponderance of each varying according to the degree of plain fact or of vividness required for the passage. A report on an international conference, a Parliamentary debate, a new law will probably be confined to facts. An eye-witness account of a volcanic eruption, a shipwreck, a riot, while less concerned with creating atmosphere than the fictional narrative, will, if well written, try to present a picture that the reader will find absorbing. Even in an account of the visit of a celebrity, the launching of a ship, the construction of a new dam, small vivid details of observation make the story come alive, though newspaper space is always restricted.

EXERCISES
A. Write a story of about 600 words on any of the following subjects.
1. You are trapped in a lift. Relate this experience.
2. Going to a concert.
3. A fire.
4. A bank raid.
5. An encounter with a very well-known person.

B. Write a newspaper report of about 500 words on one of these subjects.
1. The village of Westcote was isolated for three days by snow. A report is sent from the village when the road is open again.
2. An account of how a man rescued a child from a burning building.
3. A visit of a world-figure to your town or country which is nearly spoilt by some unforeseen occurrence.

Further subjects for essays

1. The importance of the invention of printing.
2. The way through the woods.
3. Choosing a career.
4. What is success in life?
5. Some traditions still observed in my country (or district).
6. Various kinds of courage.
7. Deserts.
8. Describe a river from source to estuary.
9. What would you regard as the greatest age in the history of your country?
10. A description of a thunderstorm.
11. The uses of a tape recorder.
12. Fortune telling.
13. The ever-changing sea.
14. Ways of telling the time.
15. State provision for the old.
16. School training for adult leisure.
17. Prefabricated buildings.
18. Describe an experience you had when lost in a fog.
19. The qualities of a personnel manager.
20. Do the means justify the end?
21. The value of the study of history.
22. Caravans.
23. On being a temporary invalid.
24. Fashion in painting.
25. A survey of one of the main economic problems experienced by my country.
26. My taste in music.
27. The emotional appeal of advertisements.
28. Inflation—its causes and remedies.
29. Children's make-believe.
30. Fashion shows.
31. The fascination a cinema has for a child.
32. A first night at the opera.
33. A portrait of a lorry-driver.
34. Buried treasure.
35. Your idea of a well-educated person.
36. Snow.
37. A young man and his motor-cycle.
38. Ice skating.
39. An evening with a record player.
40. Cousins.
41. A description of a modern building you are familiar with.
42. Give an account of the cause you think most worthy of support in the contemporary world.

43. Why would you regard it as important (or a waste of time) for ordinary people to read as much as they can about events and issues in the contemporary world?
44. The unimportance of the human race.
45. Woman's contribution to society.
46. Sleep.
47. Imaginary fears at night.
48. Wander lust.
49. The advantages of illiteracy.

Part II Reference Material

SECTION I GRAMMAR

Chapter 1

A. COLLECTIVE NOUNS

A group of living or inanimate things which are basically similar may be referred to by a collective noun.

a) EXAMPLES: a crowd of people, a litter of puppies, a range of mountains.

b) NUMBER Collective nouns may have singular and plural forms but, in the case of living things, the singular forms may themselves be regarded as singular and plural in meaning and the verb form will vary accordingly.

They are regarded as:

SINGULAR if the noun suggests a single coherent unit, that is, when every member of the group is acting uniformly.

PLURAL if the group members are showing independent individualities by disagreeing, dispersing or otherwise acting separately

(*or*) if some other idea in the sentence necessitates a plural interpretation.

Not only the verb, but also corresponding pronouns or possessive adjectives, may be affected by the number of the collective noun.

A herd of deer was making its way through the park.

The herd of cows were scattered over the field, some grazing, some lying peacefully in shaded corners, their jaws moving gently and rhythmically.

INANIMATE THINGS cannot act independently and therefore the singular collective noun is accompanied by a singular verb, pronoun and possessive adjective.

The bundle of old clothes, which was insecurely tied, has lost its covering and is now falling apart.

B. ABSTRACT NOUNS

An abstract noun expresses a QUALITY, and as such is UNCOUNTABLE.

EXAMPLES:
strength; cleanliness; patience.

Some nouns have an UNCOUNTABLE and also a COUNTABLE form.

EXAMPLES:
faith (trust)	a faith (some form of belief, possibly a religion)
speed	a speed of seventy miles an hour
interest	an interest in astronomy

Chapter 2

NOUNS

SINGULAR AND PLURAL FORMS

The nouns which probably cause most difficulty to foreign students are those which have only a singular or only a plural form or whose meaning is different in singular and plural. This is a complicated subject, but as confusion is the cause of very many mistakes, especially careful attention should be paid to it.

The following selection gives the most common of such nouns and may be used for reference. Meanings are added only when these may be unfamiliar to the student.

a) *Nouns which normally have only a singular form.* These nouns may be found very occasionally in a plural form but such forms are either rare exceptions, or have a specialised meaning, or there is a suggestion of 'kinds of', 'examples of'.

BE ESPECIALLY CAREFUL WITH: information; advice, furniture; luggage, news.
OTHERS INCLUDE accommodation; hospitality; traffic; commerce.
knowledge; ignorance; nonsense.
education; progress; behaviour.
money; change (small coins); wealth; richness; poverty; luck.
rubbish; litter (things thrown away).
childhood; boyhood; manhood.
photography; music; poetry.
biology; chemistry; arithmetic; logic; geography (and many other subjects of study).
mathematics; physics; economics; mechanics and similar nouns plural in form are yet treated as a singular idea with a singular form of the verb.
French; Dutch (and other languages).
health (notice: 'to drink healths'); safety.
violence; peace; disarmament.
generosity; patience; courage; determination; perseverance; gratitude; honesty; obedience; goodness; wisdom; stupidity; avarice (and other qualities associated with the human character).
laughter; anger; despair; strength; discipline; helplessness; protection; permission; assistance.
Christianity; Communism and all nouns used in a purely abstract sense.
Nature (the impersonal creative force); darkness; warmth; sunshine; rain ('the rains' usually refers to periodic rain in certain areas); scenery; seaside; hail; snow ('snows' is poetic).
measles; rheumatism; bronchitis; pneumonia and many other names of illnesses.
tennis; cricket; football; billiards; golf; bridge and other names of games.
electricity; oxygen (and other gases); steam; ventilation.
hunger; thirst; sleep; employment; leisure.
jewellery; millinery; footwear; hosiery; underwear; make-up; sophistication.
correspondence; stationery.
blackmail; loot; revenge; arson; manslaughter.
agriculture; aviation; architecture; vegetation.

Most gerunds have no plural form. This applies to those which indicate *the action itself* such as shopping; knitting; sewing; parking; dancing.

Those forms which express *the results of the action* may have singular and plural forms, e.g.
buildings; paintings; writings; readings ('he gave readings').
Earnings *is plural only.*

Although the word 'shopping' may also indicate the result of the action, it has no plural form.

Many commodities which are uncountable have no plural form. These include: gold; silver; ginger; hay; beef; mutton; pork; veal; poultry; china; granite; concrete; steel; rice; milk; bread; earth; Earth (though astronomers discuss the possibility of other Earths); fruit ('fruits' not common).
Certain fish such as salmon, trout and plaice; the word 'fish', together with the words 'sheep', and 'deer', have the same form for singular or plural but a plural verb is used when a plural number is referred to.

(It is rare to speak of 'fishes'. The food is uncountable.)

A few of the above words might be included in the list given under (b): e.g. discipline, but such uses are not common.

b) *nouns which may be treated as singular only but have also singular and plural forms—related meanings.* These nouns, when referring to an uncountable idea, can have only a singular form; with a related meaning which can be regarded as countable, they have singular and plural forms.

Truth is esteemed more highly in some communities than others.
We learn much from the truths taught by ancient philosophers.

(i) Often the countable forms indicate 'kinds of' 'degrees of'.

Different races thrive on different *foods*.
Compare the *literatures* of Europe and Asia.

These are further examples of words to which this differentiation may apply: ink; fat; oil (also 'to paint in oils'); butter (Danish and New Zealand butters); marmalade; speed; countryside.

(ii) In the following examples the distinction is between the commodity or quality and separate examples of it:

treatment	experience	cruelty	injustice
kindness	unkindness	weakness	illness
ability	quality	activity	formality
loyalty	falsehood	friendship	luxury
honour (notice: an honours degree)		wrong	pleasure
luxury	anxiety	sorrow	worry
crime	murder	success	failure
fear	religion	law	hope
duty	danger	government	democracy
dictatorship	marriage	ceremony	life
death	value	change	thought
absence	light	sound	noise
sight	size	pain	surprise
exercise	evil	sin	science
art	philosophy	cheese	wool

Notice: drink (to have drinks); beer (two beers, please); wine (French wines); coffee; chocolate; cake; height (to reach great heights); depth (the depths of the sea) (the depths of despair); length (dress lengths); fortune (they went to seek their fortunes); fire.

(iii) Special cases include:

space (in the universe)	a space (between things)
charity (generosity to the less fortunate)	a charity (an organisation for this purpose)
cloth (textile material)	a cloth (piece of material for certain purposes, e.g. a tablecloth, a dish-cloth)
speech	a speech
hair	a hair
Grammar (the subject)	a grammar (a book)
weight	a weight (object used for testing weight)
curiosity	a curiosity (unusual, interesting object)
waste	a waste, wastes (pl.)—wilderness
water	table waters, mineral waters, the waters of a river (poetic)
shelter	a shelter (place built for protection)
sand	the sands (pl.)—the beach
authority (right to control)	an authority—expert on a subject
power (ability to control)	a power a) a right to authority b) an important nation (various other meanings)
force (power of compulsion)	forces a) armed forces b) natural forces, e.g. the wind
right (the good and true)	a right—an action or thing one is justified in doing or having

industry (hard work or organised production)	an industry—a branch of organised production
pastry (the substance)	a pastry—a small rich cake
language (means of expression)	a language
business a) commercial matters b) regular job c) matter of one's concern	a business—a trading concern
entertainment (provision of enjoyment)	an entertainment—a performance or party providing enjoyment
dress (clothing; the art of dressing)	a dress
liberty (freedom)	to take a liberty—to behave in such a familiar way to someone as to give offence
gossip (chatter)	a gossip—a person who chatters about other people's affairs
gas (often refers to coal gas)	a gas (any gas)
sculpture (the art)	a sculpture (a carved work)

c) *Nouns with a considerable change of meaning between uncountable (singular only) and countable (singular and plural) forms* In certain examples it is possible to see some connection in meaning between uncountable and countable forms; in others the meaning in each case is quite different.

wood	a wood, woods (small forest)
iron	an iron, irons a) for smoothing clothes b) fetters (pl.)
copper	a copper a) a penny b) a large container for boiling clothes
smoke	a smoke (colloquial—act of smoking)
rubber	a rubber (an eraser)
tin	a tin (airtight metal container)
brass	a brass a) memorial tablet b) ornamental brass object
paper	a paper a) a document b) a newspaper c) an examination paper d) a learned essay
glass	a glass (a drinking vessel) glasses (spectacles)
marble	a marble (small glass ball) marbles (children's game in which the balls are used)
salt	a chemical salt health salts smelling salts
cold	a cold in the head
tea	a tea a) a cup of tea b) a meal
youth	a youth (a young man)
trade	a trade a) a form of skilled work 'to learn a trade' b) a form of productive business—'the bakery trade'
work a) labour b) employment	a) a work, works (literary, artistic, or musical production) b) the works (pl.) (a factory) c) gasworks, waterworks, road works d) a firework, fireworks
ice	an ice (an ice-cream)
relief a) freedom from anxiety or duty b) the heights of land especially as shown on map c) raising of a design	a relief (someone doing another person's job while the latter rests)
age	an age, ages (a long period)

middle age	the Middle Ages
hostility	hostilities (fighting during a war)
trust	a trust a) property administered for its future owner b) alliance of big business concerns
production	a production (a work produced in the theatre or cinema)
living (being alive)	a living a) to earn a living b) the care of a church and parish
damage	damages (pl.) (money compensation for loss or injury)
order a) fixed arrangement b) law-abiding, communal behaviour	an order a) a command b) a distinction c) a request for goods
wit (quick clever thinking or humour)	a wit (a person having this aptitude) wits (senses—out of one's wits)
sense	a sense (faculty of perception)
air	an air a) a melody b) a way of behaving
character	a character a) a person in a story b) an unusual individual c) a well-known person d) a type of letter used in writing
depression	a depression a) a climatic low pressure area b) a slight hollow c) a prolonged fall in national prosperity
reason	a reason
reaction (force contending against change)	a reaction (a response to certain stimuli)
practice	a practice a) an established form of behaviour b) the patients or clients of a professional person
flight (act of fleeing or flying)	a flight a) a journey by air b) a group of stairs
justice	a justice (a magistrate)
royalty a) quality of kingship b) royal persons in general	a royalty (payment of money for publication or performance rights)

d) In certain cases, words different in form are related in meaning, the one suggesting the abstract and/or uncountable idea, the other the concrete example. The following are among the more common:

poetry	a poem
drama	a play (a drama)
work employment	a job, an occupation
the police (pl.)	a policeman
machinery	a machine
clothes, clothing	a garment
bread	a loaf
clergy	a clergyman

e) Several nouns have plural forms only. Here are some of the more common examples:

earnings, takings (money taken in a shop); savings; surroundings; belongings.
clothes; trousers; slacks; pyjamas; braces; nylons (stockings).
scissors; pincers; pliers; shears; tongs. (Each of these five words may be preceded by 'a pair of' and followed then by a singular form of the verb.)
headquarters; premises; barracks.
alms; means (money available to a person); goods; riches; remains; thanks.
police; customs (tax on imported goods; department which collects this tax).
folk; cattle; clergy.

the wilds;   golf links.

negotiations;   minutes (notes on a meeting).

odds (chances in gambling).

contents (the things contained in something—normally plural).

ADJECTIVES OF QUALITY are sometimes used as nouns in a collective sense. They are usually plural in number.

Not enough provision is being made for the old, the sick, the poor and the needy.

The beautiful are not always the good.

THE FORM AND USE OF THE PASSIVE

CONVERSION BETWEEN THE ACTIVE AND PASSIVE VOICES

Decide the exact tense of the active form. Form the same tense of verb 'to be'. This, followed by the past participle of the verb being dealt with, gives the corresponding passive form.

EXAMPLES:

A special committee is studying the matter.

The present continuous form 'is studying' is replaced by the present continuous 'is being' together with the past participle 'studied'.

The matter is being studied by a committee of experts.

Before the end of the year they will have chosen a new President. (future perfect tense)

Before the end of next year a new President will have been chosen.

USE OF THE PASSIVE VOICE

Note:

Only verbs that can be used transitively (those that can take a direct object) can have a passive form.

1. The passive is commonly used in English when the agent is vague.

    The paper was printed yesterday.

    He has been injured in a collision and has been taken to hospital.

    The surrounding countryside is flooded.

    Cocoa, which is used in the manufacture of chocolate, is imported from Africa.

It is therefore often used instead of the third person singular pronoun 'one'. 'One says' is more often expressed 'It is said'.

    Money must be sent by registered post—not: One must send money by registered post.

In rather more formal speech, 'one' is used with an intransitive verb.

    One has to pay more attention to one's diet as one gets older.

2. Sometimes the passive is used when the agent is especially emphasised.

    This play has been attributed to William Shakespeare.

    The reply to the question was given by the Home Secretary.

Chapter 3

DEFINITE AND INDEFINITE ARTICLES

A. DISTINGUISHING BETWEEN THE ARTICLES

1. The use of the definite article implies that the following noun:

    a) has already been referred to and/or is already known.

    b) is the only one of its kind or a special example (hence its use with a superlative adjective).

2. The use of the indefinite article implies that the following noun:

    was previously unknown and is being introduced for the first time (on any succeeding appearance the noun, already known, will be preceded by the definite article).

COMPARE:
He is working in the factory. (The writer and reader know which factory is meant.)
He is working in a factory (unspecified).
The square near the Cathedral (only one square exists in this place).
A square near the Cathedral (more than one square exists—the exact one is unspecified).

3. Notice the difference the use of the indefinite or definite article followed by the word 'other' (adjective or pronoun) makes in the meaning of what is expressed.

His two dogs are completely dissimilar. One is a St. Bernard; the other is a Pekinese.
The intruders scattered when they saw the police car. One rushed upstairs; another climbed through the window; another disappeared into the cellar, while the other rushed for the back door.
Most drivers are careful. The others ought not to be on the road at all.
Some holidaymakers prefer the sea, others the country, and others like to visit foreign capitals.
(There are still some others unmentioned.)

B. THE INDEFINITE ARTICLE
1. Certain nouns are almost never preceded by the indefinite article unless

a) they are being used adjectivally to qualify another noun:
  e.g. information   an information office.
b) in a few cases, the indefinite article can suggest 'a kind of' (see 2, below),

The following nouns are rarely if ever preceded by 'a' (an) except in certain metaphorical expressions, e.g. 'a rain of blows'.

information; advice; news.
weather; rain; hail; snow; sunshine.
nature (the creative force); scenery; seaside.
health (well-being); safety; leisure; disarmament.
permission; assistance.
blame; blackmail; arson; larceny.
agriculture; aviation; transport; luggage; photography.
oxygen (and other names of gases); steam.
money; change (for money).
nonsense; rubbish.
Most names of subjects of study, e.g. biology; physics.
Most illnesses, e.g. rheumatism; appendicitis; pleurisy.
Gerunds naming the action rather than the result (but including 'shopping') e.g. riding; studying.
Games such as hockey and whist.
Traffic—though this may be preceded by the indefinite article in special uses such as 'a traffic in stolen goods'.

2. In certain cases the indefinite article may occasionally precede some of the foregoing nouns with the sense of 'a kind of':

e.g. It was a safety that depended on the temporary good-will of their enemies.

This use of the indefinite article is slightly more common with other uncountable nouns not included in the above list:

an unbelievable stupidity
a Parisian elegance
an insatiable hunger
a poverty that cries out for relief
a hospitality that exceeded any that I had experienced
a violence that appalled.

In each of these cases the indirect article suggests 'a kind of'.

Normally uncountable nouns are not preceded by the indefinite article.

3. It is sometimes necessary to isolate one example of one of the nouns given in the list under (1). For this purpose some phrase such as 'a piece of', 'a form of', 'an example of', 'a period of', 'a fall of (snow)' may be used.

   a piece of information
   a type of scenery
   an item of news
   a period of sunshine
   a case of blackmail.

4. The adjectives 'some'/'any' may be used before many uncountable nouns when a certain quantity is referred to.
   Compare:

   A cat prefers rabbit even to fish.
   (rabbit and fish are types of food)
   Blackie is hungry. I'll give him some rabbit.
   (a certain quantity of rabbit)

5. Proper nouns may be preceded by the indirect article

   a) when there is emphasis on the fact that a person is unknown to the speaker:
   A John Smith called to see you, sir.
   b) when a person is so well-known as to symbolise a certain quality:
   From your description it seems she combines the brains of an Einstein with the glamour of a Cleopatra.

6. The indefinite article may precede a noun when one single example is typical of the whole class to which it belongs:

   e.g. A dog eats meat.
   An island is surrounded by water.

7. The indefinite article qualifies a countable noun after such verbs as 'to be', 'to become', 'to seem':

   e.g. He is a doctor.

   If the following noun is a special title, no indefinite article is used:

   e.g. He became Foreign Secretary.

8. The indefinite article is used when stating the cost of things according to size or quantity:

   e.g. five shillings a yard   ⎧by the yard
        ten and six a bottle   but: to buy⎨ by the bottle
        tenpence a pound   ⎩by the pound

9. A noun qualified by a superlative adjective is always preceded by the definite article.
   But in conversation (occasionally in writing) 'most' is sometimes used with certain adjectives ('interesting', 'extraordinary', 'unusual', 'important', 'annoying' are the most common) to mean 'very'. In this case 'most' is preceded by the indefinite article:

   e.g. a most unusual event.

10. Distinguish between 'one' and 'a'. One could hardly say:
    'Has the Reverend Gentle *one* wife?'
    'A' is sometimes used as a weak form of 'one':

    e.g. a hundred;   a shilling each;   twice a day;   three at a time.

197

11. Here are some other expressions incorporating the indefinite article:
to have a cold, a chill, a sore throat, a cough, a headache, a pain, a temperature.
to be in a good temper, in a bad mood, in a hurry, in a difficulty, (but: in trouble).
to have a good time.
What a pity! What a nuisance! What a shame! (but: What fun!)
to take a seat; to make an appointment.
to tell a lie; an untruth (but: to tell the truth).
a lot of; a great deal of; a good deal of (but: plenty of).

C. THE DEFINITE ARTICLE

1.a) The definite article is used with commodities which are defined. The fact that a definite example is being referred to may only be understood:

e.g. Has the milk come yet?
(i.e. the milk we expect every morning).
The bread is on the table
(i.e. the bread we shall eat).
The coal was delivered yesterday.
The weather has changed (i.e. the weather we experience).

but: Cats like milk (undefined milk—in general).
Europeans often eat bread.

b) In certain cases the use of the definite article with an uncountable noun may suggest 'all', its omission 'some'.

Take the flowers from the vase.
Take flowers from the garden.
He gave the information to the enemy.
He gave information to the enemy.

This can also apply to countable nouns:

She put the carrots in the stew. (All that were available.)
She put carrots in the stew.

2. Abstract nouns, usually unqualified by an article if undefined, may be preceded by an article when defined. (Remember that in many cases an abstract noun and its corresponding common noun may have the same form.)

kindness	a kindness
hope	a hope

Compare these examples:

Efficiency is essential in the business world.
He showed an efficiency which they hardly expected (a kind of efficiency).
The efficiency of the staff was due to careful training (defined).
Complete obedience is expected.
The obedience of a sheep dog.
The obedience which accepts commands without hesitation.

3. While, as stated in B6, a single example, preceded by the indefinite article, may represent a whole group ('A dog eats meat'), a countable noun preceded by the definite article may become so generalised as to become the name for the whole group. 'A dog', above retains individuality, even though the suggestion is that all dogs behave in the same way; 'the dog', when so generalised, is merely the name of the species 'dog'. Generally this use has a certain scientific detachment.

Compare:

A / The telephone is essential to many people.

An / The Australian sheep farmer may own extensive areas of land.

Certain nouns preceded by the definite article in this sense may become so generalised as to acquire an additional meaning:

e.g. The Church (organised religion); the Law (the whole legal system); the Theatre (the drama); the Cinema (films); the Radio (broadcasting). 'medicine' (no article) may refer to the whole system and profession of medical practice.

4. Proper nouns may be preceded by the definite article:

a) when the person or thing referred to is regarded as very well-known:

'That was written by Dr. Johnson.'
'Was he the Dr. Johnson?'

In this case the definite article is heavily stressed when one is speaking.

b) when the person or thing is defined:

The magnetic Enrico Manfredo who is worshipped by his admirers is a very different person from the Henry Mumford his mother knows.
The Shakespeare who is revealed in the sonnets.
The Paris of the nineties.
The England of Shakespeare.

5. The definite article usually precedes names of mountain ranges (but not the names of single mountains—'The Matterhorn' is a rare exception, deserts, forests (not lakes), seas, oceans (not continents), bays, gulfs, hotels, cinemas, theatres, ships, trains, newspapers, magazines.

It precedes the names of countries only when these are in some way descriptive:

e.g. the United States, the Netherlands, the Soviet Union, the Republic of Ireland.

It precedes names of islands only when these are grouped together or the word 'island' or 'isle' precedes the name:

e.g. the Hebrides, the Canaries, the West Indies, the Isle of Wight.

A very few towns such as 'the Hague' are qualified.

6. The definite article forms part of

a) dates, as in the following example:
the twenty-fifth of December (often written as 25th December).
It is not used with most names of festivals or holidays:
Whitsun, Bank Holiday Monday, etc.

b) titles of kings, popes, etc.
Charles the First (usually written Charles I).

c) phrases used in apposition to nouns when the phrases are merely descriptive:
Mr. Ivor Storey, the editor of the 'Daily Scandal', is writing his memoirs.
If the phrase in apposition is a formal title, no article is needed.
This is Montmorency Bolingbroke, Earl of Aldgate.

d) The definite article precedes names of places if these are in some way descriptive. When they are names only, no article is needed.

the Essex marshes; the Tower of London; the Houses of Parliament; the British Museum; the National Gallery; the Royal Exchange; the Dover road (running in the direction of Dover).
Dover Road (merely a name given); Trafalgar Square; Westminster Abbey; Hyde Park; Buckingham Palace.

7. The definite article precedes each of two comparative forms which are balanced against each other:

The harder he works, the less he earns.
The sooner you leave, the earlier you will return.
The more the merrier.

199

8. The definite article precedes 'former' and 'latter' when these follow each other in the same sentence.

> Karl and Roberto share a room. The former speaks only German, the latter only Italian, and yet they never seem to ˋstop talking to each other.

9. Compare the following phrases:

a) next week   the next week   What is the difference in meaning?
last year   the last year
b) in autumn   in the autumn (usually a special autumn).
c) When a preposition governs the words 'church', 'school', 'college', 'prison', 'bed' and (in the case of 'to') 'market', the use of the definite article suggests that a definite place is being referred to. The omission of the article puts the emphasis on the *activity* carried on there:

e.g. He is in school. (He is learning.)
He is in the school. (He is visiting a certain school.)

In other cases, as for example 'the library', 'the office', 'the station', the article is always used after a preposition, (but: the Government in office—in power).

d) 'home', without an article, is the place where one lives; 'the home' refers either to the above in a very general sense:

> Children learn most in the home.

or to some kind of institution:

> The Old People's Home.

10. Meals are normally unqualified unless they are defined in some way.

> They serve breakfast at nine.

but: The breakfast we had this morning.
The Annual Dinner and Dance.

11. Musical instruments are usually qualified by the article:
to play the piano, the violin, the trumpet.

12. As the definite article refers to a known thing, or is used when there is only one possibility, it appears in such phrases as:

> at the top of;   at the foot of;   at the beginning;
in the middle;   at the side of;

Contrast: He sat in the front of the hall.
He sat in front of the Vicar (preposition).

> His house is at the top of the street.
The cat was sitting on top of the car (preposition).

13. Notice the use of the possessive adjective and not the definite article in many expressions relating to parts of the body:

> He has broken his leg.
She is combing her hair.

The possessive adjective must always precede the adjective 'own'.

> They came in their own car.

14. Phrases incorporating the definite article:

a) the Air Force; the Navy; the Army; the B.B.C.; the Common Market; the Commonwealth, but: Parliament
b) Certain very well-known books.
the Bible; the Koran; the Iliad.
c) the sky: the Earth; the world; the sea; the seaside; the countryside; the open air; the tropics; the Arctic Circle; the North Pole.
(Notice: in/on the sea—on land; land and sea.)

d) on the contrary; on the other hand; on the right; during the day; for the time being; in the end; on the whole; what is the matter? what is the time? on the radio (on television); on the air (broadcasting) (but: by air).

Notice: He talked for three hours on end (continuously).

$$\left.\begin{array}{l}\text{all}\\\text{both}\end{array}\right\}\text{ the children}\qquad\left.\begin{array}{l}\text{twice}\\\text{half}\\\text{double}\end{array}\right\}\text{ the price}$$

all the children (of a certain group); all children (everywhere).
e) North; South; East; West
   but: in (from: to) the North, etc.
f) Contrast: in a week (either; within a week; or: at the end of a week)
               in the week (not at week-ends).

D PHRASES WITHOUT AN ARTICLE
all day (all the day); by day; from day to day; day in, day out;
at dawn; in daylight; at dusk; at nightfall; at night (during the night); at work;
in need of; in honour of; in memory of; in acknowledgement of;
in answer to; in place of; in need of; in case of; in process of;
by means of; by way of; by chance; by force;
by law; by post; by car; by air; by air mail;
by bus; by rail: by train; by boat;
in gear; in second gear; in reverse;
in town (often London); in danger; in safety; in stock; in arrears;
in progress; in fact; in effect; in power; in force;
in court (in a law court); in debt; in trouble; in difficulties; in conference;
in flight; in bloom (and many more);
on foot; on horseback; on holiday; on business; on board; on land;
on the land (farming);
for example; for good (always);
to live in peace; to be at peace with;
with reference to; on condition that;
from bad to worse; from time to time; from hand to mouth;
make trouble, fun of, sense, peace, war, money (prosper);
go on strike; do overtime; give good service; (do someone a service);
have toothache, earache; (a headache);
do good; harm, right, wrong, justice to;
back to front; inside out; upside down;
head over heels; (turn a somersault); face to face;
back to back; side by side; back to front; shoulder to shoulder; arm in arm;
out at elbow; down at heel; see eye to eye; by heart; take to heart;
in 1610 (in the year 1610); at first; at last;
commit murder, suicide, etc. (but: commit a crime);
what kind of? what sort of?
Poor fellow! Good gracious!

Chapter 4

PRONOUNS AND ADJECTIVES

Much of the information that applies to pronouns refers also to the corresponding adjectives. This section is therefore arranged as follows:

A   Details applying only to pronouns.
B   Details applying to pronouns and adjectives.
C   Details applying only to adjectives.

A. PRONOUNS

1. *Personal pronouns*

1. If the first person pronoun 'I' is linked with a noun or a pronoun of another person, the noun or the other pronoun precedes the 'I'.

You and I;   Judith and I.

Remember to use the accusative case for the pronoun which is object of a verb or governed by a preposition.

The car narrowly missed my friend and me.

2. In older texts, the obsolete second person singular form; thou, thee, thine (adjective—thy) may be found.

3. In written English the complement of the verb 'to be' should be in the nominative case: 'It is I'.
This is essential when an adjectival clause qualifies the personal pronoun.

It was I who survived.

However, even in written English, expressions such as 'It was we' 'It is they', when not followed by an adjectival clause, sounds stilted and so other expressions are often used.

He wanted to know who had knocked. We told him we had.
Who cut down the cherry tree? I did.
Who's there? We are.

'It's me', 'It's them' are sometimes used in conversation.
This practice is extended to comparisons when the nominative case is grammatically correct.

He has better marks than I ('have' is understood).
I can speak more fluently than he (can).
As good as they (are).

The accusative case is sometimes used in conversation. In writing, the following verb that is often mereiy understood can be stated to avoid a stilted effect.

Her mother makes better pastry than she does.
Compare: He likes the French girl better than her.
He likes the French girl better than she does.

4. The impersonal 'one', if introduced, should not later be replaced by 'he', 'you' or 'they'. 'One's' is the corresponding adjective.

One should be careful how one chooses one's enemies.

'One' is not nearly so commonly used in English as its equivalent is in many other languages. The passive often fulfils its purpose.

One should read the instructions carefully.
The instructions should be read carefully.

5. One of the commonest mistakes in writing is the vague use of third person pronouns. The function of a pronoun is to replace a noun. If there is no corresponding noun or if there is more than one noun that might be referred to, ambiguity results.

The captain realised that the ship was off course. It caused him great anxiety.
The Council introduced a scheme to improve the library service. It has not been effective.

2. *Possessive pronouns*

1. Reference has already been made to the use of the possessive pronoun in phrases such as:

Those are colleagues of mine.
(Those are some of my colleagues.)

202

2. (i) Remember that even though these pronouns are possessive, no apostrophe should be used in 'hers', 'ours', 'yours', 'theirs'.

(ii) 'it's'—it is.   'its'—belonging to it.

3. *Reflexive and emphasising pronouns*

These are identical in form.

a) *Reflexive pronouns* are not used so extensively in English as in some other languages.

'I'm washing myself', is quite correct. It is, however, just as common to hear 'I'm washing', 'I'm having a wash', 'I'm getting washed'.

'I dressed myself' is not so common as 'I dressed', 'I got dressed'. (But: 'Three-year-old Dorothy can already dress herself'.)

Notice: 'I cleaned my teeth', 'he is hiding', 'he is getting ready'.

In the following phrases, the reflexive pronoun normally appears:

enjoy oneself;   pull oneself together;   help oneself;   excel oneself;   please oneself;   blame oneself;   teach oneself;   adapt oneself;   make oneself do something;   force oneself to do something;   hurt oneself (get hurt);   defend oneself.

Notice that 'he is mistaken' is far more common than 'he is deceiving himself'.

look at oneself;   pay for oneself;   talk to oneself;   talk about oneself;   say to oneself;   put oneself out.

All these have a definite reflexive meaning.

SOME USEFUL EXPRESSIONS (NOUNS) INCORPORATING 'SELF':

SELF—

assurance;   confidence;   control;   deception;   defence;   denial;   esteem;   indulgence;   justification;   pity;   preservation;   reliance;   respect;   satisfaction.

b) *Emphasising pronouns* may stand alone or be governed by a preposition.

He said it himself.

He did it by himself. (without help)

He lives by himself. (alone)

Between ourselves, it is likely that——.

Do it yourself.

4. *Relative pronouns*

who whom whose (that)
which (that)
what
——as

a)   *whom* is used as object of the following verb or when governed by a preposition:

One of the English novelists whom critics esteem highly is the Pole, Joseph Conrad.

Miss Florence Nightingale, whom the author refers to as a harsh domineering autocrat, was nevertheless responsible for some of the greatest reforms in history.

WHO is often heard in conversation in place of 'whom'.

b)   *Whose*

(i) That's the man whose photograph was in yesterday's paper.

(ii) WHOSE can also refer to things.

This is a play whose message will be understood by everyone

'of which', which may appear in very formal style, would appear stilted here.

(iii) WHOSE and the noun following may not be separated.

The people whose homes the hurricane destroyed are being cared for by volunteer workers.

c) *what* (RELATIVE PRONOUN) is a compound form equivalent to 'the things which', 'that which', 'those which'.

It never follows a noun directly.

What you need is a long rest.

(the thing which).

I don't think they'll approve of what he has done.

d) *Defining and non-defining clauses*

Study these examples:

(i) The train which is standing at Platform 4 will be leaving at 16.05.
(ii) The Birmingham train, which is standing at Platform 4, will be leaving at 16.05.

In (i) the clause 'which is standing at Platform 4' defines or makes clear which train is being spoken about.

In (ii) the train is known already. It is the Birmingham train and there is only one such train in the station. The clause merely adds some extra information and could easily form a separate sentence.

The Birmingham train will be leaving at 16.05. It is standing at Platform 4.

In conversation, non-defining clauses are not common. Two sentences or two main clauses joined by a conjunction are more natural.

My employer, who has a degree in Economics, also speaks five languages fluently.

In conversation this seems more natural as:

My employer has a degree in Economics and he speaks five languages fluently too.

The difference between the two kinds of clause is perhaps less easy to determine here.

(i) The advertisement which proved most effective was simple and direct.
(ii) The advertisement, which proved most effective, was simple and direct.

In (i) the clause defines which advertisement is being referred to.

In (ii) which advertisement is being referred to is known already. The clause is a piece of additional information. 'Most' means 'very'.

DIFFERENCES IN CONSTRUCTION AND PUNCTUATION

(i) The non-defining clause is separated from the rest of the sentence by commas: the defining is not.

(ii) 'Who', 'whom' or 'which' are the relative pronouns normally used in non-defining clauses.

'That' is an *alternative* pronoun to the above in defining clauses.

(iii) When the relative pronoun is object of the following verb or is governed by a preposition, it may be omitted altogether in a defining clause provided it does not immediately follow the preposition. It may not be omitted in a non-defining clause.

The policeman asked to see my driving licence, which unfortunately I had forgotten to renew (non-defining clause).

The doctor suggested that the illness $\left.{which \atop that}\right\{$ the patient was suffering from had probably been contracted in the tropics.

('which' or 'that' may be omitted altogether).

or   the illness from which the patient was suffering.

(Relative 'that' cannot immediately follow a preposition.)

204

e) *The relative pronoun 'that'* is normally used after certain expressions.
   a) a noun or pronoun qualified by a superlative.
   b) a noun or pronoun qualified by 'only'.
   c) all, everything, everybody.
   d) none, nobody, no one, nothing, nowhere.
   e) much, little, a great deal.
   'That' when object of the following verb, is often omitted.
   All that is necessary is to ask him.
   The laziest student (that) I have met.
   It is the only one (that) I could find.

f) *Agreement of a relative pronoun and its antecedent*
The relative pronoun agrees in number with its immediate antecedent.

   Edinburgh is one of those *cities which owe their* reputation to *their* romantic history.

g) *A special example of the case of a relative pronoun*
Do not confuse the case of the relative pronoun in this kind of sentence.
   Jeannette is a student *who* I think will do well in the future.

'Who' is subject 'will do', not object of 'think'. 'I think' is described as a parenthetical clause, that is a clause which, having no influence on the grammar of the rest of the sentence, can be thought of as enclosed in brackets or parentheses.

h) *Relative adverbs*
Such forms as 'where' ('in which', 'at which', etc.) 'when' ('in which'), 'why' ('for which') are known as relative adverbs.

   I know the street where (in which) he lives.
   Have you forgotten the evening when (on which) you came here?

Why can one not say?

   That's the tree where the family of robins are nesting in.
   He wants to find out the reason why you come for.

   i) A relative clause should follow its antecedent as nearly as possible. Separation from the antecedent may lead to considerable ambiguity.

   I saw a bird sitting on the branch of a tree which was highly-coloured.
   He pointed out the new secretary employed by Mr. Ferguson, who was wearing an exceptionally pretty dress.

   j) Study this example:

   He was connecting wires to a complicated type of electric plug, which requires a good deal of patience.

Here the relative pronoun 'which' refers back neither to 'wires' or 'plug': it is, in fact, unrelated. A suitable noun has to be supplied.
   ... type of electric plug, a task which requires ...

B. PRONOUNS AND ADJECTIVES

I. *Interrogatives*

   a) (i) *Pronouns:* who? whom? whose?
                      which? what?
                      whoever? whichever? whatever?

   Which goes faster?
   He doesn't know what to pack.

      (ii) *Adjectives*: what? which? whose? whichever? whatever?
   Which car goes faster?
   He doesn't know what clothes to pack.

b) As in the case of the relative pronoun, 'whom' should serve as object of a following verb or as the form governed by a preposition.

Whom will you invite?
(By) Whom was the book written (by)?

'Who' is more commonly used in these cases in spoken English but is incorrect in the written language.

c) *Whose?*
PRONOUN: Whose are these? They are Michael's.
ADJECTIVE: Whose car did you come in?
ADJECTIVE: Whose autograph album did you sign?

d) *Distinction between 'what' and 'which'* (PRONOUN AND ADJECTIVE)
'What' suggests unlimited choice.
'Which' suggests limitation of choice
Which edition have you bought?
What book have you bought?

e) *Whoever? Whichever? Whatever?*
These may be emphatic forms of the interrogative.
Whoever do you mean?
Whatever have you bought?

2. *Distributive pronouns and adjectives*

a) (i) *Pronouns:* each; everybody; everyone; everything.
either; neither.
each other; one another.
(ii) *Adjectives:* each; every; either; neither.

b) 'Everybody', 'everyone', 'everything', are more commonly used than 'all' in such examples as these:

Everybody is on holiday.
(less often: all are on holiday)
He took everything.
(uncommon: He took all).

c) *Each of these pronouns is singular in number* and must therefore be followed by singular forms of the verb, pronoun and possessive adjectives.
With certain forms [notably every(body), either, neither] plural forms often appear in conversation when there is a strong suggestion of plural meaning.

Everybody did their best but the team didn't break the record.
Neither of the parcels have arrived yet.

The *singular forms only* are correct in written English.

d) *Each other; one another*
Strictly speaking the first of these expressions refers to two persons or things, the second to three or more. 'One another' is, however, commonly used in connection with two only.
Here are some examples of their use:

They looked at each other.
They are not speaking to {each other (two) / one another (more than two)}
They live near one another.
They help each other.
They send letters to each other.

Compare the use of these expressions with that of the reflexive pronouns.

They have hurt themselves.
They have hurt each other.

3. *Quantitative pronouns and adjectives*

a) These include the following:

(i) *Pronouns:* some; somebody; someone; something;
               any; anybody; anyone; anything;
               none; nobody; no one; nothing;
               much; more; most;
               little; less; least;
               few; fewer; fewest (rare)
               all;
               one/ones;
               numerals.

(ii) *Adjectives:* some; any; no;
               much; many; more; most;
               little; less; least;
               few; fewer; fewest (rare)
               all
               a (indefinite article);
               numerals.

b) 'Some' (pronoun and adjective) and its compounds are normal in an affirmative statement.

'Any' (and its compounds), 'no', 'none' (and 'no' compounds) are normal in negative statements and affirmative and negative questions. (This applies also to the adverbs: 'somewhere', 'anywhere', 'nowhere'). Verbs such as 'deny', 'forbid', 'refuse', 'fail,' 'prevent', 'hinder', 'discourage' etc. are regarded as negative in implication. The same applies to such adverbs as 'seldom', 'rarely', 'hardly', 'scarcely', 'barely' and a condition expressing doubt or negation.

He denied any share in the conspiracy.
You have eaten scarcely anything.
You could have had some eggs if there had been any left.

In certain circumstances, however, this distinction between 'some' and 'any' does not apply.

A) 'Some' and its compounds may be used in interrogative sentences when the answer to be expected is in the affirmative.

Has someone the time?
Didn't you tell me something about him when we last met?

B) 'Any' and its compounds may be used in an affirmative statement with the suggestion of 'it doesn't matter whom, what, which, or where'.

Anyone could lift that.
Anything will do.
He'd be happy living anywhere.

OTHER USES OF 'SOME'

c) Often 'some' has the meaning 'a certain amount or number of—but not all'. The word 'some' is then emphasised in speech.

I have done some homework.
Why didn't you finish it?
I didn't know some of the new words.

Distinguish carefully between: some . . . others . . .
                              some . . . the others . . .

Some magazines are concerned mainly with politics, others with cultural topics and others with home and fashion (there are still others).
Some single people thoroughly enjoy cooking meals for themselves; the others are experts with the tin-opener (all single people have been referred to).

'The rest' could have been used instead of 'the others'.

> *Adjectival* '*some*' can have the meaning 'I don't know which'.
> 'Some friend of yours telephoned. He gave no name.'

   d) *Much* often sounds unnatural in affirmative statements and normally appears only in negative or interrogative sentences.
'A great deal of', 'a good deal of', 'a lot of', 'plenty of' are more common. 'Very much', however, is sometimes found in affirmative statements.

Young people have $\begin{cases} \text{a great deal} \\ \text{a good deal} \\ \text{a lot} \\ \text{plenty} \end{cases}$ of freedom nowadays.

I have very much to do tonight.

The adverbial 'much' with a comparative adjective is common enough in affirmative statements.

> Most people are much better-tempered after lunch.

   e) *Most, both*
> Most (of the) children.
> Both (of the) twins.

It is quite wrong to say
> The most children.
> The both twins.

   f) *Little, a little*
> *Few, a few*

'little' and 'few' have a negative sense, suggesting 'too little', 'too few', 'a little' and 'a few' have a more positive sense suggesting 'some'.

> Many cities still have ugly slums.
> Little has been done to improve them yet.
> A little has been done to improve them in the past few years.
> Few people live in desert regions as little will grow there.
> A few people live in semi-desert regions as a little will grow there.

Notice: only *a* little   only *a* few

   g) *Less, fewer*
'*Less*' indicates *quantity*
'*Fewer*' indicates *number*

> Summarise the passage in fewer than 100 words.
> He got fewer than six hundred votes.

   h) *One/ones*
This pronoun is very commonly used in English.

> I didn't take any photographs but Colin took some excellent ones.
> I don't know the name of this tree but the one over there is a birch.
> He agreed he had wanted a serious book, but not one about morbid depression.

One/ones normally follows an adjective standing alone, except in the case of a superlative form where it is possible, or a numeral where it is not.

> There are the most interesting (ones).
> He has three cousins and she has two.

   Words such as 'other' may be pronouns and need not then be followed by one/ones.

> You can have the currant cake and I'll have the other (one).

4. Demonstrative pronouns and adjectives

These include

this	that	such	the (adjective)
these	those	the former	
		the latter	

a) PRONOUN: I'll take *this*
   ADJECTIVE: I'll take this copy
   I'll take this one

b) Avoid using the plural form 'these' or 'those' with a singular noun:
   'I like these kind of cars' is wrong.
   'I like cars like these', is better.

c) PRONOUN: *Such* is life!
   (The use of 'such' as a pronoun is not common.)
   ADJECTIVE: I'm sorry it was such a trouble.
   Did he really write such nonsense?
   He has such an old car.
   That is such exciting news.
   He tells such lies.
   He makes such long speeches.

d) PRONOUN: Both shop and house are for sale. *The former* is empty but *the latter* is still occupied.
   ADJECTIVE: He speaks Spanish and Chinese. The former language is easier for him.

5. Exclamatory pronouns and adjectives

What!   How!

Notice the word order in these sentences.

What a day!
What a beautiful day it is!
What weather we are having!
How kind of you!

6. Indefinite pronouns and adjectives

Whoever	it does not matter who(m) (PRONOUN)
Whatever	it does not matter what
Whichever	it does not matter which

Whoever comes, I'm not at home.
You won't succeed, whatever you do.
You'll not be there before nightfall, whichever route you take.

Notice similar adverbial forms:

whenever	it does not matter when, at any time.
wherever	it does not matter where, in any place.
however	it does not matter how.

Come whenever you can.
Sit wherever you like.
You will not find it, however carefully you look.

NOTE: The addition of 'ever' to the pronoun, adjective or adverb may serve merely for emphasis. (See page 206.)

C. ADJECTIVES

1. Nouns used as adjectives

Many common and a few proper and abstract nouns may be used as adjectives to qualify other nouns.

a dream world; a sea story; the Surrey hills; conscience money; a North Sea port; an efficiency expert; a crime reporter.

In some cases the suggestion is that the noun qualified serves the purpose of the noun being used adjectively.

> a photograph album; a coat hanger; a travel office; an advice column (in a magazine); holiday arrangements.

Gerunds are commonly used in this way, and this suggestion of a purpose being served distinguishes them from participles, which are merely adjectival.

Compare:

GERUND	PARTICIPLE
a dancing teacher	a dancing puppet
a running track	a running commentary
a singing lesson	singing birds

Here are some other gerunds used in this way:

> a hearing aid; smelling salts; skiing equipment; a smoking compartment; a washing machine.

2. Participles

(i) Both present and past participles can be used adjectivally.
(ii) The present participle is *active* in meaning, the past participle *passive*.

COMPARE

a freezing wind	frozen food
a conquering army	a conquered army
a boring journey	a bored traveller

The use of both participles is illustrated here:

> Vast areas of land, efficiently *irrigated* and *fertilised*, could be converted into arable fields *producing* cereals.

(iii) a) Some participles seem to have almost entirely lost their verbal connections and to be regarded primarily as adjectives.

> tired; interesting; aged: are examples.

These are modified by the adverb 'very'.

b) Others still retain strong verbal associations.

> e.g. praised   recurring   travelled   rising

These cannot be modified by 'very'. Some other suitable adverb must be used:

> a highly-praised book;
> a frequently-recurring incident;
> a widely-travelled businessman;
> the swiftly-rising tide.

(iv) Beware of the unrelated participle (or any unrelated adjective)

This is a very common error in written English. An adjective must have a noun or pronoun to qualify, and a participle/adjective introducing a phrase, usually qualifies the subject of the main verb in the sentence. If this is impossible, the meaning of the sentence becomes absurd.

> Tired and desperately worried, home seemed my best refuge.
> Even when stranded in an isolated village by snow, my journey still seemed exciting.
> Being a strongly-built ship, the captain felt sure she could weather the hurricane.
> Sad at the thought of returning from holiday, the radiant sunshine made me even more reluctant to leave.

Rewrite these sentences in such a way as to clarify their meaning.

3. Comparisons

a) Be careful not to confuse the prepositions when making comparisons.

It is often *as* cold in Paris *as* in London.
It is not always *so* (as) cold in London *as* in Edinburgh.
It is usually colder here *than* in Paris.

b) 'In' often follows a superlative—always when *place* is referred to, sometimes with *groups*:

That is the finest painting $\begin{array}{l}\text{in the Gallery.}\\\text{in his collection.}\end{array}$

'Of' frequently follows the superlative when groups are referred to:

He is the eldest of the family.
He is the oldest student of his year.

c) 'More' and 'most' are used when comparing adverbs, all adjectives of more than two syllables, and participles. Some two-syllabled adjectives also form comparative and superlative forms with 'more' and 'most'; others like those ending in -ow (mellow), -y (pretty), -le (feeble) add -er -est respectively.

Notice these typical comparisons of adverbs.
The wind is blowing more strongly than I thought.
It is the basses who sing most loudly in our choir.
By travelling faster than sound, an aeroplane breaks the sound barrier.

d) *Comparisons applied to gerunds and infinitives*

GERUNDS:

Lying in the sun is pleasanter than working in a classroom.
Some students like talking better than listening.
or Some students prefer talking to listening.

INFINITIVE:

It is more enjoyable to walk along quiet country lanes than to drive along crowded roads.

e) Some adjectives cannot be compared. These include:
unique (describing the only one in existence), infinite, perfect, faultless, equal, silent (but: quieter), ubiquitous, omnipotent, omniscient, flawless, intact, irreparable.

In conversation one may hear:

This is the most perfect reproduction I have seen.

This should be: 'the most nearly perfect reproduction'.

f) *Late   Later   Latest*
       Latter   Last

What is the difference between:

The latest play at the Goldsmith Theatre.
The last play at the Goldsmith Theatre?
Trains leave for Cambridge at midnight and at 10.35 p.m.
I caught the later. I caught the latter?

g) *The intensive use of the comparative* (ADJECTIVES AND ADVERBS)

More and more people are buying cars.
You are driving more and more quickly (increasingly).
This work is getting better and better (colloquial).
The weather became colder and colder.

h) Be careful when using 'most' and 'both' as pronouns or adjectives in English.

Most students (in general).
Most of the students (majority of a certain group).

NEVER The most students. The most of the students.
NOR The both students. The both of the students. (See page 208.)
>Half the class.
>A quarter of the class.
>Some students went shopping but most (of them) went home.
>She has two maids. Both object to cleaning the stove.

(i) Adjectives preceding the noun are epithets.
Adjectives separated by the verb from the noun or pronoun they qualify are used predicatively.
Some adjectives can be used only predicatively. These include:

>alive; asleep; awake; ajar; alone.

Corresponding epithets to the first two are:

>living; sleeping.

There is no exact epithet for the other three. 'Solitary' has a slightly different meaning from 'alone'.

>The mother, who was awake . . .
>The door which was ajar, . . .
>The child, who was alone in the house, . . .

Chapter 5 VERB TENSES

FINITE FORMS—INDICATIVE MOOD

Table of tenses—Active and passive

The first form in each space is the active form of the chosen verb 'to take'. The second form is the active form of the verb 'to be'. The third form is the passive form of the chosen verb 'to take'.

	PAST	PRESENT	FUTURE	FUTURE IN THE PAST
Simple	I took	I take	I shall take	I should/would take
	I was	I am	I shall be	I should/would be
	I was taken	I am taken	I shall be taken	I should/would be taken
Continuous	I was taking	I am taking	I shall be taking	I should/would be taking
	I was being	I am being	—	—
	I was being taken	I am being taken	—	—
Perfect	I had taken	I have taken	I shall have taken	I shoud/would have taken
	I had been	I have been	I shall have been	I should/would have been
	I had been taken	I have been taken	I shall have been taken	I should/would have been taken
Perfect Continuous	I had been taking	I have been taking	I shall have been taking	I should/would have been taking
	—	—	—	—

THE USES OF THE TENSES

The present simple is used for:

1. A habitual action or state.
2. A future action—often a habitual one associated with travel.
3. The historic present whereby a story is told as if it were happening immediately before one's eyes.
   This use is far less common in English than in some languages.
   Answers to questions in literature may incorporate
   >a) Tenses associated with the present
   or b) those associated with the past.
   It is a bad mistake to waver between the two tenses.

Do not start a story in a past form and later change to the present to suggest vividness.

4. To cover a present continuous meaning in connection with such verbs as do not normally have a present continuous form.

5. In adverbial time clauses and conditions for the real future simple (see page 217).

EXAMPLES OF THE ABOVE USES

1. Habitual action: He drives to his office each day.
2. Future associated with travel: The boat leaves at midday tomorrow.
3. Historic present: When Richard II returns to England, he hears of Bolingbroke's success.
4. Continuous form of certain verbs: I want an ice-cream now.
5. In adverbial time clauses and conditions: He will come home $\begin{matrix} \text{if} \\ \text{when} \end{matrix}$ he gets hungry.

THE PRESENT CONTINUOUS is used for:

1. An action occurring at this minute.
2. An action which though possibly not actually happening at this moment goes on continually from past to future. Though prolonged the action is usually temporary.
3. The arranged future.
4. With 'always' 'perpetually' or 'constantly' to suggest a frequently occurring action. Some emotion: annoyance, surprise, etc., is often implied.

EXAMPLES OF THE ABOVE USES

1. Action happening now: It is raining.
2. Continual action: He is writing a novel.
3. Arranged future: He is addressing the conference on Tuesday.
4. With 'always': He is always asking extraordinary questions.

In connection with 4, compare:

I always make silly mistakes in dictation.

I am always making silly mistakes in dictation.

The second example suggests surprise or annoyance.

NOTICE: a) He works in an insurance office (this is his job)
He is working in an insurance office (possibly a temporary arrangement)

b) When both forms are possible, the present simple is used.
Glaciers move extremely slowly.

Verbs which normally have no continuous form in any tense

Those marked* may have a continuous form when the subject is actively doing something. See the first two examples.

Those italicised sometimes have a continuous form in conversation.

see, *hear, *smell, *taste, recognise, notice,
know, *understand, wonder,* suppose,
believe, *realise, mean, remember, forget,* forgive,
want: *wish, *need, refuse, like, love,* dislike,
seem, *appear, matter,
belong, owe, own, possess, contain,
smell: The food smells good. The cat is smelling the fish.
taste: The milk tastes sour. He is tasting the wine.
wish: I wish I were beautiful. He is wishing. (More often: 'He is making a wish'.)
appear: He appears pleasant. She is appearing in the film 'Dolores of Doncaster'.

Notice the use of 'see' to express an arranged future. I am seeing that film next week.

IN CONVERSATION one sometimes says:

> Are you understanding what I am talking about?
> I am forgetting the tragedy gradually.
> I am only wanting peace and quiet.

The present perfect simple

Both simple and continuous present perfect tenses refer to a past that is in some way connected with the present. This connection with the present is a very important feature of this tense.

They are therefore used:

1. When the present effect of an action is more important than the action itself.
2. For an action or state that occurred in the past but may be repeated in the future.
3. For an action or state which has occurred in a period of time which includes the present.
4. For an action or state which has occurred in the recent past. The adverb 'just' often appears in the sentence.
5. For an action in an adverbial time clause or condition which logically should be expressed by the future perfect tense (see page 217).

The Present Perfect forms are not used when any definite past time expression is stated or suggested. Such expressions may include 'yesterday', 'this morning' (if the time is afternoon or later), 'a second ago'. Indefinite expressions such as 'recently' and 'lately' may be accompanied by the present perfect, often in a continuous form:

> He has been travelling recently.
> Lately, he has been working hard.

EXAMPLES OF THE ABOVE USES

1. Past action with a present effect — He has been taken to hospital.
2. Past action with possible future repetition. — He has made many memorable speeches (He is still alive and can make more).
3. Action in a period of time including the present. — The weather has been mild this autumn.
4. Action in the recent past. — The servant has just sounded the gong.
5. In place of the future perfect. — When you have written your name, write the date.

The present perfect continuous

THE PRESENT PERFECT CONTINUOUS tense can be used under any of the conditions given for the present perfect simple provided that the emphasis is not on the doing of a single or repeated action but on the fact that the action continued for a certain length of time.

Often the action has been completed very recently or is still continuing.

EXAMPLES

1. I have been typing all the afternoon. Please read through what I have completed.
2. He has been making memorable speeches for the past ten years, but his party has not yet won an election.
3. It has been raining all day.
4. The servant has been sounding the gong for nearly a minute.
5. When he has been writing for a few hours he will have some more coffee.

The action may have been repeated many times:

> 'We have been attending the Municipal Concerts all this year.'

214

The past simple

The past simple always refers to an action which happened in the past and is now finished. The actual time in the past is often stated, suggested or understood.

The action may be a single one:	He sneezed violently.
A repeated one.	He always left home early.
A continuous one.	He worked for twelve hours.

Compare these examples with those illustrating the Present Perfect Simple Forms

1. I explained that several times last week but you still do not understand.
2. The servant sounded the gong five minutes before lunch was to begin.
3. After the director had dictated the letter I typed it and sent it off.
4. The late Prime Minister made many memorable speeches.
5. The weather was mild a month ago.

The past continuous tense

This tense resembles the past simple tense in that it refers to events that have already finished.

It resembles the present continuous tense in the following ways, referring to:

1. An action extending over a named moment in the past.
2. An action which, at some past time, had been arranged to happen later. Sometimes there is a suggestion that the action planned did not actually happen as expected.
3. With 'always', 'perpetually', 'constantly' to suggest a frequently occurring action in the past. The suggestion of a related emotion is not so common in the past continuous but may be there.

Other uses are as follows:

4. To contrast two actions in the past, one of which happened at some stage in the duration of the other, the latter therefore extending over a longer period than the first. This is probably the most common use.
5. To show two or more actions happening simultaneously and continuously.
6. To emphasise that an action lasted over a period.

EXAMPLES OF THE ABOVE USES

1. Action covering a certain past moment: What were you doing at the time of the the murder?
2. A past action arranged to happen later. Mrs Smith was almost distracted. She was being tried for shoplifting the next day.
He was taking the exam in June but his accident made that impossible. (this did not happen)
3. With 'always' He was always catching colds as a child.
They were always turning up without having been invited.
4. Two past actions contrasting in duration. While we were travelling along the M1, a police car forced us to stop.
5. Two simultaneous continuous past actions. While my husband was garaging the car, I was taking the parcels indoors.
6. Emphasising a continuous action. You were describing your dream all through breakfast. Don't start again at lunch.

The past perfect simple tense

This tense is often found:

a) In one of two or more clauses in a sentence.
b) In a single clause with another clause suggested.
c) In connection with a time phrase.
d) In reported speech.

215

There is usually emphasis on the fact that the action or state expressed by the verb in the past perfect tense preceded some other past idea stated or implied in the sentence.

Here are some examples:

> He did not remember my name until after he had greeted me.
> The door-to-door salesman refused to leave until the poor woman had bought something.
> 'Why did you cut the lecture?'
> 'We had heard it all before.'
> The astronaut had survived rigorous endurance tests.
> Until then he had never handled a rifle.
> It was reported that there had been an earthquake.

Unless there is some reason to emphasise the fact that one action precedes and may even determine the other, the past simple can often be used for both actions. 'Then' or 'afterwards' may give additional stress in such cases.

> He greeted me and only afterwards remembered my name.
> The cricketer hit the ball and then started to run.
> Immediately he had hit the ball, the cricketer started to run.

The past perfect continuous tense

This tense is related to the past perfect simple in much the same ways as the corresponding present perfect tenses are related—the continuous forms in each case suggesting duration of time but in other ways having the same significance as the simple ones.

> As the train approached, the signal, which had been showing a green light, suddenly changed to indicate danger.

B. OTHER FORMS

FUTURE TENSES
SHALL / WILL AUXILIARIES

Spoken Forms

'Will' is the auxiliary commonly used in all persons in statements. It is often shortened to 'll (I'll, he'll) in the affirmative and to 'won't' in the negative.

Interrogative forms
Shall I? Shall we?
Will you? he? she? it? they?
'Won't' is common to all persons in the negative.

Written forms
The forms which convey a future meaning are:

I, we shall (be)   You, he, she, it, they will (be)

WILL is used as a first person auxiliary to express:

a) a promise: I will remember to bring you a present.
b) willingness: All right. We will do it.
c) determination: I will not be bullied.

SHALL is used as a second and third person auxiliary when someone is determined that the subject will carry out an action.

You shall not leave until you have completed that job.

In a written examination, these forms should be used correctly. There is a similar use of auxiliaries in all four future tenses.

THE FUTURE SIMPLE is used for

a) An action which will take place at a later date.

216

Such difference as exists between this tense and the arranged future as expressed by the present continuous tense is shown in these examples.

Is Mr Lane there? No? Then I shall telephone again tomorrow.
I am telephoning the firm tomorrow anyhow, so I can give your message then.

The future simple can express an action the subject has only just thought of doing.

b) 'Will' can be used with all persons to express willingness. In this case it can be thought of as an independent verb 'to be willing' followed by an infinitive.

This form therefore serves for a request:

Will you bring me a newspaper, please.
(Literally: Are you willing to . . .?)

Here is a similar case:

I shall be grateful if you will return it soon.

This can be expressed in conditional form:
'I should be grateful if you would return it soon'.

THE FUTURE CONTINUOUS is used for:

a) An action which will be taking place at a certain time in the future.
Don't go this afternoon. He will be working in the garden and he may find you a job to do.
This time next week we shall be enjoying sunshine and Italian wine.
b) An arranged action in the future.

This use is almost identical with that of the Present Continuous (arranged future). With the future continuous tense, the emphasis is on future time: sometimes the more distant future is suggested.

'They will be starting on the new dam in ten years' time.'
'I shall be waiting for you in the lounge.'

THE FUTURE PERFECT SIMPLE AND CONTINUOUS

These tenses convey an action which will have been finished by a certain time in the future.

The students will have covered the whole course before they take the examination.
Before long, the play will have been running for ten years.

THE PRESENT TENSES IN ADVERBIAL TIME CLAUSES

Many adverbial time clauses (beginning with such words as 'when', 'while' 'as soon as', 'immediately', 'before', 'after', 'until') would logically be followed by a future form. In English, however, a present tense replaces the future in such clauses.
As soon as the rain stops, the floods will subside.

A logical future perfect is replaced by a present perfect form:

I can tell you no more until the committee has discussed the matter.

NOTICE
The following forms are apparent exceptions:

This is the first time it has happened.
This was the first time it had happened.
This is the last time I shall tell you.
This was the last time I would tell him.

In fact, the sentences could be written in another way which would explain the tense used:

This $\begin{matrix} \text{has} \\ \text{had} \end{matrix}$ never happened before.

It $\begin{matrix} \text{will} \\ \text{would} \end{matrix}$ never happen again.

Chapter 6

A. CONDITIONS

Conditions are of three types, the meaning being related to the tenses used in each case.

1. *Condition and result are possible*

Condition	Result
If you *eat* now	you *will* not *feel* hungry later on.
If you *are eating*	I *shall telephone* again later.
If you *have eaten* anything bad	you *will* soon *be feeling* ill.
If you *have been eating* for an hour	you *will have finished* up everything.
If you *eat* the ham	*leave* the cheese for me.
If you *eat* slowly	you *digest* your food better.
ANY PRESENT TENSE	ANY FUTURE TENSE or AN IMPERATIVE

The last example shows a present simple form (habit) used in a result clause. In this case 'if' approximates to 'when' in meaning.

2. *Condition and result unlikely or unreal*

Condition	Result
If you *ate* less	you *would lose* weight.
If you *were eating* breakfast in England	you *would be having* eggs and bacon.
If you *were to eat* only once a day	you *would save* a good deal of washing up. (you could save)
If fish *ate* grass	they *would have* to live on land.
PAST SIMPLE or CONTINUOUS TENSE	CONDITIONAL SIMPLE or CONTINUOUS TENSE
	Notice the conditional 'could'.

a) The form 'were to eat' is an alternative to the Past Simple form.

b) Study the following example:

Mother would be much happier if the twins would eat more.

In some languages, a conditional form with auxiliary 'would' commonly appears in the conditional clause. This is not normally the case in English.

But in the above example, the form 'would' in the condition may be explained as the past simple of a verb 'will' with the meaning 'be willing to'. In this case its use is in accordance with the normal tense sequence pattern.

Mother would be much happier if the twins were willing to eat more.

A similar example is:

It would help me if you would carry this bag.

c) The use of the subjunctive in this type of conditional clause is explained later.

3. *Condition and result impossible*

Condition	Result
If you *had eaten* more for breakfast (*Had* you *eaten* more for breakfast)	you *would* not *have been* hungry now.
If he *had been eating* Chinese food	he *would have been using* chopsticks.
PAST PERFECT SIMPLE or CONTINUOUS TENSE	CONDITIONAL PERFECT SIMPLE or CONTINUOUS TENSE

B. THE IMPERATIVE AND SUBJUNCTIVE MOODS

IMPERATIVE

a) The second person 'be', 'go', 'listen', etc., are the only forms.

The negative forms, 'do not be', 'do not go', etc., are abbreviated in conversation to 'don't be', 'don't go'.

   b) Certain imperatives have a colloquial use;
     'look', 'come'.
     Look! Why not have a meal at my place?
     Come, it's not so bad as you think.
   c) A near equivalent of the first person plural imperative is formed by using 'let'.
        Let's sit down!
   Negative: Don't let us argue or Let's not argue.
          (let's)

SUBJUNCTIVE

This mood is not common in English.

1. Certain forms with 'may' and 'might' are sometimes classified as subjunctives:
     He set the alarm so that he might wake early.
2. In modern English the subjunctive normally affects first and third person singular forms of the past simple and past continuous tenses of the verb 'to be'. The subjunctive may appear in the following cases especially if there is considerable doubt.
   a) 'if' in conditions of the second type:
     If I were to see that film I should have nightmares.
     If he were coming he would telephone.
   b) After 'as if' 'as though' in a clause of comparison when the comparison is obviously untrue.
     He raced down the road as if he were being chased by a mad dog.
   c) After the verb 'to wish' (where the wish is unfulfilled).
     She wishes she were less ignorant.
   d) After 'Supposing . . .' (where the supposition or hypothesis is unlikely).
     Supposing your letter were to be published . . .
3. Certain apparently illogical past forms following such expressions as
     It is time (that) . . .
   have been explained as possible subjunctive forms.
     It is time you had a haircut.
   Notice also: She wishes she could cook. Suppose it rained?
     He is walking as if he felt tired already.

C. VERBS USED AS AUXILIARIES

1. AM TO; WAS TO
   These forms suggest a strong compulsion.
   This compulsion may take the form of
   a) A very firm command:
     You are to finish your homework before you go out.
or:
   b) A very firm arrangement.
     The motorway is to be extended next year.

Was to   were to   followed by a perfect infinitive

This may suggest that the intended action did not in fact come about.

     I am worried. They were to have arrived before nightfall. What could have happened?

2. USED TO   WOULD
The use of either of these forms may suggest an action
   a) that was repeated or lasted for some time
and
   b) that occurred a considerable time ago and is certainly no longer happening.
     At one time gentlemen always used to / would always bow to their acquaintances.

'Would' replaces 'used to'

only when the action is an intended one
and (normally):
only when some period of time is stated.

In ancient times people $\frac{\text{used to}}{\text{would}}$ sacrifice animals or birds to appease the gods.

You used to like potatoes. (not 'would like')

3. GOING TO
This is used as an auxiliary only in a continuous form.
It expresses either intention:

He is going to get married.

or likelihood:

The weather is going to improve.

The past form implies that the intention was not carried out.

I thought you were going to wash up. You haven't even cleared the table.

D. NOTES ON SOME MODAL VERBS AND ON 'NEED'

CAN   OUGHT TO   SHOULD   MUST   HAVE TO   MAY   NEED TO

1. *Defective verbs*

a) CAN has only two forms: CAN (Present Simple and normally Future Simple)
COULD (Past Simple)

Other tense forms are expressed by corresponding forms of BE ABLE TO.
PRESENT PERFECT: he has been able to
PAST PERFECT: he had been able to
FUTURE SIMPLE: he will be able to
FUTURE IN THE PAST (CONDITIONAL): he would be able to

I am sorry I have not been able to locate his address for you.

b) MUST has only the single form which can express the Present or normally the Future Simple.
Other tense forms are expressed by corresponding forms of HAVE TO.
PRESENT PERFECT: He has had to move to another town.
PAST SIMPLE: Primitive man had to hunt animals for food.
PAST CONTINUOUS: was having to
PAST PERFECT: had had to
FUTURE SIMPLE: will have to
FUTURE IN THE PAST (CONDITIONAL): would have to

c) MAY   MIGHT
MIGHT expresses a past form normally only in reported speech.
My father said I might borrow his car.
MAY can express some possibility; MIGHT less possibility
It may rain so take an umbrella.
It might rain but I don't think it will.
Tense forms of MAY (permission) can be supplied by BE ALLOWED TO.
He has been allowed to leave school, but he will not be allowed to sign on as an apprentice until he is sixteen.

2. *Ought to (should)   must   have to-meanings*

a) OUGHT TO expresses a duty which may not be carried out: You ought to rest more.
b) MUST expresses a personal obligation: I must work more carefully.
c) MUST NOT—a prohibition: You must not walk on the grass.
NEED NOT there is no necessity: You need not pay for it.
d) HAVE TO—expresses an external necessity: He has to find a home.

3. *The use of a perfect infinitive after these verbs*

There is often a suggestion that the action referred to by the infinitive did not in fact happen. This implication is strong after some verbs but non-existent after others.

a) COULD You could have put it in a drawer. (This is possible)
   You could have tried harder you know. (But you didn't)

b) OUGHT TO (SHOULD) You ought to have locked the door. (But you didn't)
   Normally the action has not taken place, but this is not always the case.
   He should have left home by now.

c) MUST—with a Present or Perfect Infinitive suggests that the statement is probably true.
   It must be quite cold outside.
   That must have been a terrifying experience.

d) NEED—with a Present or Perfect Infinitive.
   You need not have bought it. (But you did)
   I didn't need to buy it. (So I didn't)

4. *Need*—Negative and Interrogative Forms

With a Noun or Pronoun Object: I don't need a coat. Do you need a drink?

With a following Infinitive: He need not go or He doesn't need to go (Present).
   He didn't need to go (Past).

Chapter 7

VERBAL CONSTRUCTIONS

One of the principal difficulties of those who wish to speak English correctly is encountered when a second verb is in some way dependent on the main verb of a clause. This second verb may appear a) in its infinitive form (with or without the preposition 'to' according to the preceding verb), b) as a gerund or c) as part of a dependent clause, often a noun clause object of the preceding verb.

a) He wants to come.
   He can come.
b) He enjoys coming.
c) He says that he will come.

As it is the gerund which almost always follows a preposition, verbs which incorporate a preposition and phrasal verbs will necessarily be followed by a gerund.

He is looking forward to travelling.
He is used to travelling. ('used' is here an adjective)
He has given up travelling.

Distinguish carefully between verbal forms which incorporate 'to', e.g. look forward to; take to; and independent verb forms followed by an infinitive preceded by 'to', e.g. want, intend, tend.

In several cases more than one construction can follow a certain verb, not always with any noticeable change in meaning.

He suggested our sitting down.
He suggested (that) we (should) sit down.

There is no logical way of learning these constructions as there seems to be no reason for each individual case. Constructions have little relation to meaning. The advanced student can only look up the normal construction, use it often enough to become thoroughly aware of it consciously, notice examples when reading and finally become sufficiently familiar with it to use it automatically.

The following table lists the more common constructions in alphabetical order. Notes corresponding to numbers follow; where there are two possible constructions and no notes, the meaning of each construction is similar enough not to need special comment. In some cases, constructions which are sometimes found are not given as these are less common and may possibly result only in confusion. The table can be used for reference.

VERB	INFINITIVE	GERUND	CLAUSE
abstain		from voting	
accuse		of cheating	
admit		(to) knowing	(that) one knows
advise	(me) to rest		
agree	to share	about sharing	(that) we should share
aim	to write	at achieving	
allow[1]	to go		
apologise		for forgetting	
appear	to like		
approve		of smoking	
arrange	to meet		that we should meet
ask	to see		if (whether) I can see
assist		in compiling	
assume			(that) he will come
attempt	to compose		
avoid		hurting	
be	(you are to obey)		
be able	to understand		
beg	to be forgiven		
begin	to search	searching	
believe		in saving	(that) he lives
beware		of losing	
bid	(to) sit down		
blame		for spoiling	
boast		of winning	(that) they have won
bother	to learn	about learning	
bribe	to support		
can	read		
cause[1]	to postpone		
cease	to struggle	struggling	
challenge	to fight		
claim	to own		(that) he owns
command	to advance		that they should advance
compel[1]	to obey		
complain		about losing	that he has lost
confess		to stealing	(that) he has stolen
confirm		writing	that he had written
consist		of preparing	
contemplate		changing	
continue	to row	rowing	
contribute		to building	
convince			someone (that) he should stay
cope		with looking after	
counsel	to withdraw		that they should withdraw
cure		of stammering	
dare[10]	to jump		
decide	to buy	on buying	(that) he will buy
declare			(that) he will stay
defer		applying	
deign	to speak		
delay		starting	
delight		in listening	
demand	to see		that he should see

222

VERB	INFINITIVE	GERUND	CLAUSE
deny		breaking	(that) he broke
describe	how to make	making	
despair		of teaching	
deter		from investing	
determine	to travel		that he would travel
detest		scrubbing	
direct	to proceed		
discourage		from smoking	
dislike	to drive	driving	
dissuade		from reading	
doubt			whether he should go
dread		losing	
dream		of living	that he would live
educate	to appreciate		
encourage	to drink	drinking	
endeavour	to create		
enjoy		dancing	
ensure			(that) it is ready
entail		planning	
entitle	to inherit		
entreat	to forgive		
envisage		winning	(that) we should win
escape		drowning	
estimate			that it will improve
evade		paying	
excel		in running	
excuse		(my) interrupting	
expect	to succeed		(that) he will succeed
fail	to realise		
fancy		winning	(that) he will be promoted
fear	to trust		(that) he must be ill
feel[2]	(something) tremble	(something) trembling (participle)	(that) something will happen
feel like		resting	
finish		eating	
forbid	to go		
force[1]	to yield		
forecast			(that) he will lose
forget[3]	to pay	paying	(that) one must pay
go on[4]	to say	speaking	
guarantee	to deliver		(that) we shall deliver
guess			what he will say
had better	wait		
happen	to remark		
hasten	to qualify		
hate	to admit	writing	
hear[2]	scream	screaming (participle)	(that) something has happened
help	(to) carry		
cannot help		smiling	
hesitate	to criticise		
hope	to see		(that) I (may) see
imagine		living	(that) he is the director
incite	to rebel		
incur		spending	
induce	to contribute		
indulge		in day-dreaming	
inform			(that) I should apply
inquire		about going	whether he should go

223

VERB	INFINITIVE	GERUND	CLAUSE
insist		on seeing	(that) I should see
inspire	to compose		
instruct	to attend		
intend	to move		
invite	to stay		
joke		about making a fortune	
keep (on)		talking	
know	how to knit		(that) the world is round
learn	(how) to drive		(that) he must obey
leave[5]	to prepare	preparing	
leave off		working	
let[1]	come		
like	to sing	singing	
should like	to come		
loathe		waiting	
long	to return		
look forward		to celebrating	
love	to dance	dancing	
make[1]	(someone) pay		
manage	to carry		
may	borrow		
mean	to finish		
mind		helping	
miss		seeing	
must	improve		
need[10, 6]	to reorganise	reorganising	
notice[2]	walk	walking (participle)	(that) he is walking
object		to meeting	
observe[2]	enter	entering (participle)	that someone is entering
offer	to help		
omit	to sign	signing	
oppose		supporting	
order	to advance		
ought	to study		
pause	to consider		
pay	to watch	for watching	
permit	to attend[1]		
persevere		in practising	
persist		in interrupting	
persuade	to change		
plan	to build		
plead	to return		that he might return
pray	to recover		
prefer	to ride	riding to driving	
prepare	to set out		
presume	to approach		(that) we may come
pretend	to understand		that he understands
prevent		(his) $\left(\begin{array}{c}\text{him}\\\text{from}\end{array}\right)$ entering	
proceed	to report		
profit		from investing	
prohibit		from entering	
promise	to reform		(that) he will reform
propose	to construct	constructing	(that) a road should be constructed
protest		against fighting	
punish		for trespassing	
read	how to use		(that) something has happened

VERB	INFINITIVE	GERUND	CLAUSE
realise			(that) it will fall
recall } recollect		meeting	(that) something happened
recommend	to buy	buying	(that) you should buy
refrain		from applauding	
refuse	to conform		
regret[3]	to report	having reported	(that) we must report
rely		on discovering	
remain		standing	
remark			(that) the weather is fine
remember[3]	to take	taking	(that) I must take
remind	to send		(that) we should bring
report		seeing	(that) sales have increased
reply			(that) he disagrees
request	to leave		(that) he should leave
resist		spending	
resolve	to achieve		(that) he will achieve
risk		damaging	
say			(that) he is hungry
scorn	to yield		
see[2]	change	changing (particle)	(that) it has changed
seek	to understand		
seem	to enjoy		
shirk		helping	
show[7]	how to make	making	(that) something can be done
sit		thinking	
smell		(something) cooking	
spend time		arguing	
stand		watching	
start	to rain	raining	
state			(that) a meeting is to be held
stay	to help		
stop[8]	to listen	listening	
stress			(that) they should bring
strive	to win		
struggle	to escape		
study	to pass		
succeed		in inventing	
suppose			(that) you are right
suspect		of cheating	(that) he has cheated
swear	to avenge		(that) he is innocent
teach	(how) to type		
tell	to fetch		
tempt	to spend		
tend	to exaggerate		
think		of changing	(that) he will change
train	to imitate		
trouble	to move		
try[9]	to capture	using	
understand	how to solve		(that) I am to write
undertake	to return		
urge	to reconsider		
unite		in defending	
venture	to suggest		
visualise		wearing	
volunteer	to carry		
vow	to return		(that) he will return
wait	to see (and see)		

VERB	INFINITIVE	GERUND	CLAUSE
want	to fly		
warn		(about) against driving	
watch²	jump	jumping (participle)	
wish	to inspect		(that) I could do it
wonder	(how) to make		how I could/should make
would rather	remain		
yearn	to travel		

1. *Make* someone *obey*: *compel, force, cause* someone *to obey*.
   let someone *help*: *allow, permit* someone *to help.*
2. *see, notice, observe, watch, hear, feel* something *happening* (action in progress).
3. *forget, remember, regret doing* something (that has already been done).
   forget, remember, regret to do something (that is to be done).
4. *go on speaking*—continue speaking.
   go on to say—finish one subject and start another.
5. *leave working*—emphasis that work is going on when the subject leaves.
   leave to work—emphasis on the fact that the work is to start or continue after the subject has left.
6. *he needs to work* harder.
   this clock needs repairing.
7. he *showed* me *how to catch* a salmon.
   the film *showed* a fisherman catching a salmon.
8. *stop doing* what is being done already *to start* something new.
9. *try to do* something difficult which has to be done.
   try doing something in the hope of achieving something more difficult as a result.
10. he dares to come, he dare not come, dare he come? (he does not dare, does he dare?)
    he needs to come, he need not come, need he come? (he does not need, does he need?)
    But, with noun or pronoun object—only: You don't need an umbrella.

THE INFINITIVE OF PURPOSE

He came to mend the roof.

A few other examples are:

    to shout to attract attention
    to work to earn a living
    to pause to rest
    to hurry to catch a train

The phrases 'so as to' 'in order to' emphasise the idea of purpose, and precede a negative infinitive.

    He walks five miles a day in order to keep fit.
    He chose his words carefully so as not to give the wrong impression.

CONSTRUCTIONS WITH ADJECTIVES

a) The commonest construction with the verb 'to be' is:
   It is interesting to study the history of one's town.
   They were anxious to help.
b) A few adjectives are followed by a gerund:
   She was busy cooking. It is worth doing.
c) Adjectives accompanied by special prepositions are followed by the gerund:
   proud of having; accustomed/used to seeing;
   exempt from paying; keen on visiting.
d) He was *too* tired *to* listen.
   He is not clever *enough* to understand.
   Would you be *so* kind *as to* wait.

226

TWO PREPOSITIONS

'Except' and 'but' (as a preposition) are followed by an infinitive without 'to'.

He promised to do anything I wanted except wash up.
He did nothing but grumble.

Chapter 8

A. SHORT ANSWERS IN SPOKEN ENGLISH

Many questions need only 'Yes' or 'No' for an answer. It is common in conversation, however, to add a subject and short verbal form.

In the case of the verbs 'have' ('possess'), 'be', 'can', 'may', 'must', 'ought', 'should', the verb itself is used.

'Have you a ticket?' 'Yes, I have.'
'Can you drive?' 'No, I can't.'

In other cases, a suitable auxiliary is sufficient, the verb itself not being repeated.
'Does he live here?' 'Yes, he does.'
'Will the shops be open tomorrow?' 'No, they won't.'

Must

These are the probable short answer forms:
'Must I register this letter?' 'Yes, you must.'
'No, you needn't.'

B. *Question tags in spoken English*

These have three main uses:

a) to confirm a preceding statement.
b) to express doubt about the correctness of a preceding statement. (In this case a question mark follows.)
c) to soften a command.

The difference between these uses becomes clear only in speech:

a) Bananas don't grow in English gardens, do they.
   (Confirmation. The voice falls from 'do' to 'they')
b) Your little boy doesn't smoke cigarettes, does he?
   (Surprised doubt. The voice rises from 'does' to 'he').
c) Bring that parcel here, will you. Sit down, won't you.

FORMATION

a) The short verbal form shown in the previous exercise is used in an interrogative form.
b) If the opening statement is affirmative, the question tag is negative.
   If the opening statement is negative, the question tag is affirmative.

EXCEPTION When it expresses anger, irony, sympathy, or some other emotion the question tag may be a mere repetition in the case of an affirmative statement.

'He uses my car, does he?'
'You think you know everything, do you?'

Notice also c) above.

Sometimes doubt is expressed by the use of the auxiliary 'do' or 'did' in the opening affirmative statement.

'You do like it, don't you?'

C. ADVERBS

Adverbs are normally formed by adding -ly to the corresponding adjective, e.g. slow, slowly.

a) Several adverbs so formed differ considerably in meaning from their corresponding adjectives.

Write sentences showing the difference in meaning and use between the following adjectives and adverbs.

bare	barely	actual	actually
hard	hardly	direct	directly
scarce	scarcely	late	lately
fair	fairly	present	presently
practical	practically	reasonable	reasonably
simple	simply	near	nearly
pure	purely	rich	richly
great	greatly	high	highly
real	really	short	shortly (notice: to stop short).

A few of the above adverbs have more than one meaning.

b) A few adjectives remain unchanged.

e.g. fast, straight, forward, backward, sideways, hourly, daily, weekly, monthly, yearly.

c) A difficulty arises in the case of adjectives ending in -ly.

A phrase is normally used in such circumstances:

silly   You are behaving in a very silly way.

friendly   He greeted me in a friendly manner.

The adverbial form can often be avoided:

He gave me a friendly greeting.

Other such adjectives are: lively, lovely, jolly, chilly, deadly, godly, ugly, kindly, gingerly, heavenly, leisurely.

d) With certain exceptions, adjectives ending in -ic, add -al before the -ly.

energetic-ally; fantastic-ally; realistic-ally; romantic-ally; characteristic-ally; enthusiastic-ally.

but public—publicly.

e) Adjectives ending in -ple, -ble, -dle, -tle, drop the -e before the -ly.

simple, simply; reasonable, reasonably; idle, idly; gentle, gently.

f) The -y ending after a consonant in adjectives usually changes to i before the -ly.

weary, wearily.

Exceptions are generally one-syllabled: dryly, shyly.

g) Notice these special cases:

(i) true, truly; good, well; difficult, with difficulty; detailed, in detail.

(ii) Certain participles: tired, bored, annoyed, surprised, interested, exciting, interesting, tiring have no corresponding adverbial form and a phrase must be used: with great interest, as if he were interested, etc. Most present participles and many past have normal adverbial forms: surprisingly, knowingly, guardedly, learnedly.

(Use each of these four adverbs in a sentence).

Chapter 1

FULL STOP, SEMI-COLON AND COLON

A. *Full stop*

    a) To mark the end of a sentence.
    b) To mark an abbreviation which may consist of several letters: Esq., or single letters: p.m., A.D., B.A.

Present-day fashion in business correspondence allows the omission of the full stop when the last letter of the abbreviated word appears e.g. Mr   Dr
The use has become optional.

B. *Semi-colon and colon*

SEMI-COLON
To divide parts of a sentence each one of which is structurally a complete sentence, in cases where the meaning requires a single sentence and the use of a conjunction detracts from some desired effect such as a dramatic pause or an effective contrast.
    The section after the semi-colon expresses ideas which carry a stage further the thought in the preceding section.

> The mist lifted a moment; immediately ahead the Captain glimpsed a reef of jagged rocks.
> The development of railways took trade from the roadside inn; motor transport in its turn, inaugurated a new prosperity and brought many more patrons.

The semi-colon may separate phrases if a very definite pause is indicated or if a verb is understood.

COLON
This may be used in a similar way to the semi-colon. The section after the colon refers back to the preceding section. It exemplifies, illustrates or explains what has gone before.

> The development of railways took trade from the roadside inn: the former stage-coach traveller, who had dined and slept several times between London and Edinburgh, now completed the journey in a few hours.

    b) To introduce a list of examples which may or may not be complete sentences in themselves.

> The regulations apply in the following cases: where the child has no surviving parent, where both parents are unable to work and where the child has been separated from the parents.
> I consider these the major nuisances of train journeys: transistor radios, freezing carriages, undisciplined children and people eating oranges.

The following section is normally separated from the preceding one by a slight pause. No colon is needed in the following example:

> Among the suspects in the murder case there were a deserted wife, a dismissed employee, an unsuccessful business rival and a neurotic intellectual.

    c) The colon may introduce a quotation.

> It was the renowned Dr Samuel Johnson who is reported to have said: 'Claret is the liquor for boys; port for men; but he who aspires to be a hero . . . must drink brandy.'

What does the line of dots signify?

Chapter 2

THE APOSTROPHE

a) To denote a letter or letters omitted.

apart from o'clock, most examples are forms of conversational abbreviation: it's (it is); isn't; I'll; he'd etc.

Remember that possessive pronouns have no apostrophe:

hers   ours   yours   theirs

Possessive adjective 'its' has no apostrophe.

b) To denote possession.
   (i) In the case of a singular noun, before the 's: the millionaire's death.
   (ii) In the case of a plural noun, after the s': workers' representatives.
   (iii) Where a plural is formed some other way than by adding -s, the apostrophe precedes the -s in the plural possessive form: men's voices; Children's Homes; people's tastes.
   (iv) When the singular ends in -s, an apostrophe 's is usually added: the actress's performance.
   In the case of proper nouns ending in -s, an apostrophe only may be added: Sinclair Lewis' 'Babbit'.
   (v) In certain words indicating a time duration:
   an hour's wait; two centuries' progress.
   (vi) Notice this use: He spent the evening at this friend's. (house)
   but: with his friend.
   I bought it at Harris's. (shop)
   (vii) Notice also: for goodness' sake.

Chapter 3

CAPITAL LETTERS

These are used:

a) For proper nouns: names of people, countries, counties, towns, mountains, seas, rivers, months of the year, days of the week, etc.
   Wednesday, the eighth of February.
b) Languages and adjectives of nationality.
   Portuguese; a Norwegian town.
c) The more important words in the names of hotels, books, newspapers, magazines, films, plays, ships.
   'The Dog and Duck Inn'; 'The Taming of the Shrew.'
d) The more important words in a title or heading:
   'The Everyday Life of the Peasant in Mediaeval Britain.'
e) The first word of a sentence and of direct speech at its first opening in a sentence.
f) I.
g) Initials of societies, degrees, decorations etc.
   R.S.P.C.C. (The Royal Society for the Prevention of Cruelty to Children).
h) The capital letter is optional for the names of the seasons and the points of the compass written as words (north, south, etc.). As initials they are capitals: N.W.

Chapter 4

COMMAS

Separates clauses, phrases or words in the following cases:

a) A list of nouns, adjectives or adverbs.
   She is trying to write a textbook, a detective novel and a travel book.

His work is methodical, accurate, well-informed and frequently entertaining.

He spoke slowly, pompously, dogmatically and, indeed, tediously.

In such cases, no comma normally precedes the conjunction.

When two or three short adjectives precede a noun, a comma is often not necessary.

He was a short dark lively man.

b) A single word or phrase which may modify the whole sentence. The comma is in most cases optional.

One should, therefore, take extra care.

This is, in effect, a result rather than a cause.

By the way, do you care for Chinese food?

c) A subordinate adverbial clause which *precedes* the main clause.

When you see the new moon, turn your money over.

Turn your money over when you see the new moon.

d) A longer adverbial phrase at the beginning of a sentence:

Throughout his horrifying ordeal, he remained unafraid.

After swimming for three hours, he felt exhausted.

This use also is optional.

e) A non-defining clause. No commas are used round defining clauses.

The Gulf Stream, which surrounds the British Isles, normally ensures a temperate climate.

The stream which is most popular with fishermen in this area is in danger of being polluted by the discharge of waste products from a projected factory.

f) Direct speech (see the following section dealing with inverted commas).

g) Phrases in apposition.

Rutland, the smallest English county, would oppose incorporation in a larger administrative unit.

This does not necessarily apply to clauses in apposition:

The fact that many teenagers approve of 'pop' music does not make it any more beautiful.

h) A word or phrase of address.

Waiter, where are my steak and chips?

That's right, sir, over there.

i) Yes and No.

Yes, I'll come.

NOTICE: A noun clause is not usually separated from the rest of a sentence by a comma.

What we said is none of your business.

He wants to know where you have been.

Happiness is what most people want.

If there are several co-ordinate clauses, these will be separated by commas, except for the penultimate one when this is followed by 'and'.

He wants to know where you have been, whom you have seen and what you have brought back for him.

Chapter 5

INVERTED COMMAS

USES

1. Round direct speech.

'Where are you going?' asked the taxi-driver.

'Victoria Station,' said his fare, 'and I'm catching "The Golden Arrow". Get a move on!'

'In all this traffic?' queried the driver. 'What do you take me for?'

NOTICE:
a) The commas are above the line in each case.
b) They may be in pairs, though single inverted commas for direct speech are not uncommon.
c) Any word or phrase normally set in inverted commas which comes inside the direct speech will have a single inverted comma inside double ones for the speech or vice versa.
d) Apart from the beginning or ending of a sentence, a comma precedes the opening of the direct speech and also ends it.
e) Questions and exclamation marks referring to the direct speech come inside the inverted commas.
   Those referring to the whole sentence come outside.
      Did he say, 'Why are you here?'?
f) A new paragraph is used for each fresh speaker.
2. Round quotations, which may be introduced by a comma.
3. Round titles of books, plays, films, pictures, etc., special names of ships, trains, public houses, newspapers and similar titles.
4. Round slang and words with a special technical meaning.

> The bus I eventually caught was a 'crawler' and took twice as long as I'd expected.
> Potters 'throw' a pot on a wheel.

Chapter 6

A. BRACKETS AND DASHES,   HYPHENS

BRACKETS AND DASHES

These are used for similar purposes, namely, to separate a word (or group of words) which is, in effect, grammatically independent of the rest of the sentence. The word (or word group) may be a definition, an alternative, a comment or an afterthought: the idea is not normally an essential part of the thought of the sentence.

> A sudden scurry caught my attention. It came from a red squirrel (a rare creature in this part of the country), who was racing panic-stricken up to a high branch.
> In the strangely silent twilight—a June night in Northern Scotland rarely achieves darkness—a figure was quietly approaching the cottage.

THE DASH also indicates an interruption in speech.

> 'But it was yesterday that I saw ——,' he suddenly paused before adding, 'I saw the new film.'

A line of dots may serve the same purpose here.

Except when the isolated word group is an independent main clause, commas may do the work of the brackets or dash as shown above but the effect of separation is not nearly so strong.

After a list of words or phrases, the dash may precede a final summarising statement.

> Crumbs, paper clips, chewing-gum wrappers, pencil sharpenings, coins and newspaper clippings—all littered the sub-editor's desk.

Be careful not to make a habit of using dashes.

HYPHEN

In many cases this is not regarded as very important in English and in such instances may be inserted or omitted according to personal whim. The following points may be useful, but are not necessarily rules.
a) by forming a compound adjective, a hyphen may change meaning slightly.
   Compare: 'a blue-lined blazer' with 'a blue lined blazer'.
b) 're-' suggests 'again' when distinction is needed.
   to re-cover a chair; to recover from an illness.

c) a hyphen may separate a 're-' prefix from a word beginning with e- and a 'co-' prefix from a word beginning with o-.
   re-enter; co-operate.
d) nouns and gerunds forming a compound noun are usually separated by a hyphen.
   dining-room; proof-reading; present-giving.
e) often a hyphen forms an adjective from a noun (or an adjective or adverb) followed by a past participle.
   home-made; semi-detached; highly-strung; fast-moving.
f) a hyphen may link a prefix with a proper or abstract noun.
   pre-Raphaelite; post-Victorian; anti-slavery; pro-Government; ex-President.
   Notice also: pre-war (but prefabricated).
g) the following are usually written as two separate words:
   fire station; bus station; post office; town hall; grammar school; hat factory; dog licence; public house.
h) the following are usually written as a single word:
   needlework; shopkeeper; playground (but recreation ground); shipbuilding; handwork; homework; headmaster; typewriter; newspaper; timetable.
i) numbers are hyphenated between tens and units:
   one hundred and twenty-three.
j) notice: traffic-warden; house-painter; mouse-trap; dog-kennel; North East.

B. THE PUNCTUATION OF LETTER HEADINGS AND ENDINGS

The conventional way of heading and ending a business letter is shown below. The punctuation marks in parentheses are optional. Both addresses may be arranged so that each line starts five spaces further to the right than the one above it.

The name and address of the person who is to receive the letter may appear after the end of the letter, still on the left-hand side.

10(,) Cream Crescent(,)
Appleburgh(,)
Devon.
3rd January, 19—(.)

A. Stone, Esq.(,)
The Blackiron Foundry Co. Ltd.(,)
Slag Street(,)
Smoketon(,)
Lancs. SM9 8ZY

Dear Sir,

Yours faithfully,
J. Greenfield
(Lt. Col. J. Greenfield)

SECTION III WORD ORDER

Chapter 1

A

English is a language in which meaning depends to a considerable extent on the order of words. This is due partly to the fact that there are few inflections (the changing of the formation and endings of words). But subtle shades of emphasis can be expressed merely by appropriate word order. Only that feeling for the language which is acquired by extensive reading and listening can produce unerring proficiency in the arrangement of words and phrases, but a knowledge of certain basic rules can ensure at least correctness in expression.

1. *Basic structure*

SUBJECT VERB OBJECT ADVERBS OR ADVERBIAL PHRASES

Interrogative structure

VERB SUBJECT OBJECT ADVERBS OR ADVERBIAL PHRASES
VERB AUXILIARY SUBJECT PARTICIPLE

Imperative structure

VERB OBJECT ADVERBS AND ADVERBIAL PHRASES

2. *Direct and indirect objects*

The INDIRECT OBJECT is normally preceded by the preposition 'to' (or 'for') when there is no direct object or when the indirect follows the direct object.

> He wrote to me.
> He spoke to me.
> He read to me.

Some of the verbs which take an indirect object are transitive and are seldom used without a direct object.

> He sold it to me.
> He bought it for me.
> I took it to him.

The indirect object is not preceded by a preposition when it precedes the direct object.

> I gave the attendant (him) the ticket.

Use of direct and indirect objects with certain verbs

a) SAY, EXPLAIN, DESCRIBE, REPORT, REPEAT, FORETELL, RELATE, EXPRESS, REVEAL, WHISPER, SHOUT (Many verbs which express the method of telling.)

When direct and indirect objects are used with these verbs, the DIRECT PRECEDES THE INDIRECT OBJECT, unless the former consists of several words. In any case 'to' always precedes the indirect object.

> He has revealed his plans to the press.
> He said hello to us.   He explained to us what he intended to do.

b) ASK

The DIRECT OBJECT normally FOLLOWS THE INDIRECT.

> I asked him the time.

c) SEND, GIVE, OFFER, WRITE, BRING, TAKE, FETCH, TELL, BUY, TEACH, and many other verbs.

The DIRECT and INDIRECT OBJECTS MAY BE IN EITHER POSITION.

(In the case of 'tell' the indirect object more commonly precedes the direct.)

> We sent him a Christmas card.
> We sent a Christmas card to him.
> He told us many legends.

When the direct and indirect objects are interchangeable in position, their order usually depends on emphasis in meaning. If the indirect object follows the direct, the emphasis may be on the indirect object.

He bought the flowers for his father and the brandy for his mother.

Chapter 2

B

3. *Adverbial expressions within a sentence*

a) (i) Remember the basic sentence order:

SUBJECT   VERB   OBJECT   ADVERB

Do not insert an adverbial expression between the verb and its object, unless the object is an extended one.

It is quite wrong to say:

Storms cause (very often) great damage along these coasts.

He wants (very much) to travel.

(The arrows show the correct position of the adverbial phrase.)

But notice: He examined with interest the microscopic drawing in the corner of the manuscript.

(ii) 'Very much' may, of course, be used adjectivally.
These plants need very much water.
(iii) What is the difference between:
Boys very much enjoy eating.
Boys enjoy eating very much.
Boys like to eat very much?

b) There is what might be described as a normal order and position of adverbial expressions in general, but, as suggested at the beginning of the chapter, the placing of such forms is very often determined by meaning, emphasis, balance or rhythm in sentence structure. A student should be really familiar with the normal order, but as he begins to acquire the feel of the language, he should be able to decide on any more suitable arrangements.

The normal order is as follows:

(i) When adverbial expressions of more than one kind are in close sequence, the normal order is:

MANNER   PLACE   TIME
He reads the newspaper methodically in the bus every morning.

It is, however, rare to have three adverbial forms in sequence.

TIME expressions often start off the sentence.

Every morning he reads his newspaper methodically while sitting in the bus.

It is sometimes possible for PLACE expressions to precede the verb.

In the bus he reads his newspaper methodically.
At the seaside children play happily from morning till night.

(ii) When two or more time adverbs, one indicating a more exact, the other (or others) a less exact time are in sequence, the expressions are arranged in order of exactness.

He was born at three o'clock on the 2nd July, 1835.

(iii) Most one-word adverbs—some of them possibly modified by 'very'—may be placed within the verbal group if they are not emphasised.

These include adverbs of frequency (always ... never); 'soon', 'now', 'then', 'next', 'immediately', 'recently', 'therefore', 'possibly', 'probably', 'certainly' and many unemphasised adverbs of manner.

Such words as 'yesterday', 'today', 'tomorrow', 'shortly', 'presently', 'directly', 'before', cannot normally be included in the verbal group.

235

The word order within the verbal group normally follows one of these patterns.

(i) *Simple present and past tenses*

AFFIRMATIVE STATEMENT

SUBJECT	ADVERB	VERB	—	—	—
He	seldom	eats	—	—	—

NEGATIVE STATEMENT

SUBJECT	AUXILIARY	ADVERBS	VERB	—	—	—
He	does	not often	eat	—	—	—

AFFIRMATIVE QUESTION

AUXILIARY	SUBJECT	ADVERB	VERB	—	—	—	
Does	he	ever	eat	—	—	—	?

NOTICE these cases in which the adverb FOLLOWS the verb in the simple tenses.

a) The verb 'TO BE'

SUBJECT	VERB	ADVERB	COMPLEMENT
He	was	still	hopeful

b) A MODAL VERB: CAN, MAY, MUST

SUBJECT	VERB	ADVERB	INFINITIVE
You	can	probably	remember
He	must	obviously	know

Exceptions to these cases include such expressions as:

'You never can tell' when the adverb is very strongly emphasised.

(ii) *Compound tenses*

These include all tenses except the Active Forms of the Past and Present Simple tenses.

The adverb FOLLOWS the first auxiliary verb.

SUBJECT	AUXILIARY	ADVERB	OTHER VERBAL FORMS
You	will	soon	be leaving

In a negative form the negative precedes other adverbs.

SUBJECT	AUXILIARY	ADVERBS	OTHER VERBAL FORMS
He	has	not yet	been questioned

The interrogative form is as follows:

AUXILIARY	SUBJECT	ADVERB	OTHER VERBAL FORMS
Has	he	often	been sailing?

Here again, special emphasis may occasionally affect word order.

I now will tell the whole story.

Chapter 3

4. *The inversion of subject and verb*

a) Contrary to the practice in some languages, the subject and verb are not normally inverted after introductory adverbs:

There at last he found contentment.

Soon after we awoke, the sleeping car attendant brought us coffee.

b) The subject and verb are inverted in a direct but not in an indirect question.

Where is Joan?

He wants to know where Joan is.

The subject and verb are inverted in question tags.

The bus stops here, doesn't it?

c) The subject and verb are inverted after certain introductory negative expressions which derive special emphasis from their position at the beginning of the sentence.

I had never before heard such a noise.

Never before had I heard such a noise.

Some of these expressions are negative in meaning even though no specifically negative word is included.

Here are a few examples:

never; never in my life; nowhere; not even then;
not until now; not until he read it in the newspaper;
in no way; in no case; under no condition; on no account;
seldom; rarely; hardly; scarcely;
only then; only if he feels like it; only in an emergency;
so (introducing a short positive answer of agreement);
neither; nor (introducing a short negative answer of agreement).

Examples:

Not until the floods had subsided could they assess the damage.
On no account may you return after midnight.
Hardly had he arrived before he started grumbling.
Only if he is seriously ill, does he ever stay in bed.
Mrs Short has a tall husband. So has Mrs Small.
They don't like fish soup. Neither do I.

5. *Word order and meaning*

Ambiguity may result from illogically arranged words, phrases or clauses.

a) Adjectival and adverbial expressions should stand as near as possible to the words they are related to.

Here are two badly arranged sentences:

He found a book in the reference library that was so useful that he bought it.
The foreman was supervising the drilling of a hole in a smart lounge suit.

b) English people very often misplace such adverbs as 'only', 'hardly', 'scarcely', 'barely', 'either', 'neither'. Each of these should be as near as possible to the word or phrase it is modifying.

These sentences show the illogical order.

He only walks as far as the station.
You can either go by boat or by train.

Chapter 3

INTRODUCTION

All great writers express their ideas in an individual way: it is often possible to determine the authorship of a literary passage from the style in which it is written. Many authors feel that the conventions of the written language hamper them and they use words freely, with little observance of accepted grammar and sentence structure, in order to convey vividly their feelings, beliefs and fantasies. Others with a deep respect for traditional usage achieve a style of classical clearness and perfection or achieve effects of visual or musical beauty by their mastery of existing forms enriched by a sensitive and adventurous vocabulary, vivid imagery and a blending of evocative vowels and consonants.

Young people often feel the need to experiment and, as a result, to break away from the traditions they have been taught. In dealing with a foreign language, however, they have to bear in mind two conditions for experiment. Any great experimental artist is fully conversant with the conventions from which he wishes to break free: he is capable of achievement in established forms but feels these are inadequate for the expression of his ideas. In the second place, he is indisputably an outstanding artist who has something original to express; otherwise the experiments will appear pretentious, even childish.

Few students can achieve so intimate an understanding of a foreign language that they can explore its resources freely and experimentally. Not all feel the need to do so. And in any case examination candidates need to become thoroughly acquainted with conventional usage as it is a sure knowledge of accepted forms that examiners look for.

The student undertaking a Proficiency course should have the ability to use simple English correctly to express everyday facts and ideas. This ability to express oneself in a foreign language on a basis of thinking in that language without reference to one's own is essential at all stages of learning. Students with extensive experience in translation who have had little practice in using the foreign language directly must, above all, write very simply at first, using only easy constructions which they are convinced are correct, forgetting for the time being their own language and rigorously avoiding translating from it.

More complex forms, more varied vocabulary and sentence structure should evolve naturally in step with the student's increasing knowledge of the language. The student introduces a certain form or construction only when he is thoroughly familiar with it and is certain that it is normally used in this way. As he achieves additional confidence, he can begin to take an interest in the use of the language to create diverse effects. He may want to convey impressions of suspense, calm, dignity, humour, of music or poetry. He will master the art of logical explanation, of exact letter-writing, of formal speeches and natural conversation and of vivid impressionistic description. But he will still write within the limits of his ability and knowledge. And, as a learner, he will still be studying and observing conventional English usage in all that he writes.

This section deals with some of the more obvious mistakes which can mar a piece of written work.

COMMON GRAMMATICAL AND CONSTRUCTIONAL FAULTS

1. *Sentences* The sentence unit is important.

It is easy to produce an incomplete sentence, especially when the idea follows closely on the one expressed in the previous sentence.

> He marched down the street protected by a dainty rose-pink nylon-covered umbrella. This being the only one he would find in the stand.

An even more common fault is the stringing together of two or more complete sentences without conjunctions or adequate punctuation.

> The almost deserted park overlooking the Adriatic was very peaceful, I dozed pleasantly. I opened my eyes reluctantly, an inquisitive but unsympathetic eye

was examining me from close quarters it belonged to a worried-looking peacock.

Show how the above sentences should be joined.

These two faults are among the most common of those made by English students as well as those from abroad. They are dealt with more fully in the various exercises on sentence construction.

Avoid also beginning a sentence with 'also'. Alternatives are 'moreover', 'in addition'. Other opening words to avoid are 'therefore' and 'especially'.

2. *Pronouns*   These are often used ambiguously (see page 202).

3. *Illogical tense changes*
This fault may occur in an essay but is more common in an answer to a question on a work of literature.

Such answers may be presented either in predominantly past forms or predominantly present ones. But do not wander haphazardly between the two.

> When his father died, the new King, now Henry V, decided to abandon all his old noisy and idle companions. When Falstaff greets him, the King therefore speaks harshly to him.

Care has to be taken also with the correct choice of tenses and also their correct sequence:

> He *said* he *was coming* soon.
> In the circumstances he *had described*, it *was* clear that ruthless action *had been* unavoidable.

4. *Wrong agreements* between subjects and verbs, nouns, pronouns and possessive adjectives, etc.

5. *Unrelated participles and adjectives*   (see page 210)
These are only a few of the grammar mistakes which frequently occur in written work. Many more are mentioned in Section 1.

Chapter 4

WRITTEN AS DISTINCT FROM SPOKEN FORMS
1. *Conversational abbreviations* are used in written English only in direct speech, or occasionally to suggest that the writer is, so to speak, talking informally to the reader. This natural conversational style may appear in letters to friends, in preparing informal talks or in writing dialogue.

In essays, summaries, business letters, answers to literary comprehension and, in fact, all exercises involving written English (unless directions require it), do not use such abbreviations as 'don't', 'didn't', 'won't', 'can't', 'I'm', 'we'll' and other similar forms.

2. *Other abbreviations* such as e.g., i.e., lbs., ozs., yds., ft., Rd., etc., are also out of place in written compositions, though they are useful in note-taking.
e.g. can be avoided as follows:

> Students from such Mediterranean countries as Greece, Italy and Spain often find English weather depressing.

and etc. in this way.

> I am acquainted with the works of Dickens, Thackeray, Trollope, Hardy, etc.
> I am acquainted with the works of various authors including Dickens, Thackeray, Trollope and Hardy.

'a.m.' and 'p.m.' are usually confined to timetables.

> Half past five in the morning; twenty to eight in the evening;

are more common in everyday English.

3. *Numbers* are not normally introduced in written English in the form of digits unless they are very complicated, are dates or are sums of money.

4. *Slang and obvious colloquialisms* should be avoided.

Adjectives such as 'awful', 'frightful', 'terrible', 'ghastly', (all with the meaning 'bad'); adverbs such as 'awfully', 'frightfully', 'terribly', 'dreadfully' (all with the meaning 'very') and 'pretty' (meaning 'fairly') are out of place in the written language. Remember that 'decent' means 'respectable'—one speaks but does not write about 'a decent meal'. The same applies to 'proper'—'She is a proper gossip'.

Other colloquialisms favoured by students, including 'fed up with', 'hard up', 'shut up!' are also inelegant. 'Lots of' is a childish expression and the word 'get' is usually avoided in cases where it has no real meaning: 'I have got a car', 'you have got to', 'he'd got to get a job quickly'.

The use of colloquialisms depends to a certain extent on the style of what is being written. A letter to a friend about one's opinion of one's lodgings could include such colloquialisms as 'digs' (lodgings), 'gets one down' (depresses one), 'clear out' (leave) and 'keep an eye on' (watch). On the other hand, such expressions would seem out of place in a more formal piece of work.

Chapter 5

CHOICE OF WORDS A

A caution against using slang leads on to stressing the importance of choosing all words carefully. Style depends fundamentally on the words used. If these are

a) dull and overworked
b) long and pretentious
c) chosen for effect without any consideration of the subject being dealt with
d) in too great an abundance
e) exaggerated
f) childish
g) with sentimental associations
h) melodramatic
i) in any other way unsuited to the job they are doing,

the work may appear lifeless, pompous, affected, verbose, ridiculous or false. To choose words wisely is no easy task.

1. *Adjectives* Avoid the weary adjectives such as 'nice', 'lovely', 'wonderful'.

Often such adjectives as 'good', 'beautiful', 'fine', 'pleasant', 'great' lack individuality, though there are of course places where these may be used with their exact meaning.

2. *Clichés*

Corresponding to the dull adjectives there are the overworked phrases. These may have once been very effective similes or metaphors: 'as poor as a church mouse' is an example. But too many people have learned and made use of these apparently interesting expressions: they serve for writers who are content with the hackneyed and stereotyped.

It is difficult for foreign students to recognise the cliché, though there is one that every student (and, to his sorrow, every examiner) seems to know: 'It was raining cats and dogs'. (This is, in fact, an expression which comparatively few English people use.)

Here are some others more commonly encountered:

'to cut a long story short', 'far and away the best', 'for good and all', 'feel in one's bones that', 'still alive and kicking', 'he would turn in his grave', 'the Machine Age', 'an irreparable loss', 'once and for all', 'complete and utter', 'a dead and alive town', 'to ring the changes', 'to be with it', 'well and truly', 'not up to much', 'the morning after', 'once in a blue moon', 'it's only human', 'this day and age', 'turn a blind eye to', 'take steps to', 'the rat race', 'traffic will grind to a standstill', 'up and coming', 'a reliable source', 'the eternal triangle', 'the psychological moment', 'put the clock back', 'a retrograde step', 'up to the eyes in', 'down to earth', 'round the bend', 'in the red', 'more or less', 'next to nothing', 'over and above'.

Even the word 'cliché' forms part of a cliché—'a cliché-ridden style'.

240

Find out the meaning of each of the above expressions as you will hear them used often enough, but avoid introducing them in written English.

Many more such expressions are given in textbooks, but some of these are old-fashioned and although known by English people, they are less often used nowadays. Such clichés include

'put one's shoulder to the wheel', 'buy a pig in a poke', 'drunk as a lord', 'brave as a lion', 'to cross the Rubicon', 'to cry over spilt milk', 'to cut the Gordian knot', 'to carry coals to Newcastle'.

It is not a good idea to learn what you think are clever phrases or idioms and drag them into your work. On the other hand it is often possible to make use of expressions drawn from what is clearly well-written prose. Such expressions may include phrases like:

to reserve judgment; to maintain friendly relations; within easy reach of; to realise one's ambitions; to give someone the benefit of the doubt; in pursuit of.

Some more colloquial expressions are almost irreplaceable:

'to split the difference', 'to cut one's losses' are two examples.

3. Avoid long pompous words, especially in groups.
The following examples are far from impressive:

We viewed with profound emotion the magnificent panorama extended before our wondering gaze.

Before the commencement of the penultimate performance of the drama, we became aware of certain manifestations of hilarity emanating from that section of the audience located in the lofty regions of the gallery. The occasion for their mirth appeared to be the semblance of a lady's stocking protruding from beneath the as yet unopened proscenium curtains.

(Translation direct from one's own language could lead to such incredible means of expression.)

Remember that the aim of the present-day BUSINESS LETTER is to present facts and opinions simply, clearly, accurately and politely. Nowadays it is not usual to 'beg to acknowledge', 'request that this matter should receive your earliest attention', 'no longer find ourselves in a position to see our way clear to'. Such elaborate and often almost meaningless formality has almost disappeared.

These would be two modern letters:

Dear Sir,
Would you please send me details of your courses in English for Foreign Students at the Northshire Technical College.
I am a German student recently arrived in England. In my own country I studied English at school for six years.
May I ask your advice about the type of course I should join?

Yours faithfully,

Dear Sir, (Mr Schwartz),
Thank you for your letter of the 6th September asking about courses in English for Foreign Students in this college. I enclose a prospectus showing the courses available.
As you seem to have a fair knowledge of English already, you may like to undertake the Proficiency course. Classes are held each week-day between 2.30 and 4.30 p.m. Enrolment can be made on any afternoon between the 15th and 19th September.
You may like to discuss your course with me when you come to enrol.

Yours faithfully, (sincerely)

4. Modern English prose is rarely sentimental. Such statements as:

It seemed that kindly Mother Nature had created so radiant a countryside to console fleetingly her sad human creatures released momentarily from their dreary existence in joyless cities.

would merely make the average English reader laugh.

241

Chapter 6

CHOICE OF WORDS B

5. Similes and metaphors, if fresh and really appropriate, can add richness and interest to your style, though too abundant a profusion of imagery is not to be recommended. Avoid the weary simile that come first to one's mind: 'as old as the hills', 'as white as a sheet', 'to work like magic', are obvious examples. On the other hand, some simile clichés still retain a certain vigour and may occasionally be effective:

> the frost-chilled wind cut through me
> with his hair lank and dripping over his forehead and his trousers and shirt clinging limply to his body, he resembled a drowned rat.

The following two descriptions show how imagery may be used:

> The old ladies in the hotel lounge appeared asleep but were silently watching his every movement. One had gaunt features and hungry eyes like those of a vulture; the second looked sleek and comfortable like a cream-contented cat, who was nevertheless intently awaiting a mouse, while the third appeared remote but harshly critical, with the cold cynical stare of an embittered parrot.
> A mean bitter crabbed day, a peering miser of a day, pinched and furtive, with thin grey whiskers of mist sprouting from wrinkled fields and blear-eyed frozen puddles socketed in furrowed tracks.

Beware of the MIXED METHAPHOR or SIMILE. The results may be peculiar.
A previous example refers to a wind which 'cuts'. It would have been odd to have referred to a 'biting wind' which 'cut'.
Making up passages of mixed metaphors can be amusing. Here is an example.

> The ship moved forward majestically, ploughing the polished ocean like a graceful castle, dwarfing the swarming fishing boats which were butting through the smoothly corrugated water like fussy ducks busily reaping the silver treasure of the sea.

But a mixed metaphor in an examination essay may not amuse the examiner.

6. Beware also of TAUTOLOGY—the repetition of an idea in slightly different words.
Here are some examples:

> So far as I am concerned, I myself personally think . . .
> The water was rushing quickly through an underground tunnel.
> We should like to draw your attention to something you have clearly and obviously failed to notice.

7. Sometimes when you read through your work, you notice that a certain word or closely related words has reappeared two or more times in a limited space. If the word is in any way conspicuous, the effect is clumsy.

> The rapid development of industry in a predominantly agricultural country almost inevitably causes problems. Industry demands a large body of skilled and semi-skilled workers. Technical workers must be supplemented by competent office workers if the industry is to be properly organised. Efficient distribution of the industrial products is the responsibility of government officials and the industrial personnel. Industrialisation is often a gradual and costly process.

8. Avoid starting an essay with a question:

> THE HAPPIEST DAYS OF MY LIFE
> Who can decide which have been the happiest days of his life?

9. Avoid the sensational, melodramatic and exaggerated. Personification, most often apparent in emotional references to Fate, Death, Hope and the like, is seldom to be recommended.

242

Here are some examples of such usage:

After years of cruel neglect and ruthless oppression, the wretched peasants rose in a desperate but doomed revolt against the tyrannical despot.

After long feverish nights of bitter self-recrimination, pacing restlessly the length of his narrow room and solacing himself with alcohol, he finally resolved that he would abandon his fruitless endeavours to expiate the injustice he had perpetrated and leave these shores for ever.

Life held no hope for him: Shame and Poverty stared him in the face.

Avoid too many adjectives, especially sensational ones.

10. Your work should *sound* pleasing. Excessive alliteration is a bad fault.

Wild waves washed the rugged rocks.

Chapter 7

SENTENCE PATTERN

1. Vary the lengths, openings and constructions of sentences.

2. Beware of the very long and complicated sentence. Structurally the sentence may be correct, but the meaning could be difficult to resolve. Moreover such a sentence is often extremely clumsy.

Many of us have become completely dependent on the public library, partly because books being expensive, we hesitate to invest in something which may give pleasure for only a few hours, though it is possible that if our reading were confined only to those books we could afford to buy, we should choose our literature more carefully and read what we had decided was worthwhile with far greater attention to detail and far more sensitive appreciation.

3. Far worse is the sentence which loses its way completely in the middle either structurally or in its meaning (or sometimes in both) and leaves the reader bewildered.

Young people of today, who are probably earning far more money than any preceding generation, are exposed to skilfully directed advertising propaganda which appeals to the dominant emotions of the young, including a love of display, which is catered for by the production of exaggerated fashions associated with various small pop groups, these being one of the characteristics of present-day entertainment, a field in which success often depends far more on clever publicity than genuine talent.

4. The dash is an insidious menace to good style. Letter writers who wish to give a carefree lively impression may become dash addicts and it is particularly attractive to young writers. The dash is, of course, a normal example of punctuation, closely related in use to brackets, but it must be used only in careful moderation.

The following sentence could have been produced by a victim of the dash:

Yesterday I saw Darlina Dobson in a new play—she is appearing now in the film 'Mad Days in Manchester'—and she was superb—though it is true that Lalimar Smythe who took the part of the rival—she was the deserted wife in the 'Sorrows of Saturday' film—was more highly praised by the critics—but they are prejudiced against Darlina.

5. A well-written essay could contain one or two direct questions which are answered by the following material, but on the whole the student is advised to avoid such personal intrusions as direct questions, exclamations and rhetorical questions (questions used only for effect, with no answer). The following example illustrates the well-meaning but unsuitable use of these forms:

There still exist countless areas in which small shabby workshops, tumbledown shacks, abandoned corrugated iron huts, scrap heaps and rubbish dumps, littered patches of ragged grass and a huddled collection of grubby small houses and prefabs cover areas several miles square. What a muddle! How can people exist in such squalid misery? With all the vast resources of modern science available, what are we doing about these dreary eyesores?

SECTION V SPELLING AIDS

Chapter 4

DOUBLING FINAL CONSONANTS BEFORE ADDED ENDINGS

1. *Monosyllables*

The final consonant is doubled when:

    a) the word has only one vowel and one final consonant
AND b) the ending begins with a vowel

> EXAMPLES: fit fitted fitting fitter fitment
> read reading reader
> start started starting starter
> EXCEPTIONS: gas gases (but: gassed); bus buses
> row rowed rowing rower; caw cawing
> box boxes boxing boxer; tax taxed
> pray praying

2. *Words with two or more syllables*

The final consonant is doubled when:

    a) there is only one vowel in the final syllable
AND b) the stress is on the final syllable
AND c) the added ending begins with a vowel

> EXAMPLES: refér reférred reférring but réference réferée (changed stress)
> háppen háppened háppening
> appear appeared appearing appearance
> defér deférred but deférment and déference déferéntial (changed stress)
> NOTICE -l is usually doubled even when the stress is on the first syllable.
> EXAMPLES: cancel cancelled cancellation
> conceal concealed; instal installation instalment
> In some cases -p and -t can be doubled though this is optional
> worship(p)er gossip(p)ing boycot(t)ed

Chapter 8

1. Final -e is dropped before an ending beginning with a vowel.
    When -c- or -g- precede the -e, however, this is retained before an ending beginning with a- or o-.

> EXAMPLES: move moving movable movement
> sane sanity sanely; wise wisely wisdom (pronunciation change)
> peaceable changeable advantageous
> If the -e is dropped in these cases, the -c has the hard k sound
> practice practical

In some cases when -able is added to a word ending in -e, both forms, with and without the -e-, can be found

> likable likeable; ratable rateable

2. -y changes to -i- before -es, -ed, -er except when a vowel precedes the -y. It does not change before an -ing ending.

> EXAMPLES: envy envied envying; happier happiest; fly flies;
> enjoyed: play plays
> Single syllables often keep the -y before -er and -est
> dry, dries dried but dryer dryest or drier driest
> Notice these: die died dying, dye dyed dyeing; ski skiing

3. Single-syllabled verbs ending in -ay:
   a) with one first consonant: lay laid; pay paid; say said
   b) otherwise: played prayed stayed strayed

4. i before e except after c. This applies when the sound is i:
   EXAMPLES: niece field hygiene priest
   EXCEPTIONS: seize weir weird Sheila

5. e before i when the sound is ei, ai, e.
   EXAMPLES: rein weight height their
   Notice: friend.

6. *Dis-* is added to the existing word.
   appear disappear; satisfied dissatisfied

SECTION VI   REPORTED SPEECH

Chapter 5

STATEMENTS

Students will almost certainly already have experience of conversion between direct and reported speech. Here are the main rules summarised:

1. *Tense changes*

In a formal exercise, it is usual to introduce the reported speech with a verb in the past simple tense. 'He said . . .' 'He told me . . .' etc.

DIRECT SPEECH		REPORTED SPEECH
Present Simple	becomes	Past Simple
Present Continuous	becomes	Past Continuous
Present Perfect Simple⎫ Past Simple ⎬	becomes	Past Perfect Simple
Present Perfect Continuous⎫ Past Continuous ⎬	becomes	Past Perfect Continuous

Future Tenses change to their corresponding Future in the Past tenses.

One of the difficulties of changing from reported to direct speech is the fact that each of the past perfect tenses in the former has two possible corresponding tenses in the latter. The student has to be guided by the way in which the verb is being used and a knowledge of the uses of tenses is important in deciding.

2. *Pronouns and possessive adjectives*

Nouns and third person pronouns and possessive adjectives do not normally change.

A first person pronoun or possessive adjective normally becomes a third person pronoun or possessive adjective.

A second person pronoun or possessive adjective normally becomes a first or third person pronoun or possessive adjective, the person depending on the opening phrase introducing the reported speech.

He said, 'You are right'.
He told me I was right.
He told them they were right.

3. *Words and phrases*

Here again the change is controlled by the meaning. The following list gives suggestions but other forms may be more suitable in certain cases.

DIRECT SPEECH		REPORTED SPEECH
today	becomes	that day; the same day.
yesterday	becomes	the day before; the previous day.
tomorrow	becomes	the day after; the following day.
the day before yesterday	becomes	two days before.
the day after tomorrow	becomes	in two days' time.
this; these	becomes	that; those; (the).
now	becomes	then; at that time; immediately; at once.
here	becomes	there; in that place.
ago	becomes	before.
last week	becomes	the week before; the previous week.
next week	becomes	the week after; the following week.

4. *Must*

'Must' may be used in direct speech in four different ways and therefore has four corresponding forms in reported speech.

a) *Habit   must—had to*
   'I *must* always change my shoes as soon as I go indoors.'
   Jones said that he always *had to* change his shoes as soon as he went indoors.

247

b) *Future action   must—would have to*
'You *must* pay duty on this camera.'
The customs officer said *I would have to* pay duty on the camera.
c) *A permanent arrangement—No change*
'The system depends on the fact that water *must* find its own level.'
The engineer explained that the system depended on the fact that water *must* find its own level.
d) *A prohibition   Must not—'was not to' or 'must not'*
'You *must not* go out without a coat.'

His mother said that he $\frac{was\ not\ to}{must\ not}$ go out without a coat.

5. Ought to, should, used to—No change

'That form *ought to have been* completed yesterday.'
The official told me that the form *ought to have been* completed the previous day.
'You *should have told* me.'
He said *I should have told* him.
'I *used to live* on the Yorkshire moors.'
He stated that he *used to live* on the Yorkshire moors.
or   He stated that he *had once lived* on the Yorkshire moors.

6. Conditions

The tenses in the second and third types of condition do not change.

a) 'If it *rains*, the garden party *will be postponed*.'
It was announced that if it *rained*, the garden party *would be postponed*.
b) 'If it *rained*, the garden party *would be postponed*.'
It was announced that if it *rained*, the garden party *would be postponed*.
c) 'If it *had rained*, the garden party *would have been postponed*.'
It was announced that if it *had rained*, the garden party *would have been postponed*.

Chapter 6

1. Question forms

Two types of question can be distinguished:

a) Questions beginning with an interrogative pronoun or adverb:
'Who signed Magna Carta? Why did he sign?'
b) Questions beginning with an interrogative form of the verb:
'Must we learn Grammar? Do you think it is really necessary?'

IN BOTH CASES: the reported question is written as a statement, with the subject before the verb.

In the second case, the word 'whether' ('if') precedes the indirect question.
a) The teacher asked who had signed Magna Carta and why he had signed.
b) The students asked whether they had to learn Grammar. They wanted to know whether the teacher thought it was really necessary.

2. Commands

The imperative in a direct command should appear as an infinitive in an indirect command.

'Hurry up, Elizabeth!'
Mother told Elizabeth to hurry up.
'Don't leave the camp.'
The officer forbade the soldiers to leave the camp.
'Please don't forget.'
She begged me not to forget.

248

3. Exclamations

There is no rule to aid one in changing these into reported speech. Their form will depend entirely on their meaning.

'What beautiful weather!'
He commented on the beautiful weather.
'How kind of you!'
He acknowledged my kindness.

Some exclamations are elliptical, that is to say, certain words are understood. An example of this is 'How interesting!' which written in full, might be: 'How interesting your news is!', in reported speech: 'He told her how interesting her news was.'

4. Special words and expressions

Certain words and expressions appearing in direct speech cannot be expressed exactly in reported speech. These include: 'please', 'thank you', 'Oh!', 'Now then!', names of people addressed, 'Really!', etc. They have to be conveyed in reported speech by some other means.

'I should like some tea, please.'
She said politely that she would like some tea. She asked politely for some tea.
'Help! I am drowning!'
He yelled for help as he was drowning.
'Now then! What is all the trouble about?'
The policeman addressed me sharply and asked what all the trouble was about.
'My dear Watson, the solution of the problem is obvious.'
With some condescension, Holmes told Watson that the solution of the problem was obvious.

In all such cases the student must rely on his own intelligence, common sense and initiative.

5. Introductions

It is possible that only the words spoken are given, in which case the student has to supply an opening phrase suited to the subject of the direct speech. The verb should be in the past simple tense.

'Run for your lives!'
The leader of the gang ordered them to run for their lives.
'You need a long quiet holiday.'
The doctor suggested that I needed a long quiet holiday.
'I am sorry I am late. My car was held up in a traffic jam.'
The student apologised for his lateness. He explained that his car had been held up in a traffic jam.

6. Changing groups of sentences

When several sentences have to be changed into reported speech, there is no need to repeat the introductory verb when the various sentences are of the same type and deal with the same subject. If the sentences are of different types (e.g. statement, question, command), each new type of sentence has to be introduced by an appropriate verb.

'Dickens must have created more fantastic characters than any other author. What a brilliant imagination he had! How many novels did he write?'
One of the students declared that Dickens must have created more fantastic characters than any other writer and expressed his admiration for the author's brilliant imagination. The student wanted to know how many novels Dickens had written.

7. Confusion of pronouns and possessive adjectives

Owing to the tendency of first and second person pronouns and possessive adjectives to change in reported speech to corresponding third persons, very great care must be taken not to confuse the meaning of the passage by ambiguity.

Study these examples:

The inspectors' report addressed to the teachers read as follows: 'Your methods are orthodox, adequate but uninspired.'

In reported speech this could become:

In their report addressed to the teachers the inspectors stated that their methods were orthodox, adequate but uninspired.
'I need a new suit,' said the business executive to his friend, 'the one I am wearing does not suit me.'
The business executive told his friend that he needed a new suit. The one he was wearing did not suit him.

This could be made clear in this way:

The business executive was speaking about the suit he was wearing which did not suit him. He told his friend he needed a new one.
Express the first example more clearly.

8. *Conversational abbreviations*

These do not appear in reported speech.

9. *Arrangement*

When a conversation has to be reported in indirect speech, the original paragraphs are retained and appropriate introductory phrases are inserted. However, in the conversation below, this will obviously not apply.

I once overheard part of a conversation at a small station in Hampshire between a French girl and a booking office clerk.

"A ticket for Victoria, please."
"Single or return?"
"Single, please."
"First or second class?"
"Second class, please."
"That will be eighty pence."
"But I have only fifty pence. Will you take French money?"
"Sorry, I can't."
"Is there an exchange office here?"
"You can change it at the bank."
"But the banks are closed now. Oh dear! How difficult! I must catch this train."

My own train arrived at that moment and I never learned whether the French girl reached Victoria.

REPORTED SPEECH:

I once overheard part of a conversation at a small station in Hampshire between a French girl and a booking office clerk. She wanted to go to Victoria and, in reply to the clerk's questions, asked for a second class single ticket.

When the clerk told her that the ticket would be eighty pence the girl said that she had only fifty pence and asked whether he would take French money. The clerk regretted he could not and told the girl, who wanted to know whether there was an exchange office on the station, that she could change the money at a bank. But the girl remembered that the banks were closed at that time and expressed great anxiety about this difficulty as she had to catch that train.

My own train arrived at that moment and I never learned whether the French girl reached Victoria.

Chapter 7

CHANGING FROM REPORTED TO DIRECT SPEECH

1. *Tenses*

Remember that the past perfect simple tense in reported speech has two possible equivalents in direct speech: present perfect or past simple. The same applies to a

250

past perfect continuous tense which may become a present perfect continuous or past continuous form.

The tense used will, of course, depend on the meaning of the passage.

2. *Pronouns*

Pronoun and other word changes normally reverse those given for direct to reported speech conversion, but their form will be determined by the meaning.

3. *Punctuation*

Inverted commas, *commas* and *paragraphing* will be used in accordance with normal punctuation rules.

4. *The speaker*

In direct speech, reference to the speaker often follows the words spoken.

> 'He said he had been looking everywhere for me.'
> 'I have been looking everywhere for you,' he said.

Often terms such as 'he said', 'they asked', etc., break up the direct speech.

> He asked whether I really thought it possible that a research station could be established on another planet.
> 'Do you really think it possible,' he said, 'that a research station can be established on another planet?'

When there is a noun subject, the verb in such cases may precede the noun.

> 'That matter will be dealt with in the next session,' stated the Minister.

Such inversion is rare with pronoun subjects.

5. *Colloquial abbreviations*

Conversational abbreviations will probably be introduced into the direct speech.

> The air hostess told the passengers they would be landing in ten minutes.
> 'We'll be landing in ten minutes,' said the air hostess.

6. *Special forms*

The remarks listed previously which relate to the conversion from direct to reported speech (pages 247–50) apply in reverse.

Test Papers

PAPER 1

COMPOSITION (3 hours)

Answer the questions 1, 2 and 3. You should spend about the same amount of time on each.

Section A

1. Either a) Having spent many pleasant years in a well-loved house, you have to move to another one. Relate your feelings and reactions as you take up life in your new home.

   or   b) Sounds I enjoy hearing.

2. Either a) Nowadays a number of young people insist on spending a period of time wandering from place to place providing for their needs as best they can. In what ways can they benefit from this type of experience and what may be some of the harmful or unpleasant sides of this existence?

   or   b) In what ways are human beings and birds interdependent?

Section B

3. Read the following passage and then answer the questions below.

Denis Carew watched her go. That was something like a car, he reflected, un-enviously. When earlier he had inquired about the possibility of getting mechanical assistance to release Atalanta from her gelid prison, he had been told he could abandon any such absurd hope. Too many and too valuable cars were in the same
5 plight as his own for any labour to be available at the moment. The garage at Plowford had merely looked over its shoulder to throw out this information and the same went for the first Maidment garage he approached; but Mr Gladstone at the Blue Garage in the High Street promised that, if her owner could beguile her as far as his premises, he'd see about doing a bit of spit and polish, face-lift, underpinning,
10 the lot. On the other hand, if she was unable to proceed under her own steam, she was as safe with her nose jammed against a tree-trunk in Nightingale Lane as anywhere.
Denis, disagreeing but having the wit to keep his mouth shut, got a lift to Nightingale Lane, hired a spade and got to work. He proceeded slowly because he didn't
15 want to scrape any more paint off his darling's complexion than he could help, and she wasn't one of these heavily-made-up girls at the best of times. Two of her tyres seemed to be wedged in a ditch some vandal had half-filled with broken glass, rotten tins and various forms of flotsam likely to do a car harm, but though he cut his own hand and, in his own parlance, bled like a pig, removing half a broken milk-bottle,
20 she hadn't suffered. True, she'd need a new bumper and front-view she looked more like a pekinese dog than she had before, the same rather squashed appearance, so far as he could judge without removing all the snow, and though both her front lamps had perished, one way and another it could have been a lot worse. The main thing was whether she could be coaxed to amble as far as Maidment under her own
25 steam. Carefully he loosened the snow all round her, working her gently back and forth, throwing up miniature balls of the stuff as he released her wheels, rubbed the worst of the snow off the roof and windows—no sense in keeping a dog and barking yourself and you could be sure the garage bill wouldn't be a fleabite—but what a surprise Mr Gladstone was going to have when the job was finished. A bit of spit and
252

polish had the same effect on Atalanta as a permanent wave on a not-very-young 30
woman with straight hair.

Anthony Gilbert, The Fingerprint, Collins

a) What do you gather from the passage had recently happened to Denis' car?
b) 'That was something like a car, he reflected unenviously' (lines 1–2). What in other words was Denis's opinion of the car being referred to?
c) 'The garage at Plowford had merely looked over its shoulder to throw out this information.' (line 5). Describe what had in fact happened when Denis was given the information.
d) What does the expression 'spit and polish' in line 9 suggest about the treatment the car would get?
e) 'if she was unable to proceed under her own steam' (line 10). What in fact would the car be unable to do? Suggest also a probable origin for this expression.
f) 'and she wasn't one of those heavily-made-up girls at the best of times' (line 16). What impression does this statement give of the normal condition of the car?
g) Suggest what 'it' in line 23 is referring to and why this vaguely-used pronoun is quite suitable here.
h) What is the general meaning of the proverb 'no sense in keeping a dog and barking yourself' and how is it used here?
i) In about 30 words describe Denis's feelings towards his car.
j) What impression does the style of this passage give of the kind of person Denis was?

PAPER 2

Section A

In this section you must choose the word or phrase which best completes each sentence. Write the numbers 1-40, each on a separate line, and beside each number, write the letters **A, B, C, D** and **E.** Then cross through the letter before the word or phrase you choose in each case. Give one answer only to each question.

1. An Arctic blizzard swept through the now —— city streets.

    A lonely **B** deserted **C** neglected **D** isolated **E** insulated

2. I —— this book to all who enjoy an exciting story.

    A recommend **B** praise **C** approve of **D** compliment
    E appreciate

3. The lawyer gave advice to poor people for a very small ——.

    A payment **B** cost **C** fee **D** wage **E** contribution

4. I hurried to —— Smith so that we could discuss some of the new plans as we were walking

    A come up with **B** overtake **C** reach up to **D** catch up with
    E go along with

5. The congregation listened in reverent attention to the bishop's ——.

    A sermon **B** speech **C** lecture **D** discourse **E** conference

6. It was his —— to retire from business the following year.

    A intention **B** opinion **C** meaning **D** advice **E** hope

7. There is a very —— rule forbidding smoking in bed.

    A severe **B** strong **C** heavy **D** hard **E** strict

8. This is my business and you have no right to ——.

    A intervene **B** interfere **C** interrupt **D** disturb
    E break in

9. You have taken —— far too many responsibilities.

    A in **B** on **C** out **D** upon **E** to

10. I found the missing file —— on the top shelf.

    A laying **B** lain **C** lying **D** resting **E** deposited.

11. I was told that this material would not —— in the wash but it has.

    A dwindle **B** shrink **C** decrease **D** contract **E** reduce

12. I realised it would be far too —— to walk alone through those ill-lit streets after dark.

    A bold **B** heroic **C** risky **D** daring **E** courageous

13. The jury returned a(n) —— of 'not guilty'.

    A sentence **B** charge **C** summons **D** verdict **E** evidence

14. The student waited with some slight —— while his teacher stood reading his exercise.

    A dread **B** terror **C** apprehension **D** horror **E** despair

15. The police have asked for the —— of the public in tracing the whereabouts of the escaped convict.

    A partnership **B** co-operation **C** union **D** association
    E alliance

254

16. The very idea of her winning the beauty competition is quite ——.

A abrupt   B absurd   C awkward   D abnormal   E futile

17. The widely-publicised demonstration did not after all ——.

A come off   B go off `   C get on   D break out   E put on

18. —— he fails his final examination, he is still sure of a University place.

A if   B in case   C although   D even when   E even if

19. To a large extent slavery was —— during the past century.

A stopped   B prevented   C abolished   D uprooted
E removed

20. —— of half-starving wolves were roaming the snow-covered countryside.

A flocks   B herds   C packs   D swarms   E shoals

21. As the sky darkened it soon became obvious that a violent thunderstorm was
——.

A imminent   B instantaneous   C immediate   D simultaneous
E eminent

22. To what extent will future scientific discoveries make possible the —— of the
human life span?

A magnification   B increase   C expansion   D prolongation
E growth

23. Is a person to be more highly —— for his courage or for his self-sacrifice?

A estimated   B assessed   C esteemed   D gauged
E reckoned

24. His parents gave him many expensive toys as some form of —— for his lame-
ness and inability to play active games.

A prize   B remedy   C bribe   D reward   E compensation

25. The firm should make a substantial profit —— satisfactory labour relations are
maintained.

A unless   B with the result that   C provided that   D even if
E in case

26. A half-savage mongrel went —— the tramp as the man approached the farm.

A at   B against   C about   D upon   E for

27. No hazard or difficulty could —— the two mountaineers from their intention of
reaching the summit.

A dilate   B defect   C deflect   D deflate   E defeat

28. He set one alarm-clock for five o'clock and the other for five past so as to ——
that he did not oversleep.

A assure   B ensure   C insure   D reassure   E safeguard

29. The dentist had to —— the tooth as it was badly decayed.

A extract   B release   C pull off   D extricate   E eradicate

30. I hope you are not —— that I obtained this money dishonestly.

A implying   B involving   C denoting   D inferring
E deducing

31. The townspeople were always so well-behaved and —— that the police had an
idle life.

A systematic   B orderly   C methodical   D meticulous
E scrupulous

32. Under certain conditions of stress, some people —— qualities they had never
known they possessed.

A uncover   B expose   C express   D reveal   E show up

33. The evening's entertainment was —— by an electrical power cut.

   A curtailed   **B** condensed   **C** abbreviated   **D** abridged
   E compressed

34. The cathedral is —— in the centre of the city.

   A positioned   **B** placed   **C** situated   **D** stood   **E** localised

35. The fire was —— by the time the firemen arrived.

   A in   **B** off   **C** out   **D** away   **E** finished

36. The interpreter gave only a —— version of the old man's long rambling account.

   A minor   **B** minimum   **C** miniature   **D** marginal
   E condensed

37. All members of the staff should —— in the canteen for special instructions.

   A assemble   **B** unite   **C** merge   **D** amalgamate   **E** combine

38. I know him —— but I have never actually spoken to him.

   A by sight   **B** at sight   **C** on sight   **D** in sight
   E from sight

39. That evening he reached the theatre late, only just —— time to dress and make up.

   A on   **B** in   **C** by the   **D** with   **E** at the

40. He lives —— his office.

   A out of   **B** far from   **C** apart from   **D** a long way from
   E distant from

Section B

In this section you will find after each of the passages a number of unfinished statements about the passage, each with four suggested ways of finishing it. You must choose the one which you think fits best. Write the numbers 41–60 and beside each the letters **A, B, C** and **D.** Then in each case, cross through the letter you choose. Give one answer only to each question. Read each passage right through before choosing your answers.

FIRST PASSAGE

Eskimo villages today are larger and more complex than the traditional nomadic groups of Eskimo kinsmen. Village decision-making is organised through community councils and co-operative boards of directors, institutions which the Eskimos were encouraged by the government to adopt. They have been more readily accepted in
5 villages like Fort Chimo where there is an individualistic wage ethos and where ties of kinship are less important than in the rural village such as Port Burwell, where communal sharing between kinsmen is more emphasised. Greater contact with southern Canadians and better educational facilities have shown Fort Chimo Eskimos that it is possible to argue and negotiate with the government rather than to
10 acquiesce passively in its policies.

The old-age paternalism of southern Canadians over the Eskimos has died more slowly in the rural villages where Eskimos have been more reluctant to voice their opinions aggressively. This has been a frustration to government officials trying to develop local leadership amongst the Eskimos, but a blessing to other departments
15 whose plans have been accepted without local obstruction. In rural areas the obligations of kinship often ran counter to the best interests of the village and potential leaders were restrained from making positive contributions to the village council. More recently, however, the educated Eskimos have been voicing the interests of those in the rural areas. They are trying to persuade the government to recognise
20 the rights of full-time hunters, by protecting their hunting territories from mining
256

and oil prospectors, for example. The efforts of this active minority are percolating through to the remoter villages whose inhabitants are becoming increasingly vocal.

Continuing change is inevitable but future development policy in Ungava must recognise that most Eskimos retain much of their traditional outlook on life. New schemes should focus on resources that the Eskimos are used to handling as the Port Burwell projects have done, rather than on enterprises such as mining where effort is all too easily consigned to an unskilled labour force. The musk-ox project at Fort Chimo and the tourist lodge at George River are new directions for future development but there are pitfalls. 25

Since 1967 musk-oxen have been reared near Fort Chimo for their finer-than-cashmere undercoat which can be knitted. But the farm lies eight kilometres from the village, across a river, and it has been difficult to secure Eskimo interests in the project. For several months of the year—at the freeze-up and break-up of the river ice—the river cannot be crossed easily, and a small number of Eskimo herdsmen become isolated from the amenities and social life of Fort Chimo. The original herd of fifteen animals is beginning to breed but it will be difficult to attract more herdsmen as long as other employment is available within the village. 30 35

The Eskimo-owned tourist lodge near George River has been a success. American fishermen spend large amounts of money to catch trout and Arctic char, plentiful in the pure sub-Arctic rivers. The lodge is successful because its small size allows its owner to communicate with his employees, fellow villagers in George River, on a personal basis. This is essential when Eskimos are working together. If the lodge were to expand its operations, the larger number of employees would have to be treated on a more impersonal and authoritarian basis. This could lead to resentment and a withdrawal of labour. 40

The population growth of northern Ungava is rapidly outstripping the resources for hunting and fishing and the Eskimos are drifting into unskilled labour and a dependence on the receipt of welfare. It is, therefore, 'farming' and tourism that could save the region but development projects must take adequate account of Eskimo values. 45 50

David Riches *Three Life Styles for Ungava Eskimos*, from 'Geographical Magazine' April 1973

41. People are more favourably disposed to the village councils in places where
   A they are more accustomed to working independently for a living
   B they are already accustomed to co-operating
   C people in general are better educated
   D there is already communal ownership of goods

42. An acquaintance with outsiders has taught the Eskimos that
   A they can achieve greater independence
   B they can stand up for their rights
   C they can gain by opposing the government
   D they should not accept anything the government decrees

43. What was the attitude of Canadians towards Eskimos in the past?
   A they were a useful source of unskilled labour
   B the Canadians had the responsibility of looking after them for the Eskimos' own good
   C they should be encouraged to carry out useful government projects
   D they should be kept under firm government control

44. The Eskimos' uncritical acceptance of outside control has
   A caused considerable annoyance to the government
   B been general welcome to the officials in charge
   C caused difficulties to those trying to encourage responsibility
   D caused problems to officials administering these territories

45. According to the passage more government assistance is needed for the Eskimos in
   A providing schools
   B safeguarding their traditional means of livelihood

C   encouraging agricultural production
D   promoting industrial job possibilities

46. Future plans for this area should have regard to
    A   adaptation to existing conditions
    B   a general development of local resources
    C   the provision of opportunities for large-scale employment
    D   the recognition of the necessity for change

47. The two new projects mentioned should be suitable for this area but
    A   they may involve certain dangers
    B   certain possible difficulties have to be considered
    C   so far they have shown little success
    D   there are only untrained workers available to carry them out

48. Why is the Fort Chimo scheme not very popular?
    A   this kind of work does not appeal to Eskimos
    B   at certain times the work can be dangerous
    C   the location of the scheme has certain drawbacks
    D   too few people are involved in it

49. Under which of the following conditions might more people be ready to work on this scheme?
    A   if this were the only work they could find
    B   if the project itself had some chances of success
    C   if the type of work were more suitable
    D   if the men employed were less apprehensive of the flooding river

50. Why are the tourist lodge employees contented?
    A   they can hope for improved conditions in the future
    B   the lodge scheme is a worthwhile one
    C   they can feel they are individuals in a closely-knit group
    D   the proprietor is an Eskimo from their own village

SECOND PASSAGE

A full moon was shining down on the jungle. Accompanied only by an Indian guide, the American explorer and archaeologist Edward Herbert Thompson—thirteen hundred years after the Mayas had left their cities and made a break for the country farther north—was riding through the New Empire that they had built for
5 themselves, which had collapsed after the arrival of the Spaniards. He was searching for Chichen-Itza, the largest, most beautiful, mightiest, and most splendid of all Mayan cities. Horses and men had been suffering intense hardships on the trail. Thompson's head sagged on his breast from fatigue, and each time his horse stumbled he all but fell out of the saddle. Suddenly his guide shouted to him. Thompson
10 woke up with a start. He looked ahead and saw a fairyland.
    Above the dark treetops rose a mound, high and steep, and on top of the mound was a temple, bathed in cool moonlight. In the hush of the night it towered over the treetops like the Parthenon of some Mayan acropolis. It seemed to grow in size as they approached. The Indian guide dismounted, unsaddled his horse, and rolled out
15 his blanket for the night's sleep. Thompson could not tear his fascinated gaze from the great structure. While the guide prepared his bed, he sprang from his horse and continued on foot. Steep stairs overgrown with grass and bushes, and in part fallen into ruins, led from the base of the mound up to the temple. Thompson was acquainted with this architectural form, which was obviously some kind of pyramid.
20 He was familiar, too, with the function of pyramids as known in Egypt. But this Mayan version was not a tomb, like the Pyramids of Gizeh. Externally it rather brought to mind a ziggurat, but to a much greater degree than the Babylonian ziggurats it seemed to consist mostly of a stony fill providing support for the enormous stairs rising higher and higher, towards the gods of the sun and moon.
25 Thompson climbed up the steps. He looked at the ornamentation, the rich reliefs. On top, almost 96 feet above the jungle, he surveyed the scene. He counted
258

one—two—three—a half-dozen scattered buildings, half-hidden in shadow, often revealed by nothing more than a gleam of moonlight on stone.

This, then, was Chichen-Itza. From its original status as advance outpost at the beginning of the great trek to the north, it had grown into a shining metropolis, the heart of the New Empire. Again and again during the next few days Thompson climbed on to the old ruins. "I stood upon the roof of this temple one morning," he writes, "just as the first rays of the sun reddened the distant horizon. The morning stillness was profound. The noises of the night had ceased, and those of the day were not yet begun. All the sky above and the earth below seemed to be breathlessly waiting for something. Then the great round sun came up, flaming splendidly, and instantly the whole world sang and hummed. The birds in the trees and the insects on the ground sang a grand Te Deum. Nature herself taught primal man to be a sun-worshipper and man in his heart of hearts still follows the ancient teaching."

Thompson stood where he was, immobile and enchanted. The jungle melted away before his gaze. Wide spaces opened up, processions crept up to the temple site, music sounded, palaces became filled with revelling, the temples hummed with religious adjuration. He tried to recognise detail in the billowing forest. Then suddenly he was no longer bemused. The curtain of fancy dropped with a crash; the vision of the past vanished. The archaeologist had recognised his task. For out there in the jungle green he could distinguish a narrow path, barely traced out in the weak light, a path that might lead to Chichen-Itza's most exciting mystery: the Sacred Well.

C. W. Ceram *Gods, Graves and Scholars*, Gollancz

51. The territory which Thompson was exploring
   A had been abandoned by the Mayas about thirteen hundred years previously
   B had been occupied and developed by the Mayas about thirteen hundred years before
   C had been deserted by the Mayas as soon as the Spaniards arrived
   D was conquered by the Mayas thirteen hundred years ago

52. Thompson was repeatedly almost dismounted because
   A it was too dark to see where he was going
   B his horse was cantering dangerously
   C he was too worn out to concentrate on riding properly
   D the trail was unfamiliar to him

53. The guide shouted at Thompson
   A to wake him and so prevent him from falling off
   B to warn him that they had reached their destination
   C because the guide was excited by the superb view
   D because he was a long way ahead and had to let Thompson know his whereabouts

54. What was Thompson's first reaction to the scene ahead?
   A he remained in the saddle for several minutes spellbound
   B he immediately jumped down and went forward
   C he waited until his bed was ready and then dismounted
   D he rode to the mound and stared at the structure before him

55. The mound reminded Thompson of similar Egyptian constructions because of
   A its shape
   B its purpose
   C its very great antiquity
   D the means of access to it

56. What gave Thompson the impression that the pyramid was probably not a tomb?
   A the shape was wrong
   B it was too big

C it was in fact some kind of ziggurat
D it appeared to him to be merely a solid base

57. Thompson made his way towards the temple cautiously because of
A the darkness
B his interest in the surrounding ruins
C the condition of the steps
D his close examination of the sculpture on the way

58. What suggestion is made about the former purpose of the various ruins he could see?
A they had formed part of the capital of a new Mayan kingdom
B they were what remained of a temple to sky gods
C they were what was left of the starting-point from which the Mayans had moved to new territory
D they were what remained of the farthest city reached in a large-scale Mayan migration

59. Thompson believed that man is instinctively a sun-worshipper because
A the worship of the sun-god had clearly been the function of the temple
B all living things celebrate the sunrise
C the sunrise is the most magnificent of all phenomena
D it is natural for man to worship the sun and he has always done so

60. What abruptly ended Thompson's dream of the past?
A the realisation that this was only a time-consuming fantasy
B the glimpse of an important clue to future discovery
C a resolution derived from his fantasy that he must learn more about this great past city
D the locating of the mysterious Sacred Well

PAPER 3

Answer all questions

Section A

1 Write down each of the numbers 1–20 and beside each one suitable word that could fill the space indicated by the number.

A good deal of research is being —— (1) out nowadays —— (2) the causes of juvenile crime. It is obvious —— (3) one of these is an unsatisfactory home background. The father or even —— (4) both parents may be involved —— (5) some form of criminal activity and the growing child —— (6) conflict with the authorities for granted. The parents may be —— (7) bad terms with each other or even separated and the child is subjected to constant emotional strain which may make him —— (8) seek some kind of outlet in violence and serious crime.

—— (9) cause of teenage crime may be boredom or discontent. —— (10) the boy of low intelligence who scarcely knows —— (11) to read, there is the better-educated but spoilt middle-class youth who —— (12) his parents as outdated humbugs. The police —— (13) considered to be domineering bullies —— (14) purpose and delight it is to suppress ruthlessly all who challenge the meaningless dogmas of —— (15) society. Some of these youngsters pride themselves —— (16) being anarchists or revolutionaries —— (17) others find a certain fulfilment in —— (18) banks and shops, taking —— (19) in gang warfare or even beating up harmless individuals whom for some reason or —— (20), they happen to take a dislike to.

2 Complete each of the following sentences in such a way that it means the same as the sentence printed before it.

Example: The museum curator gave him permission to take photographs of certain exhibits.
  The museum curator said ....
Answer: The museum curator said that he might take photographs of certain exhibits.

  Man cannot exist without air, food and water.
1. Air, food and water are ....
  Mr Cinnamon suggested that the garage might be painted green.
2. "How ....
  We had not expected we should have so much difficulty in finding the house.
3. The house ....
  He had no idea of how difficult the climb would be until he was halfway up the mountain.
4. Only when ....
  We all wished that the weather would turn cooler.
5. We all wanted ....
  It was quite unnecessary for you to carry all that shopping home yourself.
6. You ....
  "I am sure he is innocent," she said.
7. She expressed her ....
  "Somebody will be taking my photograph tomorrow," he said.
8. He said that he ....
  Further progress was impossible because of the deep snowdrifts.
9. The deep snowdrifts ....
  Mr Carroway blamed his wife for their late arrival.
10. Mr Carroway said that it ....

261

3 Suggest one word or phrase which could fill each of the blanks in these sentences.

Example: He crept up the stairs without his shoes on .... to disturb his sleeping family.

Answer: so as not,   in order not

1. He said he could not speak much German yet but he hoped he .... to speak more fluently by the end of the course.
2. She kept her dog on a lead till she reached the park as otherwise he .... run over in the busy streets.
3. The concert was .... started at eight o'clock but the conductor of the orchestra did not come until a quarter past.
4. The child gazed speechless at the giraffe. It was the first time in his life he .... such an extraordinary animal.
5. "Would you prefer to sunbathe or to go for a walk?"
   "Oh, I'd rather .... for a walk as it's far too hot for walking."
6. As he had no head for heights, he dared .... to the top of the ladder.
7. This picture is believed .... painted by Goya.
8. He took a whole bottle of tablets with him in .... be seasick.

4 For each of the sentences below, write a new one as similar as possible to the original sentence but using the word given in capital letters.

Example: Do you live far from here?
     WAY

Answer: Do you live a long way from here?

1. He very seldom gets up before ten.
   HARDLY
2. Unfortunately few people have been very interested in preserving these lovely old cottages.
   INTEREST
3. Would you mind moving your car as it's in my way.
   KIND
4. I think that the cat from next door might have stolen the fish.
   SUSPECT
5. Do sit down and describe your new house to me.
   WHAT
6. We found the weather so cold that we stayed indoors the whole time.
   SUCH
7. We have appointed Mr Clove to the post of Senior Research Chemist. You drew our attention to his exceptional qualifications in science yesterday.
   WHOSE
8. You should do as much as you can during your two days in Paris.
   MAKE
9. I am asking you about Edinburgh because you used to live there.
   REASON
10. I feel sure you will be able to pass the examination.
    CONFIDENCE

Section B

5 Read the following passage and then answer the questions which follow it.

Man's chief offence against nature has been to damage the earth's natural covering of vegetation without replacing it with a system of farming able to maintain the fertility of the soil. Man the farmer penetrated new lands in many directions, and the forests and grasslands were vulnerable to his various activities.

5   The roots of plants help to bind and protect the all-important soil and keep it in place. Falling dead vegetation and animal-remains ensure a regular return of nutrients to the soil. If kept in good condition a layer of soil acts as a sponge and regulates the movement of water in the area. Also, green plants perform a further vital function on our planet. Carbon-dioxide is taken in by the leaves in the daytime

10 because it is one of the raw materials needed for the making of food substances

such as sugars and starches in the green cells during the process known as photo-synthesis. At the same time oxygen is given out. The carbon-dioxide given out by the living world during respiration is thus used and turned into valuable plant products of all kinds. In this way a healthy balance of gases is maintained in our atmosphere.

As farming spread through Europe, Africa and Asia, this natural balance in the 15 biological world was altered in a variety of ways. Cultivators needed to ensure that crops received maximum sunlight and rain and the minimum of competition from other plants. They therefore cleared the land as completely as possible of the previous vegetation

The 'slash-and-burn' method, as it is called, was developed very early in the 20 history of agriculture, and present-day primitive Dyaks of Borneo, in the East Indies, still provide us with an example of this type of farming. They clear the tropical rain forest of their land with methods very similar to those used by the New Stone Age people in Europe five or six thousand years ago. The bark of the trees is cut so that they gradually die. Other vegetation is also cut down and, when it has dried 25 out, is burned. This leaves gaps of bare soil between the dead trees, which now cast little shade. In these gaps the seeds are planted and from them harvests of a sort are finally removed.

After a year or two the harvests begin to get smaller and smaller because the plant food in the soil has been used up. The soil becomes exhausted and the community 30 moves on to the next area to deal with that in the same way. The forest soon invades the abandoned plots and to some extent fertility is restored. During the period of clearance, however, valuable soil will have been lost by erosion, and this is especially serious in hilly areas in the tropics where rainfall may be frequent and heavy. While populations were low and stable little permanent damage was done, but with a 35 steady increase in the size and number of human communities the forest and soil have little time to recover.

Forest felling and the burning of vegetation was frequently practised in New Zealand by nineteenth-century immigrants from Europe, who 'opened up' the country for farming. Such activities loosened the hold the vegetation had upon the 40 soil, resulting in rapid, widespread erosion as the soil that had accumulated over the centuries was carried away by the rainwater draining off the land.

1. Suggest what various things the earth's 'natural covering of vegetation' (lines 1–2) mainly consists of.
2. What are two different meanings of the phrase 'in many directions' as it is used in line 3 ?
3. Explain the exact significance of the word 'return' in line 6.
4. What function of a sponge is being referred to in the words 'a layer of soil acts as a sponge' (line 7) ?
5. In what sense is the writer using the word 'our' in line 9 ?
6. What is the meaning of 'raw materials' (line 10) when this expression is used in connection with industry ?
7. Explain how the respiration of living creatures and the food production of plants are interdependent.
8. What does the expression 'in this way' (line 14) refer to and what other word in the four lines before or after it has a similar meaning ?
9. Why was it necessary to ensure that crops received 'the minimum of com-petition from other plants' (lines 17–18) ?
10. Explain why one of the early methods of vegetation clearance was known as the 'slash-and-burn' method.
11. Explain what the word 'this' in line 26 refers to.
12. How would the meaning have been changed if in the expression 'cast little shade' (lines 26–27) the word 'a' had preceded 'little' ?
13. What kind of harvests are suggested by the phrase 'of a sort' (line 27) ?
14. Explain the meaning of the word 'exhausted' in line 30. This word can have another meaning. Explain this other meaning and then suggest how the two different meanings are in fact connected.
15. Why did people who carried out the 'slash-and-burn' method of cultivation have to keep moving from place to place ?

16. 'valuable soil will have been lost by erosion' (line 33). Explain how in fact the soil is lost.
17. 'this is especially serious in hilly areas' (lines 33–34). What two differing meanings can the first four words have in this context.
18. In what way does the passage suggest that land-clearance by nineteenth-century New Zealand immigrants differed from that carried out by primitive peoples practising the 'slash-and-burn' method?
19. Why are the words 'opened up' in line 39 enclosed in inverted commas?
20. In a paragraph of not more than 100 words explain the stages by which methods of cultivation have resulted in the permanent destruction of soil fertility.

Section C

6 The following letter has been written to his parents by a fifteen-year-old English boy attending a vacation course in German at the Sprachfreude Language School in Southern Germany.

The school issues a prospectus in English, which is sent to English schools and colleges. Prepare that part of the prospectus which incorporates the information given in the letter. Gather all the relevant ideas you can find in the letter, paragraph them suitably and write in a style appropriate to a publicity prospectus intended in the first place for teachers and lecturers.

The beginning of the prospectus is written for you. Write another 125–175 words.

Dear Mum and Dad,

I've been here a week now and I'm having a super time. The family I'm staying with speak almost no English—Ernst, who's two years younger than I am, speaks just a little—so I have to use my German. Of course we speak German too when we talk to the pupils from other countries—about 60 of them, from France, Sweden, Italy, Greece and lots of other places. A few of them are quite old but most of us are still at school.

I have a room to myself and the food isn't bad when you get used to it. The town's just on the edge of a mountain lake where we can swim (there's also a town open-air swimming-pool) and we go sailing and even water-skiing. The school takes us on excursions. We've been nearly to a mountain-top by funicular and for one or two walks and next week we're going to visit an old castle by coach. They've got three German students to look after us on excursions and the three of them organise entertainments in the evenings sometimes. But the family takes me round a lot in their car and sometimes we visit their relatives and friends. And it's German that's spoken all the time.

The lessons are all right too. We've got only twelve in our class and the maximum for a class is fourteen. The teachers are all young—they could be students on holiday —and we don't learn any grammar but we talk and discuss most of the time. We often have lessons in the garden. I don't know that I'll get any better marks at school now but I can certainly speak much more easily and understand too.

One of the boys was taken ill yesterday in class but they've got a special doctor for the school and he was there in twenty minutes. I don't think he's really very ill because I saw him swimming this afternoon.

I've already made several friends and we'll correspond when the course is over— in German of course. In fact I've invited a Dutch boy to stay with us next summer —you don't mind, do you?

There's a film show and discussion in the school in half an hour so I'd better stop. I hope you're both all right.

> Yours,
> Gavin

THE SPRACHFREUDE LANGUAGE SCHOOL, TANNENBERG

The Sprachfreude School offers holiday courses in German for visitors from other countries who wish to improve their knowledge of the language and especially their spoken fluency. . . . .
. . . .

PAPER 4

Section A

Specimen Photograph

Give a general description of what you can see in this picture.
What things in it do you find attractive or unattractive?
Why would you like or dislike to live in one of these houses?

What are some of the advantages and disadvantages of living in a small town?
What may be some of the traffic problems in a small town?

265

Imagine the type of person who might be living in one of these houses and describe him or her.

Many towns nowadays have large areas of slums. What are some of the things being done to clear these slums?

Section B

Specimen set of topics

Choose one of the following topics and prepare to give your views on it, for 1¼ to 2 minutes, when asked to do so by the examiner. You may make notes, but do not try to work out a whole speech.

1. My idea of a really well-educated person.
2. What career would you regard as a really interesting one and why?
3. The points I would look for in a really good car, or an ideal kitchen or an ideal husband or wife.

Section C

A specimen dialogue

(Prepare to read the part of Webb. The examiner will read the other part.)

WEBB: Good evening, Inspector. Nice to see you. Please sit down. May I offer you a drink?

INSPECTOR: No thank you. Sorry to disturb you when you're writing.

WEBB: Not at all. I've been working long enough. How can I help you?

INSPECTOR: Well, you may have heard of the bomb they found at 'The Three Horseshoes' last night.

WEBB: Oh yes, I was down there earlier today. Nearly empty the place was, and Mr and Mrs Bassett very upset about it. But it didn't go off so what's the trouble?

INSPECTOR: We've still got to find who planted it.

WEBB: I suppose so. Well, I don't see how I can help. Hardly likely to have put it there myself. Or is that what you're thinking, just because you know I've got a prison record?

INSPECTOR: Twice inside, I think sir. Once for arms smuggling and once for beating up someone in a quarrel.

WEBB: So that *is* it. And so you consider me the most likely suspect. All right. Long ago I defended myself violently against an attacker. But why should I now try to destroy the premises of a good friend, where I like to spend much of my spare time?

INSPECTOR: I heard something about a disagreement between you and Mr Bassett, a rather angry one.

WEBB: Who told you that? Whoever did is a liar. I suppose some old woman heard me arguing and exaggerated it into a violent quarrel. I don't deny that I've got a loud voice and I do blow up at times. But not with Bob Bassett and I'm not a potential murderer.

INSPECTOR: Where were you then yesterday evening at eight o'clock?

WEBB: What's that got to do with you? You come here interrogating me, accusing me of scheming wanton destruction and murder, without one scrap of evidence all because I've been wrongly punished previously for two quite different things.

INSPECTOR: You haven't answered my question, sir.

WEBB: Well, if you particularly want to know, I was here in this room, writing as usual. No, nobody was here with me. No, nobody telephoned or called or otherwise checked on me.

INSPECTOR: You're usually at 'The Three Horseshoes' at that time. Why not yesterday evening?

WEBB: Look here, Inspector, I've had enough of this. I was here and I've nothing more to say. Do you want me to telephone my solicitor?

266

INSPECTOR: That might be a good idea. As you were seen not a hundred yards from 'The Three Horseshoes' at ten to eight yesterday evening. By a very reliable witness.

WEBB: They couldn't have done. Because there wasn't anybody who could have seen me as I wasn't there. Who told you that lie?

Section D

Specimen set of five situations

1. You have parked your car by a meter but find you have no change, so you leave the car for five minutes while you go off to get some. When you get back a parking warden is writing a ticket. How do you try to dissuade him from doing this?
2. As you are about to leave a shop, you notice that the assistant has given you the wrong change. Explain this to him.
3. There is some small item you want to buy in England but don't know the English name for. You go into a shop and try to discover whether you can get it there by describing it.
4. You have to find a friend who has a single room in a large flat in a very extensive building. You know neither the number of the flat nor the name of the main occupier, so you knock at a door chosen at random. Explain the situation and describe your friend in the hope that the person you are speaking to has seen him or her and knows which flat he or she lives in.
5. For some very good reason you have to delay paying the rent for your room or flat for a week or two. Explain the situation to your landlady and ask whether in this case, you may pay later.

Appendix I

EXPRESSIONS INCORPORATING CERTAIN COMMON WORDS
Explain the meaning of each of the following expressions and use it in an interesting
sentence. Round brackets indicate expressions used normally in the spoken language.

a) TOUCH
in touch; out of touch with; (touch and go); touch typing; to lose one's
touch; to have a sensitive touch; to get into touch with; to keep in touch
with; to lose touch with; to be touched by something; a touching scene; to
touch one's hat to; (to be slightly touched); to touch up a photograph; to touch
on a subject; finishing touches; a touch of the sun; a touch-down; touch-lines.

b) BACK
to be back; back to front; a back view; to talk behind a person's back; to
put one's back into work; with one's back to the wall; a back in football;
a back number of a periodical; there and back; to back a horse; to have
backers; a back-room scientist; to back down; to back out of.

c) TIME
once upon a time; at the time; in time [two meanings]; out of time; in no time;
on time; overtime; for the time being; olden times; time and again; two at a
time; an egg timer; good timing; a timepiece; a timetable; a time-server;
summer time; Greenwich mean time; in record time; time and motion study;
half-time; time is up; a good time; the time of one's life; to beat time; to keep
time; to keep good time; to mark time; to spend time; to pass the time; to pass
the time of day; to gain time; to lose time; to waste time; to save time; to make
time; to make up for lost time; to serve one's time; to take time; (to do time
[slang]); to take time off; to bide one's time; good timing; waltz time; three-
four time; time-honoured; timeless; timely; to time something; ill-timed;
five times four.

d) WAY
by the way; by way of [two meanings]; in the way; in a way; out of the way;
an out-of-the-way place; way in; way out; on the way; to go out of the way to;
nothing out of the way; to be under way; anyway; this way; to get one's own
way; to want one's own way; do it my way; to have a way with one; to lose
one's way; to find one's way; to ask the way; to make way for; in some ways;
in a bad way; to pave the way for; ways and means; a motorway; a one-way
street; a right of way; a wayfarer; wayside; to waylay.

e) SIGHT
at sight; at first sight; at the sight of; to shoot at sight; by sight; in sight; out of
sight; on sight; a horrible sight; what a sight!; to see the sights of London;
(to look a sight); to come into sight; to lose sight of; to lose one's sight; to
catch sight of; second sight; foresight; an oversight; insight; sightseeing; a
sightseer; short-sighted; long-sighted; far-sighted; to sight land; the sights of a
gun; to sight-read music.

f) MEAN MEANS
by means of; by all means; by some means or other; by fair means or foul;
a means to an end; a means test; a person of means; mean annual rainfall; to
mean well; well-meaning; to mean to do; a mean thing to do.

g) CUT
a short cut; a good cut of meat; to get one's hair cut; a cut in salary; to cut an
acquaintance (dead); to cut a scene of a play; to cut a figure; to cut a lesson; to
cut a pack of cards; (that cuts both ways); to cut down expenses; to cut off

the gas; to be cut off from help; to cut off a corner; to cut out a garment; not cut out for; to cut out smoking; cut out of a will; to have one's work cut out; to cut in; to cut into a conversation; (he's very cut up); (to cut up rough); to cut short a speech; (to cut it fine); cut glass; cut flowers; cut and dried; cut prices; a cut finger; a cutting remark; a cutting.

h) CLASS
this is first-class work; a second-class compartment; in a class of its own; class distinctions; the working classes; class war; a classless society; evening classes; the top class [or form]; not to be classed with; to outclass; to classify.

i) CROSS
cross-roads; a crossword puzzle; cross-stitch; to cross-question; to cross-examine; a cross between; the Red Cross; the Southern Cross; the Victoria Cross; the George Cross; to make one's cross; noughts and crosses; to cross swords with; to be crossed in love; cross-country; a crossed cheque; to cross one's mind; cross-legged; to be cross; a level crossing; a pedestrian crossing; a rough crossing; a cross-section; at cross purposes; cross-eyed.

j) FAIR
a fair; a trade fair; fair weather; fair-haired; fair-skinned; a fair copy; fair treatment; a fair attempt; a fair number; a fair offer; fair play; fairly good; a fair share; fair words.

k) HELP
a home help; self-help; to be a help; a mother's help; a great help; help yourself; help-yourself service; (she can't help it); to help out; that doesn't help; (it can't be helped); a helper; helpless.

l) HAND
at hand; by hand; in hand; hand-in-hand; to hand; to hand over; to take in hand; on one's hands; off one's hands; out of hand; to hand out; a handout; a hand at cards; a hand of a clock; a hand in a factory; at first hand; second-hand; (hands off); (hands up!); (not to do a hand's turn); (to keep one's hand in); (to have one's hands full); to shake hands with; the upper hand; to lay hands on; hand in glove with; a handshake; a golden handshake; a hand-kerchief; a handful; a handbag; handiwork; handwriting; a handcuff; handy; handed down; underhanded; overhand; to have a hand in.

m) HEAD
the head teacher of a school; (heads or tails?); (unable to make head or tail of); head over heels; from head to foot; ten shillings a head; to keep one's head; to lose one's head [two meanings]; to shake one's head; head first; at the head of; over the heads of; a head-waiter; a head wind; to head a ball; to head a delegation; to head west; a heady drink; a headstrong youth; a headlight; a heading; a headland; to make headway, to fall headlong; headquarters; a head-on collision; a headline; a headache; a head-dress; ahead; overhead.

n) LINE
a branch line; the 'up' line; a telephone line; a party line [two possible meanings]; write me a hundred lines; to take a strong line; a clothes line; lines of poetry; marriage lines; (What's your line?); a new line in frozen foods; the enemy lines; in line; in line with; out of line; to draw the line at; to read between the lines; a line of business; to forget one's lines; a lined face; unlined notepaper; a lining; a liner; to underline.

o) LAND
an aeroplane lands; (to land on one's feet); by land; on land; overland; to work on the land; a land worker; a landlord; a landlady; a landowner; a landing in a house; a landing-stage; land-locked; a landmark; a landscape.

p) SENSE
a sense of proportion; a sense of direction; a sense of humour; common sense; a sixth sense; out of one's senses; to come to one's senses; (what's the sense of doing that?); in a sense; to make sense; to sense danger; nonsense; senseless; sensible; sensitive.

q) LIGHT
(May I have a light?); high lights; a spotlight; limelight; a searchlight; torch-light; a nightlight; a light year; to come to light; to throw light on; to get light;

lighting-up time; light reading; to make light of; light-hearted; light-headed; light-fingered; a lighthouse; a lighter; lightning.

r) PLACE
to lose one's place in a book; to return to one's place; a market-place; in place; out of place; to take place; to take the place of; to know one's place; it's not my place to; in place of; (I can't place him); to replace; to displace; four places of decimals.

s) DOG
a dog's life; a cat and dog life; an underdog; (to go to the dogs;) at the dogs; a shaggy dog story; to dog someone's steps; dog-tired; dog-eared; dogged by misfortune; dogged (adjective).

t) MIND
a mind of one's own; to bear in mind; to make up one's mind; to change one's mind; (to have a good mind to); on one's mind; an open mind; presence of mind; to the mind's eye; to give one's mind to; a state [frame] of mind; to go out of one's mind; (Never mind); (I don't mind); (mind what you're doing); (mind the doors); (mind your own business); to mind children; absent-minded; feeble-minded; broad-minded; mindful of; do you mind?

u) POWER
the Great Powers; the power of speech; nuclear power; power politics; in power; out of power; to gain power; at the height of his power; a power station; powered by electricity; to overpower; powerful; powerless; $x^4 = x$ to the fourth power.

v) WEIGHT
to lose weight; to put on weight; overweight; underweight; weightless; a pound weight; a paperweight; (a weight off one's mind); a weighing-machine; to weigh up the chances; to weigh a person up; one consideration outweighs another; certain considerations have great weight; to weigh anchor; a weighty argument.

w) UP
(it's up to you); (up to no good); (up to mischief); (what have you been up to?); (not up to much); (not feeling up to the mark); (not feeling up to it); (it's all up!); (is he up yet?) (up and doing); to eat up; to use up; (fed up with [slang]); upside down; to walk up and down; (the ups and downs of life); to jump up and down; up to town; the up-line; (quick on the uptake); up country; up-to-date; upstream; upstairs; upkeep; uprising; upheaval; (on the upgrade); an upright man; to stand upright; to uproot; to go up to University; (up with the rebels!).

x) DOWN
(to have a down on); to talk down to; to look down on; to burn down; to let someone down; to get down to work; to put something down to; to be down for a course; the North Downs; a down quilt; an eider-down; sundown; a downfall; a downpour; downstairs; downhill; down to earth; down-hearted; downright; down and out; (down in the mouth); a down train; downcast; downtrodden; a downward trend; to come down from University; (down under).

y) SIDE
a football side; (to make money on the side); to be on the wrong side; side by side; sideways; on all sides; off side; to take sides; on their side; to look on the bright side; at the side of; a side of bacon; an outsider; a side-line; to side with; a side effect; a side-saddle; side-whiskers; a side-car; a sideboard; a side-show at a fair; a siding; a sidelong glance; a many-sided person; eight-sided; an aside in a play; to take someone aside.

z¹) OUT
out for a walk; he is out; a batsman is out; a fire is out; out in one's reckoning; inside out; to wear out; worn out [two meanings]; to catch out; to fall out with a friend; radioactive fall-out; an outpatient; the outskirts; an outhouse; an outsider; an outing; an outcry; an outburst; the outset; output; an outbreak; a prison break-out; outlook; a walk-out; way out; an out and out rogue; out at elbows; out of date; outdoor; out of doors; to outgrow; outweigh other

271

considerations; to outstay one's welcome; to outdo; the outgoing president; outstanding; outlying districts; outstretched; outspoken; an outboard motor.

z²) IN

(to know the ins and outs); (to have it in for someone); (to be in for trouble); to get in [be elected for Parliament]; the train is in; fall in with someone's wishes; way in; income; influx; instep; inlet; inset; intake; inborn; ingrown; ingrained; inland; an innings.

Appendix II

PRONUNCIATION AND SPELLING DISTINCTIONS

a) Notice the differences in stress between nouns, verbs and adjectives in the following lists:

NOUN	VERB	ADJECTIVE
présent	presént	preséntable
éscort	escórt	
récord	recórd	
áddict		addícted
cóntract	contráct	
súbject	subjéct	subjéctive
óbject (objéction)	objéct	objéctive
súrvey (survéyor)	survéy	
cónduct	condúct	
prógress	progréss	progréssive
áttribute	attríbute	
cónvert	convért	convértible
próject (projéction)	projéct	
súspect	suspéct	
próduce	prodúce	prodúctive
pérmit	permít	
díscount	discóunt	
cónflict	conflíct	

Notice these pronunciations: estimate (éstimit) (noun) and estimate (éstiméit) (verb)

b) Notice these spellings:

NOUN	VERB
advice	advise
device	devise
prophecy	prophesy
licence	license
practice	practise

c) CONFUSION BETWEEN SUFFIXES
The following are a few examples which cause great confusion:

-ABLE
accountable; adjustable; advisable; agreeable; amenable; applicable; arable; blamable; capable; comparable; desirable; despicable; favourable; indispensable; inexplicable; irreconcilable; irreparable; irreplaceable; irrevocable; movable; notable; operable; peaceable; portable; predictable; realisable; reasonable; regrettable; retractable; unmistakable; usable; valuable; veritable.

-IBLE
accessible; admissible; audible; convertible; defensible; eligible; flexible; imperceptible; incompatible; indivisible; intelligible; legible; permissible; responsible; sensible; susceptible.

273

Here are some of the more common words ending in -ance (-ant) or -ence (-ent).

-ANCE -ANT
acceptance; accountant; ambulance; assistance; assurance; attendance; extravagance; grievance; importance; insurance; lieutenant; maintenance; occupant; performance; relevance; sergeant; tolerant.

-ENCE -ENT
absence; confidence; convalescence; correspondence; dependence; difference; efficient; existence; insistent; preference; presence; providence; reference; reverence; residence.

Index

276